The BBC Proms Guide to Great Choral Works

Nicholas Kenyon has been Director of the BBC Proms since 1996. He was a music critic for *The New Yorker*, *The Times*, and the *Observer*, and was Controller, BBC Radio 3, from 1992 to 1998, responsible for the award-winning Radio 3 seasons 'Fairest Isle' and 'Sounding the Century'. He wrote the history of the BBC Symphony Orchestra and edited the influential volume *Authenticity and Early Music*. In 2001 he wrote a new edition of his biography of Simon Rattle. He is now Controller, BBC Proms, Live Events and Television Classical Music, and was appointed a CBE in 2001.

in the same series

THE BBC PROMS GUIDE TO GREAT CONCERTOS
edited by Nicholas Kenyon

THE BBC PROMS GUIDE TO GREAT ORCHESTRAL WORKS
edited by Nicholas Kenyon

THE BBC PROMS GUIDE TO GREAT SYMPHONIES
edited by Nicholas Kenyon

THE BBC PROMS GUIDE TO

Great Choral Works

edited by Nicholas Kenyon

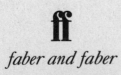

faber and faber

First published in 2004
by Faber and Faber Limited
3 Queen Square London WC1N 3AU

Typeset by Faber and Faber Limited
Printed in England by Bookmarque Ltd, Croydon

A CIP record for this book
is available from the British Library

ISBN 0–571–22096–7

10 9 8 7 6 5 4 3 2 1

Contents

List of contributors

Nicholas Anderson 303
Clifford Bartlett 182
Julian Budden 234, 294, 297
Anthony Burton 101, 152, 204, 206, 271
David Cairns 23, 33, 47, 52, 59
Andrew Clements 1
Misha Donat 195
Malcolm Hayes 306
Andrew Huth 89, 203, 213, 226, 252
Stephen Johnson 105, 108, 112, 177, 281
Jonathan Keates 125
Lindsay Kemp 7, 10, 14, 17, 119, 121, 129, 130,
    135, 191
Nicholas Kenyon 222
Hugh Macdonald 40
Malcolm MacDonald 66, 69, 161, 238, 286, 289
David Matthews 166, 278
Gerard McBurney 216
Diana McVeagh 94
David Nice 257
Roger Nichols 231
David Osmond-Smith 28
Stephen Pettitt 261
John Reed 248
Philip Reed 77, 81
Paul Reid 245
Denby Richards 199, 207
Lionel Salter 263
Robert Stein 163
Andrew Stewart 4, 91, 98, 116, 210, 211, 276
Nicholas Temperley 170
Wendy Thompson 175, 291
John Tyrrell 156

Introduction

What is choral music? The answer would seem to be obvious, epitomised by those vast gatherings of choral societies at great festivals, pounding out the massive masterpieces of the repertory with a thousand voices. In the Royal Albert Hall in London, where the BBC Proms take place annually, there is an engraving entitled 'The Choral Festival on Saturday Last at the Royal Horticultural Society's Gardens, 10 July 1869' showing endless serried ranks of choristers in the open air, stretching as far as the eye can see, controlled by a tiny bowler-hatted conductor: the picture encapsulates a peculiarly powerful English cultural activity, where the participation of amateur choral singers in great musical occasions became a distinctive tradition that still thrives today, whether at the Three Choirs Festival, or on the first night of each BBC Proms season.

Yet it would be quite wrong to imagine that all the extraordinarily varied works in this volume of notes were to be performed in anything like this way. We know that Handel's *Messiah* was performed at its premiere in Dublin and at performances for the Foundling Hospital in London during the composer's lifetime with quite modest forces. But already by the Handel Commemoration of 1784 the piece was being performed in Westminster Abbey by a choir of 275 and an orchestra of 248. By the Great Handel Commemoration Festival of 1859 (to celebrate the centenary of his death) there was a chorus of 2765 and an orchestra of 460. There were even larger gatherings in America, where the Boston Handel and Haydn Society presented a festival in 1857 with a *Messiah* featuring between 600 and 700 voices, and a 'Grand National Celebration of Peace' in 1869 featured the 'Hallelujah Chorus's with no less than 10,000 voices and 500 instruments.

The spirit behind these great choral gatherings was expressed by a writer in the *Musical Examiner* in 1843, who

asked, 'Who ever heard of a choir too large for Handel? . . .
Not though nations should be formed into choirs, and the
genius of thunder were to swell the harmony till it shook the
very spheres, would the true votary of Handel cry "Hold,
enough!"' This was inspiring, but it was not long before true
votaries of Handel did begin to cry 'Hold, enough!' in no
uncertain manner. Performances using forces more closely
approaching Handel's own proportions became fashionable,
and the revival of eighteenth-century music in the twentieth
century created a radically new performing style in this country from 1950 onwards in the work of John Tobin, Charles
Mackerras and Basil Lam. This was not just about size of
forces, but about articulation, ornamentation, rhythmic con-
ventions – all part of the move to relate performance style to
individual composers, whereas the choral tradition tended to
merge all works into one. (My favourite evidence of this is
that when I once wrote an article for the *Sunday Times* referring to *Elijah*, and a sub-editor changed it to read 'Handel's
Elijah', the paper then printed a correction saying that 'the
Messiah referred to is of course Mendelssohn's'!)

The reaction against convention was even more extreme in
the case of Bach and earlier choral music, where the case was
made that this was not music for many voices, or even few
voices, but essentially for solo singers each of whom performed a vocal line on their own. This was evidently true in
the madrigal and consort repertory (though it was not the
norm for the English church music tradition), and the
Monteverdi Vespers is the earliest major work in this book
which springs from that consort tradition. But the Bach
Passions and B minor Mass? It was in 1980 that the American
scholar Joshua Rifkin unveiled his theory that these pieces
were conceived, and should be performed now, by one singer
to a part, and recorded the B minor Mass in this way. He has
only just followed this up with the full scholarly exposition
that was promised, and some brilliant performances by
Andrew Parrott (whose recent book *The Essential Bach Choir*
is the best account of the reasoning behind the argument) and

Paul McCreesh's recent recording of *St Matthew Passion* have kept the controversy alive with exciting and challenging music-making.

It is difficult not to see in these attacks on conventional practice a thinly-veiled irritation with inherited tradition. The assumption that cheerful participation by large numbers of not especially well-trained singers in these pieces is basically a good thing (and therefore could not morally be objectionable) is a difficult one to challenge. And it is also evident that the temper of our times generally favours performance textures of clarity and lightness which massive choral societies simply cannot provide. Is our current preference for small-scale precision stimulated by accurate history or modern taste? The story of choral music performance is subject to this fluctuating balance just like every other part of the repertory. (The most fascinating recent discussion of the tension between musical taste and musicological history is Daniel Leech-Wilkinson's important book *The Modern Invention of Medieval Music*.) Perhaps we are now reaching a stage where different performance traditions can exist simultaneously, with Beecham's monster re-orchestrated *Messiah* sitting happily beside Mozart's late eighteenth-century version in German, as well as purist re-creations of the text of a single *Messiah* performance on a precise date in Handel's lifetime with the exact performing forces of the time.

Another story this book tells in the margins, as it were, is the fascinating one of how the tradition of choral writing has reinvented itself in the twentieth century. Other countries will have their own examples, but this is one area where Britain has led the way. The Victorian oratorio was in danger of becoming extinct, falling like a dinosaur under its own weight. But Elgar's *The Dream of Gerontius*, with its powerful text and supremely imaginative music which hints at Wagner, gave a massive hope to the genre at the start of the new century. Without *Gerontius*, Walton's *Belshazzar's Feast* would not have been possible in the 1930s, nor without that, Britten's *War Requiem* in the 1960s (with its highly original textual structure but with musical echoes back to Verdi) would not have captured the imagination of a new generation of singers and record-buyers. Beyond that, there is Tippett's *The Mask of Time* from the 1980s, paradoxically a massive statement about the impossibility of massive statements in our age, which felt exactly right at the end of the millennium when it began the 1999 BBC Proms at the climax of the broadcast festival of twentieth-century music, 'Sounding the Century'.

The place of choral music in the BBC Proms, where all these programme notes had their origin, is a curious and interesting one which needs to be more fully researched. Henry Wood created the Proms in 1895 as an orchestral festival, in contrast to the many choral festivals that existed in Victorian England. He did not need to mount accounts of the big choral works because they were regularly heard elsewhere, and so none of this repertory – apart from isolated solo arias taken from choral works – was heard in the early years of the Proms. (The most bizarre evidence of this is that Beethoven's Ninth Symphony was performed without its choral finale until 1929!) It was not until Malcolm Sargent took over the season in 1950, by which time the Proms had moved from the bombed-out Queen's Hall to the larger Royal Albert Hall, that the staple choral works were first heard: Verdi's Requiem became a regular from 1956 onwards, Elgar's *The Dream of Gerontius* from 1957. The revolution that William Glock wrought in Proms programming during the 1960s, which is often thought of as consisting entirely of contemporary music, was actually just as prominently a revolution that brought choral music to the season: endless riches of Bach cantatas, Haydn's *Creation* and *Seasons*, Mozart's Requiem and other masses, Monteverdi church music, Berlioz, as well as the twentieth-century choral repertory – Janáček, Messiaen, Henze. Glock's successors have been happy to follow in this vein, and we have introduced 'new' choral works both ancient and modern to the Proms each year.

Much of that rich repertory is reflected in this volume, which aims to bring together the most authoritative and accessible accounts of the most popular choral works (however one defines that term) which have been performed at the Proms in recent times. We have not, within the confines of this Pocket Guide format, been able to include the texts and translations of these works, but we hope they provide a concise guide to listening, whether on the radio and TV or on disc.

Acknowledgements

I would like to thank Edward Bhesania for his expert help in the preparation of this volume, and for writing the new composer biographies. Mark Pappenheim, who originally commissioned many of these notes for BBC Proms Publications, has had much input into their shape and consistency, and gave advice on the content of the volume. Sarah Breeden oversaw the project for BBC Proms Publications, and Hannah Rowley has tirelessly assembled the notes. At Faber, Belinda Matthews has been far more than an editor: a collaborator, constant supporter and enthusiast for the project as it was assembled against the unforgiving deadlines of a Proms season. Above all, our thanks go the many outstanding authors who have allowed their work to be reprinted in this new format.

Nicholas Kenyon
Director, BBC Proms

John Adams (b. 1947)

John Adams has been described as the composer who gave minimalism a human face, and he has developed a popular appeal beyond that of many of his contemporaries, absorbing a wide range of eclectic musical influences. Even as a Harvard undergraduate in the 1960s, Adams had embraced jazz and rock for their directness of expression. On moving to California he experimented with electronic music. In the late 1970s he produced his first important works incorporating minimalist processes – *Phrygian Gates* (1978) and the string septet *Shaker Loops* (1978, later revised for string orchestra). An association with the San Francisco Symphony (1978–85) led to large-scale orchestral works, including *Harmonium* (1980–1), with choir, setting texts by Donne and Dickinson; *Grand Pianola Music* (1982) featuring two piano soloists, and *Harmonielehre* (1984–5). His two full-scale operas, *Nixon in China* (1987) and *The Death of Klinghoffer* (1991), took scenarios from current affairs, marking an engagement with world events that continued with his rock-oriented 'songplay' *I Was Looking at the Ceiling and then I Saw the Sky* (based on the LA earthquake in 1994), and *On the Transmigration of Souls*, commissioned by the New York Philharmonic to mark the first anniversary, in 2002, of the September 11 terrorist attacks.

∾ *Harmonium* (1980–1)

1 Negative Love
2 Because I Could Not Stop for Death
3 Wild Nights

In the mid-1970s the American composer John Adams underwent what he has described as 'a diatonic conversion – like a born-again Jesus freak'. It was by no means the first of his stylistic turnabouts. Adams had been educated firmly within the Harvard tradition, studying composition there with Leon Kirchner and deriving much also from Roger Sessions's presence at the university in 1968–9. Yet those academic certainties had been undermined subsequently by an encounter with the writings of John Cage; his parents gave him a copy of *Silence* as a graduation present, and its subversive thinking – with the emphasis on the primacy of sound itself rather than its organisation – was sufficient to knock Adams off the traditional career rails of Harvard music graduates. He moved to the West Coast, worked at the San Francisco Conservatory, and identified himself with the post-Cage generation of American composers that included Robert Ashley and Alvin Lucier. To that aesthetic he added some of the techniques of early minimalism, but the attraction of consonance was already growing. There was no need to revisit the highly organised world of atonality that he had left behind in the East; instead of evoking the conventional icons of modernism he looked back to the symphonic tradition, to Wagner and Sibelius, and especially to Beethoven.

Harmonium was the first celebration of that diatonic renewal, and Adams has defined its starting point as the experience of overhearing a radio broadcast of the cantata *Calm Sea and Prosperous Voyage*, and revelling in its soft-edged celebrations of unalloyed G major. It chimed in with the first image he had had for the piece, of 'a single tone emerging out of a vast empty space and, by means of a gentle unfolding, evolving into a rich pulsating fabric of sound'. That was how *Harmonium* would eventually begin, with the repetitions of a single note and a single choral syllable, which gradually pulls in more pitches and syllables until a word and a tonality are defined.

In those early stages, however, the precise nature of the piece was still vague. Commissioned by the San Francisco Symphony Orchestra to write work for the opening of a new concert hall, Adams first contemplated a textless choral piece, using just syllables and phonemes. But the discovery of John Donne's 'Negative Love' provided the necessary literary impulse. Adams was fascinated by the poem's evasiveness:

'Every time I read it, it seemed to mean something different.' He went on to match its meditation upon the nature of love with two poems of Emily Dickinson, one of which contemplates death, while the other, 'Wild Nights', allies love and death in a single furious image. While the Dickinson offered Adams the compositional guide of a rigid formal scheme, the Donne poem by contrast was uni-directional, aimed always at its final lines.

Adams sets 'Negative Love' as a steadily building musical mass, always gaining in tempo and harmonic momentum. 'The poem really is about the humility of love, and my response was to see it as a kind of vector, an arrow pointing heavenward.' By radically slowing down the rate of harmonic change in his music, Adams had discovered, modulations could take on a far more significant, almost numinous role; each new key opened new expressive territory that was quite independent of melody. So the treatment of the two verses, separated by an instrumental interlude, is targeted towards the last two lines; when they are reached, the circle is completed, and the music can return to the opening mood and tempo. 'To date,' says Adams, 'I still consider "Negative Love" one of the most satisfying architectural experiments in all my work.'

Dickinson's 'Because I Could Not Stop for Death' offers maximum contrast: the modulations are sudden rather than gradual, the musical images distinct and sharply characterised rather than steadily evolving. Again, though, key changes provide the expressive weight, mirroring what Adams calls 'the cinematographic unfolding of imagery' as the poet imagines herself taken up by Death for a journey over her past life.

'Wild Nights' begins with a massive crescendo, and is driven along by rapidly repeated arpeggios; but it has to end in tranquillity: Dickinson's Eden was the sea, observes Adams, 'the universal archetype of the Unconscious, an immense nocturnal ocean of feeling where the slow, creaking funereal carriage of the first poem now yields to the gentle, unimpeded "rowing" of the final image'.

© Andrew Clements

Gregorio Allegri (1582–1652)

Allegri was born in Rome, where he trained as a chorister before singing as a tenor at the church of S. Luigi dei Francesi. He received lessons in counterpoint from a pupil of Palestrina, and from 1607 to 1621 joined the cathedral at Fermo as a singer, composer and beneficiary priest. Between 1618 and 1621 he published two sets each of concertos and motets, some of which came to the attention of Pope Urban VIII, leading ultimately to his appointment in 1629 to the papal choir at the Sistine Chapel. He remained in this post until his death, writing a number of works fashioned with the Sistine Chapel's acoustics in mind – among them four masses, two settings of the Lamentations of Jeremiah, and the popular *Miserere* on which his current reputation largely rests. A devout Christian, he was described by the early nineteenth-century scholar Karl Proske as 'a model of priestly piety and humility, a father to the poor . . . rescuer of suffering humanity'.

∾ *Miserere* (*c.*1638)

Of all the symbolic acts associated with the Holy Week liturgy, one of the most powerful is the snuffing-out of fifteen candles during the Office of Tenebrae, the nocturnal service observed on Maundy Thursday, Good Friday and Holy Saturday. *Tenebrae* is the Latin word for 'darkness', and served as the perfect term for a service that began with the fading of daylight and concluded when the fifteenth candle, symbolic of the light of Christ, was carried behind the high altar and finally extinguished.

In 1831 Mendelssohn wrote to Carl Friedrich Zelter about the three Tenebrae services he had attended that year in the papal chapel in Rome.

A death-like silence prevails . . . For an hour and a half
previously a single line of chant has been heard, almost
without variation; and now the *Miserere* commences, with
a chord softly breathed out by the voices, causing everyone to feel in his heart the Power of Music. The best
voices are reserved for the *Miserere*, which is sung with
the greatest variety of effect, the voices swelling, dying
away, and rising from the softest piano to the full strength
of the choir. No wonder it excites deep emotion in every
listener . . .

The plainsong Tenebrae services were punctuated by
polyphony (melodic writing in several simultaneous voices)
at two points: one early in the service and the other – a setting of Psalm 50, 'Miserere mei, Deus' – at its conclusion.
Allegri's *Miserere*, composed specifically for the papal choir
(most probably in 1638), became the stuff of legend thanks
to the papal composer Giuseppe Baini, a character described
by Mendelssohn as 'the craftiest priest one can imagine'.
Baini's romantic fantasies, dressed up and published in 1828
as historical biography, helped construct the myths of
Palestrina as 'the saviour of church music' and of Allegri's
Miserere as the most preciously guarded of all musical jewels,
exclusive property of the Pope and his famous chapel choir.
According to Baini, Palestrina and nine other composers
created falsobordone (or simple polyphonic) settings of the
odd-numbered verses of the Miserere Psalm from the late
sixteenth century until 'this competition to write the
Miserere ceased in our College when the setting by Allegri
appeared'. Archival evidence, however, suggests that Allegri's
work was not an immediate success, was revised in 1641 and
again (posthumously) in 1661, and only established its pro-
longed series of annual performances after 1662.

The straightforward, chant-like chordal delivery of the
Psalm text for five voice parts is punctuated in Allegri's work
by a quartet of solo voices, placed at a distance from the main
choir, their florid music adorned by a high-rising part for

soprano voice. A castrato in the papal chapel choir would almost certainly have taken the top line, adding his own *abbellimenti* (or embellishments) to the received notes of Allegri's composition. It was these *abbellimenti* that were so jealously guarded by the papal singers; yet, although apparently never written down, they were almost certainly 'fixed' by the early eighteenth century. According to another legend, it was the fourteen-year-old Mozart who first broke the Vatican's hold on Allegri's work by transcribing it from memory after hearing it sung by the Sistine Choir.

In the 1930s, the German musicologist Robert Haas (best known as one of the editors of Bruckner's symphonies) published a version of Allegri's *Miserere*. Although questionable in its scholarship, the Haas version was adopted by Sir Ivor Atkins for his English-language edition, published in 1951, and brought to a worldwide audience thanks to the 1963 recording by the Choir of King's College, Cambridge.

Andrew Stewart © BBC

Johann Sebastian Bach (1685–1750)

Born in the German town of Eisenach to a musical family, Bach was a chorister, then a violinist, before taking his first organist post at Arnstadt while still a teenager. It was in Weimar, as court organist from 1708, that Bach began to produce cantatas regularly, and wrote many of his great organ works, as well as organ transcriptions of concertos by Vivaldi. In 1717 Prince Leopold offered him the position of Kapellmeister at Cöthen, where he wrote the 'Brandenburg' Concertos, the Four Orchestral Suites and the violin concertos, and married his second wife Anna Magdalena, who bore him thirteen children. Bach's heavy duties in his final job, as Kantor of the Thomasschule in Leipzig from 1723 until his death, involved for some years the writing of a new cantata each week, as well as teaching Latin and music, choir training, and directing the music for church services. During these years he also wrote and revised the *St John* and *St Matthew Passions*, and in later years he drew his art together in such major works as the Mass in B minor, *The Art of Fugue*, the *Musical Offering* and the *Goldberg Variations*. His densely contrapuntal idiom became unfashionable soon after his death until the early nineteenth century, when a revival of interest in his music began that has lasted to the present.

❧ *Magnificat* in D major, BWV 243 (1723; rev. *c.*1728–31)

1 Magnificat
2 Et exultavit spiritus meus
3 Quia respexit humilitatem
4 Omnes generationes
5 Quia fecit mihi magna
6 Et misericordia
7 Fecit potentiam

 8   Deposuit potentes
 9   Esurientes implevit bonis
10   Suscepit Israel
11   Sicut locutus est
12   Gloria

One can only wonder at the busy atmosphere that must have pervaded the crowded Bach household in Leipzig during the mid-1720s, as the composer's vast body of cantatas, much of it of the highest quality, was created, copied and prepared. Twice a year, however, there was some respite; cantatas were not required for Sundays in Advent or Lent, and the resulting rest period, with more time both to compose and to rehearse, offered Bach the chance to plan something more ambitious. The period leading up to Christmas 1723 was the first of these opportunities, and Bach took it gladly. On Christmas Day two new works were performed: a Sanctus for chorus and orchestra, and a rich and varied *Magnificat* in E flat major.

Despite the importance of the vernacular in Reformation liturgies, Latin still had a role to play in Lutheran worship. Part of the Latin Mass, for instance, was included in the main weekly service, the Hauptgottesdienst, at which Latin motets might also be heard. Motets were also sung at Vespers, and although here the Magnificat was sung on ordinary days in German to a short chant known as the *tonus peregrinus*, on important feast days it could be replaced by a more sophisticated Latin setting.

Bach's 1723 Christmas setting certainly came into this category. Scored for five soloists, five-part choir and an orchestra consisting of trumpets and drums, recorders, oboes, strings and continuo, it had twelve discrete numbers and an unusually high proportion of tricky choruses, making it notably more elaborate than anything he had hitherto composed for Leipzig. It also had four extra interpolated movements on texts designed to link it specifically to Christmas, but these were removed when Bach revived the work around the end of the 1720s, thus rendering it suitable for use on any occasion. Bach's revision did not stop there, however; he also transposed the work into D major, replaced the recorders with flutes, substituted oboes d'amore for oboes in two movements, and made a number of small changes to the melodic lines.

Bach divides Mary's exultant song of thanksgiving (taken from Luke's Gospel) into single verses and allocates a separate movement to each, a scheme which gives him freedom to respond to the words with unusual immediacy and variety. But the Magnificat is not a long text, and Bach – who may well have been given a fixed time-slot in the service – writes no movement longer than ninety-two bars and most shorter than fifty, a rare economy resulting in what, by his standards, is a remarkably concise work.

The first movement is a sparkling chorus whose joyous spirit, lent brilliance by trumpets, recalls the atmosphere of many of the cantatas Bach composed for festive occasions. After this come solos for the two soprano soloists: 'Et exultavit' (soprano 2) is basically a lighter, gentler continuation of the sentiment of the opening, but 'Quia respexit' (soprano 1) brings a change as a solo oboe d'amore helps to conjure a mood of quiet humility, before being interrupted by the chorus's sudden, clamorous fugal treatment of the words 'omnes generationes'. Such a literal dramatic stroke was not an innovation on Bach's part (Monteverdi had done something similar more than a century earlier), but it is certainly effective.

A pompous bass solo ('Quia fecit mihi magna') is then followed by a tender duet ('Et misericordia') for alto and tenor, ending with a nice illustrative touch as the tenor suggests the fear of God in tremulous repeated notes.

'Fecit potentiam' is another sparkling chorus, growing to a memorable climax before being followed by two more solos: 'Deposuit potentes', in which the tenor depicts in graphic terms both the fall of the mighty and the exaltation of the meek; and 'Esurientes implevit bonis' for alto, which ends with a single bass note cheekily depicting just how empty the rich have been sent away.

The work now begins to build towards its conclusion: the beautiful 'Suscepit Israel' is a still gathering-point overlaid by a haunting oboe intonation of the traditional *tonus peregrinus* chant, and the fugue 'Sicut locutus est' brings a measure of solid seriousness before a magnificent threefold 'Gloria' leads to a reprise of the opening chorus at the words 'Sicut erat in principio' ('As it was in the beginning'). Again, this last is not an original move, but it makes a fittingly jubilant end to this uplifting and most perfect of Bach's choral compositions.

© Lindsay Kemp

❧ Mass in B minor, BWV232 (assembled c.1747–9)

'The greatest musical work of art of all times and nations.' Few people today would disagree much with the view of Hans Georg Nägeli, the first publisher of Bach's B minor Mass, despite the almost two hundred years of musical history that have passed since he put it forward. To Parry this was 'the mightiest choral work ever written', while for the philosopher and organist Albert Schweitzer it was 'as enigmatic and unfathomable as the religious consciousness of its creator'. All this for a Mass compiled and adapted by a sexagenarian composer with failing health and eyesight, largely from the music composed during forty years of providing for the Lutheran liturgy; a work whose diverse origins have prompted some commentators to doubt its claim to the status of a unified whole, and others to criticise it for unevenness; and a work, above all, whose very reason for existence remains a tantalising mystery.

Tantalising, because the fact is that when Bach prepared the score of the Mass in the late 1740s, adding a Credo, Benedictus, Osanna, Agnus Dei and Dona Nobis Pacem to an already-existing Kyrie, Gloria and Sanctus, there can have been no prospect of its receiving a complete performance. True, the Lutheran liturgy did allow for the use of the Latin Mass; Luther's original purpose in advocating the use of the vernacular in church had not been to banish Latin, but simply to ensure that an alternative was available where that language was not understood. Latin settings continued, therefore, to be heard in Lutheran churches until well into the eighteenth century, though usually it was only the Kyrie–Gloria unit or the Sanctus that would receive an elaborate setting, and even then not on the same occasion.

Bach, it seems, cannot have intended his complete Mass for use in Leipzig, or indeed in any other Lutheran centre. And although Lutheran composers (Bach included) did write masses for Catholic patrons, at well over 100 minutes in length this huge piece is simply too big to be included in any service. Lutheran or Catholic, no liturgy can contain it.

Numerous other theories, variously plausible, have been put forward: that Bach compiled the Mass for (though never actually presented it to) Frederick the Great of Prussia, the recipient in 1747 of the *Musical Offering*; or that he prepared it as a presentation to the learned Corresponding Society of the Musical Sciences, for whom he had earlier composed a number of contrapuntal test-pieces. But the more one looks at it, the more the answer to the question 'Why did Bach write the B minor Mass?' appears to be that he did it purely for his own satisfaction. Or, to put it more romantically, he wrote it for posterity.

The image of the composer before Beethoven's time is often that of the resourceful pragmatist providing music to meet specific needs or circumstances. It is easy to view Bach, who during the 1720s speedily produced cycles of cantatas to cater for at least three entire Leipzig church calendars, often happily reusing material from earlier works in the process, as an especially skilful example of a composer writing primarily to order. Yet in his fifties and sixties, when his duties as Leipzig Kantor had become less demanding, he increasingly directed his activities towards the composition and organisation of cycles of works displaying great musical erudition but no discernible practical usefulness other than to demonstrate his own prowess in a particular musical field. Placed in the context of works such as *The Art of Fugue*, then, the giant, liturgically unwieldy B minor Mass begins to look more and more like a final statement of Bach's abilities as a composer of sacred vocal music, and perhaps of his Christian faith as well.

By rescuing from all periods of his career music that would otherwise have remained rooted to its original, distinctly earthbound circumstances – a monarch's nameday, or the election of a town council – Bach was leaving his musical testament; by linking it to a sacred work that could not be performed as part of a service, he was producing what has been called a 'universal Christian artwork', a Mass which – though, for all the composer knew, it might never be heard – was nevertheless public, for all and about all. It is a breadth of vision which makes the requirements of the Leipzig town council or of the Elector of Saxony look small indeed.

Yet it was to that same Elector, Friedrich August II, that, in 1733, Bach sent a copy of the Kyrie and Gloria – which were later to become the first two main sections of the B minor Mass. The Elector's court in Dresden was one of the most prestigious musical establishments in Europe, and Bach, whose relations with his Leipzig employers had recently been under strain, was hoping with this carefully prepared mass to win the honorary title of Court Composer. Many of its features – five-part choral writing, florid solo vocal lines, even the use of a solo horn in the Quoniam – appear calculated to satisfy Dresden's musical preoccupations. Yet it must be remembered that, like Bach's other settings of the Kyrie and Gloria (the four short, so-called 'Lutheran' Masses of the 1730s), it was constructed from pre-existing material – indeed, it is thought that each and every one of its movements is an adaptation of some lost original.

The Credo (or *Symbolum Nicenum*, as Bach entitled it) was almost certainly compiled at the same time as the complete Mass in the late 1740s, and some of it may even have been composed specially. The choruses 'Credo in unum Deum' and 'Confiteor unum baptisma' both show the skills in classical or *antico* polyphony – here based on Gregorian plainchant melodies – which Bach perfected after assiduous study during the late 1730s and early 1740s. And the layout of the entire section also matches the organisational rigour demonstrated by such late works as the *Musical Offering* and *The Art of Fugue*. With the Crucifixus as its focal point, the section pans out symmetrically with two further choruses, two solo numbers and two linked pairs of choruses, and it is a mark of Bach's adaptive genius that the central panel of three choruses – in which even the Crucifixus is borrowed from a cantata composed in 1714 – is perhaps the most moving and dramatic sequence of the entire Mass.

The Sanctus was originally written for performance on its own on Christmas Day 1724; for many people it is the highlight of the B minor Mass. It is tempting to suggest that this sumptuous and magisterial movement for six-part chorus is what Shaw was referring to when he wrote of 'the stupendous march of Bach's harmonies'. After such a climax, the remainder of the Mass brings something of a relaxation: the Osanna is an uncomplicatedly joyful movement for double choir which Bach adapted from the opening chorus of his 'dramma per musica' *Preise den Glücke*, taking care as he did so to preserve momentum by omitting its orchestral introduction; the Benedictus is a lyrical still point of great beauty; and the Agnus Dei (borrowed from the *Ascension Oratorio* of 1735) evokes the sacrificial lamb with warmth and nobility. The Mass is then brought to its dignified but inexorable close with a reprise for Dona Nobis Pacem of the music of the Gratias.

This concept of a prototype super-denominational mass is an attractive one, especially for those who long for the best Baroque music to be understood as being about life, death, love, pain, faith, the individual – all the things most great music is about. To learn of Bach's extensive reuse of earlier music in the B minor Mass might dent that ideal for some, but that is to ignore the degree to which the art of recycling extant music formed part of the technical armoury of the Baroque composer. For Bach, at least, it certainly was an art, a procedure which appears to have been not so much an expedient as an aim in itself, perhaps even a system of self-reference every bit as consciously applied as that of a Shostakovich or a Strauss. For those for whom a masterpiece must be sanctified by originality, the extensive recycling found in the B minor Mass is no doubt problematic, especially given the work's spiritual flavour. But for those who relish the skill, care and discernment with which Bach selected and reworked his material to produce both a personal manifesto of his faith and a compendium of his choral–orchestral art, the piece is a never-ending source of wonder.

© Lindsay Kemp

∾ *St John Passion*, BWV 245 (1724; rev. 1725, 1732, 1749)

Today, it is hard to imagine either of Bach's two great surviving Passions – the *St Matthew* and the *St John* – ever being mistaken for an opera. For many people, believers and agnostics alike, attending a Passion performance is a vital and meaningful part of Holy Week, an act often invested with something of the sombre reverence of a religious celebration. And sure enough, Bach composed his Passions to be performed in church on Good Friday, one of the most important days in the Church calendar, when, instead of enjoying a relaxing interval drink between the work's two parts, listeners would have endured a gruelling sermon.

Yet, in composing Passions of this particular type, Bach was slotting into a tradition of increasingly dramatised musical settings of the Gospel texts relating the events leading to Christ's crucifixion – a tradition that went back to early Christian times, but had gained particular strength in northern Germany during the previous century. The evolution from the first chanted Passions to elaborate compositions involving solo singers with named roles, choirs and orchestras certainly shows a strong trend towards the theatrical, as the theologian Christian Gerber recognised when he complained in 1732 that 'if some of those first Christians should rise, visit our assemblies, and hear such a roaring organ together with so many instruments, I do not believe that they would recognise us as Christians and their successors'. Gerber had also written of an unidentified Passion performance at which 'all the people were thrown into the greatest bewilderment . . . An elderly widow of the nobility exclaimed: "God save us, my children! It's just as if we were at a comic opera."'

Nevertheless, for all that the *St John Passion* is a strikingly dramatic work – for instance, in its vivid depiction of Christ's trial in Part Two – and while the presence in it of urgent recitatives interlaced with arias and choruses to words adapted from those which the poet Barthold Heinrich Brockes and others had already furnished for even more openly operatic Passions by Keiser, Telemann and Handel is presumably just the sort of thing to which Gerber objected, it seems unlikely that in composing music for his first Good Friday service in Leipzig's St Nicholas's Church in April 1724, Bach was actually setting out to be theatrical. After all, at the time of his appointment the previous May to the job of Kantor of St Thomas's School – a post which carried with it responsibility for organising the music at all Leipzig's four main churches – Bach's new employers, the town council, had specifically stipulated that he should 'so arrange the music that it shall not last too long, and shall be of such a nature as not to make an operatic impression, but rather to incite the listener to devotion'.

In fact, the *St John Passion* is more complicated than that. Bach's achievement was to devise a work which is more than two hours long, with a detailed and complex yet utterly coherent construction, which tells its well-known story in four parallel and mutually supportive strands. At its core is the narrative, the text of the Gospel itself, sung in recitative by a tenor representing the Evangelist, with Christ's words sung by a bass; in addition, the smaller roles of certain other characters (Peter, Pilate, the Maid and the Servant) are taken by solo voices, while the utterances and exclamations of the crowd are voiced, succinctly but sometimes with almost hysterical intensity, by the chorus.

As a foil to this narrative element, there are the episodes provided by the eight arias, in which the action stops and a relevant emotion or reaction is explored; these are where the most reflective moments in the Passion are to be found, enhanced and coloured by accompanying solo instruments, including two violas d'amore in the bass arioso 'Betrachte, meine Seel', and a viola da gamba (associated in Bach's time with mortality) in the superb alto aria which announces Christ's death, 'Es ist vollbracht!'.

The third strand is the meditative and communal element represented by the chorales. These would have been extremely familiar to Bach's contemporaries, and while their role as points of entry was probably not literal in the sense of the congregation actually joining in, they would certainly have provided listeners with moments of recognition and identification.

Finally, there are the great choruses that frame the work like massive structural pillars: the first, the very opening movement, is a harrowing depiction of Christ's agony and humiliation, but one which, at the same time, reminds us that within this is contained his ultimate glory; the second, 'Ruht wohl', almost at the very end, is a moving and consoling farewell to God's earthly incarnation.

Given Bach's fondness of order and formal logic, it would be reasonable to assume that a number of elaborate organisational conceits were set into play within the *St John Passion*, Bach's largest single work at the time of composition. Attention has been drawn by some scholars to the groupings of numbers around certain moments key to the particular message of John's Gospel, such as the chorale 'Durch dein Gefängnis' (telling how we receive freedom by Christ's captivity), about which a symmetrical pattern of choruses, chorales and recitatives pans out symmetrically. A similar scheme, this time involving a pair of strophes from a

Passiontide chorale, surrounds 'Es ist vollbracht!' (the second of them appearing embedded in the bass aria 'Mein teurer Heiland'). Bach's key scheme for the work, both symbolic and dramatic, has likewise been remarked upon. More immediately effective on the listener, perhaps, is his telling use of internal cross-reference: the crowd choruses of the trial scene gain in intensity through the sensation of repetition, and one, 'Sei gegrüßet, lieber Judenkönig!' ('Hail, King of the Jews!'), surely makes mocking reference to the melodic line of the earlier soprano aria 'Ich folge dir gleichfalls', which had declared unswerving allegiance to Jesus.

The *St John Passion* was long seen as a poor relation to the larger, later and better-known *St Matthew*. Recently, however, its popularity has grown, a testament to an increasing realisation among both performers and listeners that this is a work with its own character and ambitions. Bach himself certainly liked it enough to perform it again on a number of occasions, the last as late as 1749. Maybe it does not reach quite so far into the listener's soul as the more contemplative *St Matthew* but, as a gripping depiction of the emotionally charged events of Holy Week, it ultimately appeals with greater directness to our human emotions and sympathies.

Lindsay Kemp © BBC

❦ *St Matthew Passion*, BWV 244 (1727)

In 1879 the English composer Ethel Smyth attended a performance of the *St Matthew Passion*, given in Bach's own church of St Thomas's, Leipzig. She later recalled the impression it made on her:

> I despair of giving an idea of the devoutness of the audience . . . It was not only that the church seemed flooded with the living presence of Bach, but you felt as if the Passion itself, in that heart-rending, consoling portrayal, was being lived through as at no other moment of their lives by every soul in the vast congregation.

Smyth's reaction is one we can recognise without much difficulty today. The *St Matthew Passion* is still performed more often than not during Holy Week, and such occasions continue to be invested with something of the sombre reverence of a religious celebration. Despite the fact that it rarely any longer forms part of an actual service, the work is for many a vital and meaningful component of the Easter experience.

This continuing impact is in spite of the fact that Bach's great masterpiece is more widely known today than ever before. In the composer's own time it would not have been known outside Leipzig, the town in which he lived and worked for the last twenty-seven years of his life, and even there it received no more than a handful of performances under his direction. After his death it lapsed into obscurity, at a time when, if Bach was remembered at all, it was as a famous organist and master fuguist, not as one who could stir the emotions or inspire religious feeling. Only when Mendelssohn rediscovered it and performed it in Berlin in 1829, to general acclaim and wonder, did it begin to enter into wider consciousness. Yet even today, when time and dissemination through recordings have made it familiar to a greater number of people, the *St Matthew Passion* is a work that can affect its listeners profoundly in live performance, as if it and the story it tells were being heard for the first time. 'It is not given only to believers to be moved by it,' wrote the Bach scholar Malcolm Boyd of the work, and while it is true that the same might be said of the emotional tenor of Holy Week itself, there is no denying that there is a monumental and sustained power in this music that is equalled by few other works of man. Boyd goes on: 'Bach's supreme achievement is a work of profound humanity, and the most monumental dramatic masterpiece before Wagner's *Ring*.' One could add that it is a piece in which audiences may still feel – as, one senses, did Ethel Smyth – to be in the presence of a musical deity: Bach himself.

When Bach became Leipzig's Kantor in 1723, the tradition of performing sophisticated Passion settings of the sort represented by the *St Matthew* as part of Good Friday Vespers was just two years old in the town. Previously, a much older species of purely biblical Passion had persisted there, in which the words of the Evangelist and individuals in the story were delivered in plainchant, and those of the crowd by a chorus singing in simple chordal style. In this matter Leipzig lagged well behind the more cosmopolitan cities of North Germany, where the modern oratorio-type Passion, with instruments accompanying an assortment of recitatives and arias setting lyrical, non-Gospel texts, had been current since the end of the previous century. By 1721, however, progressive members of Leipzig's Town Council were looking to update the town's church music, and Johann Kuhnau, the ageing and conservative Kantor, had been persuaded to produce a concerted Passion that went some way at least towards the newer, more operatic style. Kuhnau's death the following year gave the Council the opportunity to install a more genuinely forward-looking Kantor, and after Bach's appointment the performance on Good Friday of a large-scale oratorio Passion with instruments became established Leipzig practice. The performances alternated between the town's two main churches, St Thomas's and St Nicholas's, and Bach's first Passion, the *St John*, was heard in St Nicholas's in April 1724. His second, the *St Matthew*, probably received its first performance in April 1727 in St Thomas's.

The Council can hardly have anticipated what Bach gave them, however. The *St Matthew Passion* is a piece conceived on a scale without precedent, longer than any previous work of its kind, and written for larger forces – two choruses, two orchestras, and an extra group of sopranos (or boy trebles) for the opening chorus – than almost any other of its composer's works.

The work's construction, too, is detailed and complex, presenting the story, as does Bach's *St John Passion*, in four parallel strands. At its core is the narrative material, the text of the Gospel itself sung in recitative by a tenor representing the Evangelist, with Christ's words sung by a bass, also in recitative but this time accompanied by a portentous 'halo' of string chords; in addition, the smaller roles of certain other characters (Judas and Pilate, for instance) are taken by solo voices, while the utterances and exclamations of the crowd are voiced, succinctly but tellingly, by the chorus. As a foil to this narrative element, there are the reflective episodes provided by the numerous arias (and one duet) in which the action stops, as in Baroque opera, and a relevant emotion or reaction is explored; all of these have texts furnished by Bach's contemporary, Christian Friedrich Henrici (known as Picander). The third strand is the meditative and communal element represented by the chorales; these German hymns would have been extremely familiar to Bach's contemporaries, and while their role as 'entry points' may or may not have been literal in the sense of the congregation actually joining in, they would certainly have provided them with moments of recognition and identification. Finally there are the momentous choruses that frame the work, acting as massive structural pillars and bearing mass witness to the events as they unfold before us.

Perhaps the most striking thing to emerge from all this – not least because it is not something we are used to associating with Bach – is the dramatic force of the work. The old description of the *St Matthew Passion* as 'the best opera Bach never wrote' may be glib, but there is no denying that the composer here demonstrates a musico-dramatic skill that one could wish he had had more opportunities to apply elsewhere. It runs deeper, furthermore, than such obviously theatrical moments as the rending of the temple veil or the crowd scenes. The sequence from Christ's prayers on the Mount of Olives through to the end of Part One, for example, is superbly handled. Jesus's announcement to the sleeping disciples that the hour of his betrayal is at hand accelerates the drama and propels it forcefully into the next scene, where a soprano–alto duet ('So ist mein Jesus nun gefangen') seems to watch Christ's arrest in horror-struck slow motion before exploding into the turbulent chorus 'Sind Blitze, sind Donner in Wolken verschwunden?'. The scene ends powerfully with the Evangelist starkly relating how the disciples forsook Jesus and fled.

It is true that the constraints of the Gospel text elsewhere pose problems of momentum – surely no opera libretto would ever bother with the fleeting contribution of Pilate's wife, for instance – but such oddities must be viewed in the context of Bach's overall dramatic pacing of the work, in which the reflective movements play just as vital a part as the recitatives. Peter's denial is moving enough as it is related by the Evangelist, with his deeply expressive melisma on the word 'weinete' ('wept'); but how much more heart-rending the whole scene becomes when we hear the alto aria that immediately follows. And who could deny the dramatic impact of the soprano's interruption of the trial scene, answering Pilate's enquiry 'What evil has he done?' with the mock-ingenuous 'He has done good to us all'?

In the end, perhaps the finest and most meaningful achievement of the *St Matthew Passion* is exactly this way in which Bach blurs the distinction between the work's several layers, between the lyrical and the dramatic. The great opening chorus has, in addition to its architectural role, a dramatic element in the form of a dialogue between the two choirs, with the first urging the faithful to witness Christ's troubles, the second answering with cries of 'Whom?', 'How?', 'Where?'. It thus becomes a huge tableau, in which the early twentieth-century Bach scholar C. S. Terry saw 'a band of Roman soldiers; in their midst the Man of Sorrows staggering under the Cross's burden: a sad procession moving forward slowly: Zion and her daughters in the distance awaiting it expectant.' And in what is perhaps the key moment of the entire work, the words of the centurion and those around him – 'Truly this was the son of God' – are magnified by Bach's brief but fervent choral setting into a universal statement of Christian doctrine: from being simply part of the story, it becomes an expression of timeless religious faith.

It is this meeting of worlds – Bach's with that of the New Testament – that lies at the heart of the *St Matthew Passion*.

Its multiple layers of musical and dramatic argument, and the way in which the emphasis shifts constantly between them, help to support its vast span; but it also lifts the work high above the level of functional church music and turns it into one of the profoundest creations of Western art.

© Lindsay Kemp

Ludwig van Beethoven (1770–1827)

Beethoven left his native Bonn in his early twenties for Vienna, where he became established in fashionable circles as a composer, piano virtuoso and improviser of considerable ability. His first works developed the classical models of Haydn and Mozart. As early as 1796, he recognised signs of his impending deafness, and his subsequent suffering and alienation, as well as his creative resolve, were disclosed in his 'Heiligenstadt Testament' of 1802. His 'middle period' was characterised by a broadening of form and an extension of harmonic language which reflects his proto-Romantic expressive tendencies; this period produced the Symphonies Nos 2 to 8, notable piano sonatas, several string quartets and his only opera, *Fidelio*. From 1812 to 1818 he produced little music, but his later years saw the mould-breaking 'Choral' Symphony and the *Missa solemnis*, as well as an exploration of increasing profundity in the more intimate genres of the string quartet and piano sonata.

∾ Mass in D, *Missa solemnis*, Op. 123 (1819–23)

1 Kyrie
2 Gloria
3 Credo
4 Sanctus
5 Agnus Dei

For Beethoven, the composition of the *Missa solemnis* was the supreme challenge of his life. The occasion for which it was intended may have been the enthronement of his friend and patron Archduke Rudolf as Archbishop of Olmütz in March 1820; but from the first Beethoven saw it as something far transcending earthly ceremonial. It would be a summing-up of Western liturgical music, the last word on ancient, ever-present concerns central to the human spirit, and at the same time an expression of his own beliefs and feelings, his personal reaction to God the maker of all things visible and invisible.

In the event the Mass was nowhere near ready for the service of installation, and was not completed until more than two years later. Other preoccupations intervened, and other compositions, including the three final piano sonatas Opp. 109, 110 and 111, and the *Diabelli Variations*. More than that, the Mass itself demanded time: time to study the works of his predecessors – not only the Viennese Masses of Haydn and others but also Bach and Handel and, beyond them, Palestrina – and to solve the special problems it posed, problems not answerable to a deadline.

Chief among them was the sheer variety of ideas and emotions contained in the Mass, particularly in the Gloria and the Credo. Earlier composers might have been content to glide over them in the interests of musical continuity; Beethoven was not. But, given his determination to make the music faithfully reflect every shade of meaning, the task he set himself was formidable: how to discipline the abundance of musical imagery generated by his passionate response to the text of the Mass and shape it into coherent musical form. He must do full justice to its fundamental truths – the juxtaposition of the awesome grandeur of God and the littleness of deluded, erring humanity, the mystery of the Incarnation, following straight on from the celebration of 'the Father by whom all things were made', the miracle of the elevation of the Host and the descent of the godhead, succeeding the Hosanna's hymn of praise, and the final prayer for peace – yet not be overwhelmed by the intensity of emotion they aroused in him. His mission was to write a work which fulfilled the promise of the words that he inscribed on the first page of the score – 'From the heart: may it go to the heart' – while remaining true to his lifelong principles of order and unity.

It was perhaps inevitable that the result should have seemed to many, for a long time, eccentric, quirky, alarmingly and wilfully unorthodox, and altogether too extreme for comfort. Beethoven could have retorted that comfort was not what he was concerned with, and that the Mass, of all subjects, demanded extreme measures. Certainly, the music's continual shifts in dynamics and mood and its unremitting intensity of expression made, and still make, merciless claims on the stamina, technique and musical understanding of its performers. Beethoven's answer to that would have been the one he gave when his violinist friend Ignaz Schuppanzigh complained of the difficulty of the late quartets: 'Do you suppose I consider your wretched fiddle when God speaks to me?' And God speaks to him more directly in the *Missa solemnis* than in any other of his works.

Its unorthodoxy, however, is largely the invention of critics. The musical gestures of the work are rooted in tradition (sometimes in a tradition by then forgotten: some of the most inspired strokes look back to the pre-Baroque). Right from the outset, in the dotted rhythm derived from the word 'Kyrie' that dominates the opening movement, Beethoven declares his allegiance to immemorial practice. The uprushing scales at the beginning of the Gloria translate the prescribed gestures of the liturgy quite literally: the priest raising his arms in jubilation, then lowering his head at 'adoramus te' (duly reflected in an abrupt, awed pianissimo). What musical idea could render 'Et incarnatus est' with less quirkiness than the remote, austere sound of the Dorian mode (prompted by a sixteenth-century treatise consulted by Beethoven in the library of Archduke Rudolf)? What could be more apt than the incomplete chord on which the Crucifixus comes to its brief, hushed rest, before the shout of 'Et resurrexit'? In both these cases the momentous news is announced by the tenors – another bow to the past.

What Beethoven does with it is another matter. His 'Kyrie' has the choir starting half a bar early, on the weak beat – so that the trumpets and drums, entering on the strong beat, give the prayer added force – and then the soloists emerging dramatically from the body of choral sound like a religious equivalent of the solo woodwind phrases at the beginning of the Seventh Symphony. The Gloria's scales are the 'rushing mighty wind' of Pentecost. Again, earlier composers may have emphasised the 'et' that occurs so often in the Creed, but Beethoven the dramatist uses it in such a way as to evoke a stammering, incredulous wonder. In his hands the conventional rising scales at 'Et ascendit in coelum' ('and ascended into heaven') bring before us the very joy of the disciples running like mad things to share the news with the whole world.

If the often frowned-upon noises of warfare in the 'Dona nobis pacem' are not new – Haydn's 'Mass in Time of War' provided only the most recent precedent – Beethoven gives them a fierce immediacy unequalled before. We see the swirl of dust of the advancing column, before the martial fanfares sound, and later the terrifying 'club-footed march' (in Joseph Kerman's phrase). Yet these images, far from intruding, bring finally into the open a persistent feature of the score. The pulsation of trumpets and drums is prominent from the first page of the Kyrie, and recurs throughout, even in the quietest, most devotional passages. The whole work, in a sense, is a 'mass in time of war'.

How otherwise? Beethoven's Mass could not conceivably satisfy those who liked their religious music to be consoling. There was no consolation to give. The human race made it impossible. His final movement could only be, as the composer wrote in the score, 'a prayer for inner and external peace' – for an end not merely to the warfare that had been part of so much of the life of his time but to the whole senseless ferocity of the human race. The frenzied orchestral fugue to which, with a sudden shift of perspective, the choir's exultant repeated 'pacem' gives way suggests the human ant-heap seen from the viewpoint of God. It leads inexorably to the second irruption of war and the desperate cry, 'Lamb of God, grant us peace'.

The urgency of that cry is a central reality of the *Missa solemnis*. It rises up behind the noble breadth of the Kyrie, and we hear it from then onwards. Hence the length of the

'Qui tollis', a slow movement in the midst of the generally fast-moving Gloria, and the pleading, impassioned character of its musical expression. Beethoven can offer no more than gleams of hope, visions. Visions of heaven opening, in the coda of the Credo; visions of blessing, in the serenity of the Benedictus, with its celestial violin solo, spinning ceaselessly, and its beautiful choral unisons; visions of pastoral tranquillity, in the memorable passage for staccato strings and woodwind, ascending and descending, in the penultimate page of the work. But he is too truthful to crown his Mass with a grandly decisive conclusion. The distant drum-taps of war continue to punctuate the whispered 'pacem' almost to the end. When they have faded and the last 'Dona nobis pacem' ('Grant us peace') has sounded, Beethoven allows himself just a couple of chords to round off all the grandeurs and sublimities that have gone before.

© David Cairns

Luciano Berio (1925–2003)

Berio was one of the twentieth century's great modernists, who radically developed the fields of music theatre and electronic music. He was born in the Ligurian town of Oneglia and attended the Milan Conservatory before encountering avant-garde experimentalism. He directed the Italian Radio (RAI) electronic music studio in Milan, early fruits of which included *Thema (Omaggio a Joyce)* (1958) and *Différences* (1958–9), an early fusion of live players and electronic music. He wrote a number of innovative vocal works for his first wife, soprano Cathy Berberian, most calling for 'extended' vocal techniques (as in *Sequenza* III, 1966). From 1962 to 1971 he taught in the US and later moved to Paris to direct electroacoustic music at IRCAM, Boulez's computer-music research centre. Between 1977 and 1984 he collaborated with Italo Calvino on his two major operas, *La vera storia* and *Un re in ascolto*. His inventive series of instrumental *Sequenzas*, begun in 1958 with *Sequenza* I for flute, ended in 2001 with a fourteenth sequenza, for cello. His alternative ending to Act III of Puccini's *Turandot* was given its staged premiere in 2002. He died in 2003.

◆ *Coro* (1975–6)

Coro was written for Cologne's Westdeutscher Rundfunk during 1975–6, and somewhat extended in the subsequent year. It is a setting, for a 'chorus' of forty voices and forty melodic instruments, plus piano, electronic organ and two percussionists, of a series of folk texts interleaved with fragments from Pablo Neruda's trilogy *Residencia en la tierra* (1933–47). Each vocalist is associated with an instrumentalist, and the two are placed side by side so as to create a fully integrated *tutti*, used for setting almost all of the Neruda fragments. This can then be broken down into chorus plus orchestra, a great variety of chamber ensembles, or duets from individual vocal– instrumental couples. Berio has so positioned his eighty-four performers that he can create an interplay between differing ensembles all over the stage – thus revitalising the experiments with acoustic space that he had initiated in such major works of the late 1950s as *Allelujah II* or *Tempi concertati*.

The folk texts come from a wide variety of sources. Those from North and South America, Polynesia and Africa are sung in a simple, literal English translation, but later sections of the work introduce Croatian texts sung in French, Persian texts sung in German, and Italian dialect texts and a fragment from the Hebrew Song of Songs both sung in their original languages. Their common themes of love, death and work are placed in a more disquieting perspective by the Neruda fragments. These summarise one of the most significant developments within Neruda's work, for they juxtapose the intensely subjective imagery of the 1933 *Residencia en la tierra* – here represented by fragments from 'Débil del alba' and 'Colección nocturna', each beginning with the words 'El día', and respectively evoking dawn and dusk – and the emergent political commitment of the 1947 *Tercera residencia*. This latter collection is represented by the final lines of 'Explico algunas cosas', a fierce denunciation of right-wing atrocities in the Spanish Civil War. But Berio sets aside the explicit accusation of Neruda's original:

> Treacherous
> generals:
> see my dead house,
> look at broken Spain:

in order to write his own 'canto general' against the destruction wrought on innocent lives. Thus the thrice-repeated final line of Neruda's poem:

> *Venid a ver la sangre por las calles*
> (Come and see the blood in the streets)

is reiterated obsessively by the *tutti* throughout the first half of *Coro*. Only at the end of the work do we discover that this phrase is the answer to a question:

> *Preguntaréis por qué esta poesía*
> *no nos habla del sueño, de las hojas,*
> *de los grandes volcanes del país natal?*
> (You will ask why this poem
> does not speak to us of dreams, of leaves,
> of the great volcanoes of [the poet's] native land)

Despite the rich variety of folk texts interleaved between the Neruda fragments, Berio does not employ any original musical folk material apart from one Croatian melody. In this, therefore, *Coro* differs from such earlier folk-based works as *Folk Songs* (1964), *Questo vuol dire che* (1970), *Per la dolce memoria di quel giorno* (1974), and *Voci* (1984). Instead he uses a variety of techniques derived from folk sources but reinterpreted in terms of his own musical language. One specific and striking example of this process of adaptation is Berio's reworking of the 'hocketing' demonstrated by the Israeli ethnomusicologist Simha Arom as the fundamental technique of the wooden trumpet bands of the Central African Republic. Within these bands each instrument plays a single note in a complex rhythmic pattern – the result suggesting to Western listeners a jubilant anarchy devoid of any audible metric basis, although in fact it depends upon a highly organised set of rhythmic counterpoints proliferating from an unsounded 'central' line. Berio transfers this process to the orchestral brass, but rationalises it in relation to a clearly audible semiquaver pulse, thus creating a distinctive texture that first appears in section IX, and returns in XI, XVI, XXV and XXVI. (Although this hocket technique first appears in conjunction with an African folk text, no sustained attempt is made to match texts of a given geographical provenance with musical techniques from the same area.)

The sheer variety of resources, punctuated by the vast block chords characteristic of many of the Neruda sections, gives the work a mosaic-like surface. But beneath it Berio is careful to coordinate a satisfying large-scale framework. The first eight sections, in which individual voices predominate, culminate in the first extended setting of Neruda. (It is also the first to combine a fragment from the 1933 collection with the ubiquitous 'venid a ver . . .') In the next eight sections (IX–XVI) the voices are generally treated as an ensemble (despite XIII and XV for solo voices), and the orchestra, having established its hocket technique in IX, develops it extensively in XI. Hocket also marks the end of the group, and the singers underline the halfway point by taking up the words of the opening section.

Although this synthesis rounds off the first half of the work, Berio is careful to avoid an exaggerated climax that would underline the work's symmetries too forcefully. Even so, the second half mirrors the overall structure of the first: eight sections (XVII–XXIV) alternating solo voices with *tutti*, and finally seven sections (XXV–XXXI) where massed resources predominate, but where two solo sections intervene. The first group is mainly concerned with love poetry, and introduces new languages – French, and later German and Italian. Indeed, the final section of this group, XXIV, combines texts in different languages for the first time. The final group continues the multilingual mix but emphasises its parallels with the second group by immediately restoring the hocket technique (XXV), and then gradually transforming it into something less ebullient and more disquieting. It thus helps to establish the 'alrededor de llanto' (environment of lament) that permeates the final sections of *Coro*.

But despite the shadow that descends over the work at the end, Berio intended *Coro* as a celebration – a musical equivalent to the Festival dell'Unità with which Italy, every year, explores the diversity and richness of cultures around the world. The lines from Neruda's *Colección nocturna* from which Berio selected a fragment for *Coro* would serve as a fitting epigraph to the work:

There is something from every living being in the atmosphere: close inspection of the air would disclose beggars, lawyers, bandits, postmen, seamstresses, and a little of each occupation, a humbled remnant wants to perform its own work within us.

David Osmond-Smith © BBC

Hector Berlioz (1803–69)

One of the most imaginative and individual composers of the nineteenth century, Berlioz inherited a French love of instrumental colour and put it at the service of his vivid imagination. Indeed Berlioz encapsulated the essence of the Romantic artist: headstrong, with a turbulent emotional life, he was strongly drawn to literature; his music was inspired by Shakespeare (*Romeo and Juliet*, *Beatrice and Benedict*, as well as his overture *King Lear*), Goethe (*The Damnation of Faust*), and Byron (*Harold in Italy*). His epic opera *The Trojans*, based on Virgil's *Aeneid*, represents the pinnacle of the French grand opera tradition. He was one of the leading conductors of his day and published much vivid musical criticism. Among his writings is a famous and influential treatise on orchestration.

∾ *The Childhood of Christ*, sacred trilogy, Op. 25 (1850–1854)

1 Herod's Dream
2 The Flight into Egypt
3 The Arrival at Saïs

Alone among Berlioz's major works, *The Childhood of Christ* came into being not in response to a clear and fully formulated plan, but gradually and haphazardly, over a period of several years. One evening in 1850, at a party, while the other guests were playing cards, Berlioz's friend, the architect Joseph-Louis Duc asked him to write something for his album. Berlioz complied:

> I take a scrap of paper and draw a few staves, on which in a little while an Andantino in four parts for organ makes its appearance. I am struck by a certain character of naive, rustic devoutness in it and promptly decide to add some

words in the same vein. The organ piece disappears and turns into a chorus of the shepherds of Bethlehem saying goodbye to the child Jesus at the moment when the Holy Family set out on their journey to Egypt.

The card-players, who interrupt their whist to listen to it, are amused by the archaic flavour of both words and music, and Berlioz includes the piece at his next concert, passing it off as the work of a forgotten seventeenth-century Master of the Sainte-Chapelle, whom he christens Ducré as a gesture to his friend Duc. In the meantime the 'Shepherds' Farewell' has been joined by two other movements, also conceived (in the composer's words) 'in the manner of the old illuminated missals': an overture on a modal theme and a piece for solo tenor describing the Holy Family resting at an oasis.

The resulting work, 'The Flight into Egypt', later to form the central section of *The Childhood of Christ*, seems then to have been put on one side and forgotten. It was not till three years later that it was performed in full, in Leipzig. Only then, it seems, did Berlioz decide to take his 'naive, rustic' composition really seriously. A sequel, 'The Arrival at Saïs', was written early in 1854, and the 'sacred trilogy' was completed in July (at the suggestion of the British music publisher Frederick Beale) with the addition of an introductory section, 'Herod's Dream'. The whole work was performed in Paris the following December. It had taken four years to grow from its first chance seed.

One reason was Berlioz's reluctance to commit himself to large-scale composition during these years. He deliberately suppressed the urge to write a symphony, ideas for which kept coming to him. Once it was written, he would be impelled to have it performed and therefore to spend money (including a large copyist's bill) which he hadn't got. The failure of *The Damnation of Faust* and the heavy debts he had incurred because of it had had a profoundly discouraging effect on him, and he had vowed never to risk putting on a big work in Paris again. *The Childhood of Christ* could only

come into the world by stealth. When, to his surprise, it was
received enthusiastically by critics and public alike, and
actually made a profit, he was naturally delighted. The work
was hailed as a masterpiece. It seemed he had finally become
respectable. He found himself praised for the very qualities
he had always been told he lacked – charm, gentleness, economy of means, simplicity of utterance, melodiousness. Those
who, like the poet Heine, had written him down as a freak,
obsessed with the macabre and the gigantic, now hastened to
recant.

All this, though gratifying, was somewhat two-edged.
Berlioz could not help regarding the extraordinary success
of his little oratorio as 'insulting' to his other works; he
understood the irritation the painter Salvator Rosa felt when
people kept praising his smaller landscapes: 'sempre piccoli
paesi!' *The Childhood of Christ* was a 'piccolo paese' beside *The
Damnation of Faust*, which Paris had taken no interest in, or
beside the monumental *Te Deum*, composed five years earlier
and still awaiting performance.

Even more galling was the suggestion that he had changed
– that he of all people, for whom artistic integrity was the
religion of his life, had altered his style, even adapted his
approach to suit the public. 'I should have written *The
Childhood of Christ* in the same style twenty years ago . . . The
subject naturally prompted a naive and gentle kind of music';
and, in the nearest he ever got to a direct statement of his
artistic aims, he went on to emphasise his preoccupation with
'passionate expression', that is, 'expression bent on reproduc-
ing the essence of its subject, even when that subject is the
opposite of passion, and gentle, tender feelings are being
expressed, or the most profound calm'. This applied to sacred
music exactly as it applied to secular; an oratorio should be as
true to its subject, as expressive, as an opera.

Faithful to these principles, the composer of *The Childhood
of Christ* remains a dramatist. Though it is not a work for the
stage, and the delineation of character is stylised 'in the manner of the old illuminated missals', the approach is the same.

He is, as ever, concerned to express the essence of his subject and to present it as he naturally sees it, in dramatic terms. The work is conceived as a series of tableaux in which we are shown the various human elements of the story: the uneasy might of Rome, the world-weariness of Herod, the blind fanaticism of the soothsayers, the joys and griefs of Jesus's parents, the shepherds' friendliness and the busy welcome of the Ishmaelite household.

The tableaux are juxtaposed in a manner which (as with *The Damnation*) it is tempting to call cinematic. An example is the transition from Herod's rage to the peace of the Bethlehem stable. We see as though in angry close-up the fear-distorted faces of Herod and the soothsayers, like faces in a Bosch or Bruegel crucifixion. Then the nightmare fades, the picture dwindles, and the manger comes into focus. In the epilogue it is again as though the glowing family circle of the Ishmaelites were growing faint and blurring before our eyes. The moment has come for the narrator to close the book and draw the timeless moral; and the composer, having shown us the loving kindness of his good Samaritans, tracks away from the scene, causes the picture to fade by means of a series of very quiet, still unisons, surrounded by silence. The purpose of this strange passage is to separate us from the scenes we have been witnessing, to make them recede from us across the centuries and return to the ancient past from which they have been evoked. This distancing process, by removing us from the action, achieves the necessary transition to the final meditation on the meaning of the Christmas drama.

Everything is visualised. In Part Three, when the Holy Family, having trudged across the desert, reach Egypt hungry and exhausted and beg in vain for shelter, the musical imagery brings the scene before us. The plaintive viola motif, the wailing oboe and cor anglais, the fragmentary violin phrases, the agitated tremor of cellos and double basses, Mary's panting utterances, Joseph's long, swaying melody constantly returning on itself, the tap of the drums as he timidly knocks, the shouts of 'Get away, dirty Jews!' which

brusquely interrupt the prevailing 3/8 metre – all this combines to make a vivid and poignant 'expression of the subject'.
Nor is it only the sufferings of the refugees from intolerance
and persecution that arouse the composer's compassionate
understanding. He illuminates the loneliness of the tormented Herod and the forlornness of the soothsayers, whose
gloomy choruses and weird cabbalistic dance in 7/4 time
express the sense that superstition is at once sinister and
ridiculous, to be pitied.

Such music was not unfamiliar to the public that had followed Berlioz over the years. What surprised it was the
'Shepherds' Farewell' and the trio for flutes and harp, the
charm of the little overture which represents the shepherds
gathering at the manger, the purity of the narrative of the
Holy Family at the oasis, the hushed beauty of the unaccompanied chorus which concludes the work. The Berlioz of the
cartoonists was given to augmenting his army of musicians
with reinforcements from the nearest artillery depot. Yet here
he was, using a handful of instruments as though to the manner born. Part Two of the work is written for a chamber
orchestra of strings and six wind, without bassoons or horns;
Part Three requires only slightly bigger forces; and even Part
One, in which trombones appear, is sparingly scored.

Though the public was wrong in thinking that all this was
uncharacteristic of him, it was right in sensing something
special about the achievement. In composing the work,
Berlioz did not repudiate his past methods and principles;
but these would not have been enough by themselves to
carry him successfully through the hazardous task he had set
himself. The subject was full of pitfalls; it bristled with
opportunities for sentimental religiosity. Nineteenth-century
religious art is not notable for truthfulness of feeling; for all
its striving after purity, it frequently suffers from the cold
touch of artificiality, combined with a cloying sweetness. *The
Childhood of Christ*, miraculously, is free of such defects.
Maybe something of the beautiful austerity of the first inspiration was sacrificed when the scale and scope of 'The Flight

into Egypt' were enlarged so as to make a full-length oratorio. Even so, the music avoids taking the short step into
sentimentality, and in the most perilous places, like the scene
in the stable, never seems in danger of doing so. Its naivety is
a natural naivety.

The explanation lies in the make-up of Berlioz's style. The
purity the subject demanded did not have to be sought; the
archaic flavour that permeates much of the score came quite
easily to him – it was in his musical blood. One element in the
formation of his style was the folk music of his native
Dauphiné and the noëls and other popular chants he heard in
his boyhood (the first six notes of the tenor's 'Les pèlerins
étant venus' in 'The Flight into Egypt' are identical to those
of the ancient liturgical chant 'O filii, o filiae'). Another influence was the composer Jean-François Le Sueur, his teacher,
whose biblical oratorios had once had a great appeal for him,
and whose interest in modal music – most uncommon in that
period – was passed on to his pupil. Berlioz often resorted to
modality for particular expressive effect; so that when the
subject suggested a more systematic use of modal inflections,
he could meet the need without falling into pastiche. It was
an extension of his natural style. By the time 'The Flight into
Egypt' was composed, the development of music had left
such things so far behind that Berlioz felt it prudent to guard
against possible misinterpretation by printing an asterisk
alongside the theme of his overture, with a warning that the
seventh of the scale was to be read as a natural, not as the
usual sharp. The piece is certainly untypical of its time. But it
is pure Berlioz, as are the long, chaste melodic lines and sweet
serenity of the narrator's account of the Holy Family resting
in the shade of some palm trees, while the child sleeps surrounded by kneeling angels.

How are we to account for the sharpness of vision and the
unclouded truthfulness of feeling that made the music of this
scene as fresh as the spring water gushing up from the desert?
Beyond the possession of a musical style able to encompass
such simple sublimities lay something else: the memory of

childhood beliefs. They had once been central to his life. As a boy, his first musical experiences had come to him in the context of the Church. By the time he wrote *The Childhood of Christ* he had long ceased to be a Christian in any conventional or even unconventional sense. But the past, increasingly, dominated him. It was a time of looking back, of returning to the sources of his artistic being. The intensity of recollected feeling was such that in composing the work he could momentarily re-enter a world in which the personages and events of the Christmas story, as they first stamped themselves on a sensitive and precocious child, were once again vibrantly alive. The pang of regret gives a sharpness, a touch of melancholy to his retelling of it. No sentimental recovery of belief is involved. It is an act of piety in the Roman sense. His mind remains sceptical. But his imagination believes. He remembers what it was like to have faith. And at the end, having re-enacted the age-old myth, and stepped out of the magic circle again, he can only pay tribute to the power of the Christian message and, agnostic as he is, bow before the mystery of Christ's birth and death.

Part One: Herod's Dream
The narrator sets the scene: Palestine shortly after Christ's birth, and the hopes and fears already in the air. A Roman detachment patrols the empty streets of Jerusalem. Their march is briefly interrupted as two soldiers discuss the strange terrors of King Herod. Alone, unable to sleep, Herod reflects on the solitariness of his life and on the dream that haunts him, of a child who will overthrow his power. He consults his soothsayers and learns that his throne will be preserved only if all the children lately born in his kingdom are put to death. He gives orders for the massacre of the innocents. The scene moves to the stable in Bethlehem and Mary and Joseph worshipping the child. In a vision they are warned by angels of the danger to Jesus, and are told to leave at once and travel across the desert to Egypt.

Part Two: The Flight into Egypt
Shepherds gather at the stable. They say goodbye to the Holy
Family. The narrator describes Mary, Joseph, the baby and
the donkey resting at an oasis, watched over by angels.

Part Three: The Arrival at Saïs
The narrator tells how, after great hardships, the travellers
reach the city of Saïs. They knock at many doors but are driven
away. At last, half fainting from hunger, they are hospitably
received by an Ishmaelite. Like Joseph he is a carpenter, and he
invites them to stay and live with him and his family. The
grateful pilgrims take their rest, entertained with music by the
children, and then retire to bed. In an epilogue the narrator
tells of their long sojourn in Egypt, their return to Palestine,
and the child's fulfilment of his redeeming mission. Narrator
and chorus pray that mankind's pride may be abased before
such a mystery and its heart filled with Christ's love.

© David Cairns

∾ *The Damnation of Faust*, dramatic legend, Op. 24 (1845–6)

'Shakespeare and Goethe: the silent confidants of my torments; they hold the key to my life.' So wrote Berlioz to one
of his closest friends in 1828, the year in which these twin literary passions most ardently consumed him. And although
Shakespeare was to penetrate the more deeply into his soul,
Berlioz recognised at once in Goethe a spiritual brother, a
poet who articulated the still half-formed yearnings of his
twenty-four years. Goethe couched in words precisely those
feelings that Berlioz strove so passionately to capture in
music. Few artists of his generation escaped the spell. *The
Damnation of Faust* is one of the finest and probably the most
personal of the countless Faust settings that the nineteenth
century produced.

It was in Gérard de Nerval's translation of *Faust* that Berlioz
first encountered Goethe, probably in the spring of 1828.

'This translation,' he wrote, 'made a strange and deep impression upon me. The marvellous book fascinated me from the first. I could not put it down. I read it incessantly, at meals, in the theatre, in the street.' Nerval's translation was in prose, with certain scenes, ballads, hymns and songs in verse: it was these that Berlioz set, beginning with the Ballad of the King of Thule, sketched in a carriage in September 1828, with modal inflections to match what he called his 'Gothic' song. Almost involuntarily seven more settings followed, and the composer yielded to the temptation to have these *Eight Scenes from Faust* engraved and published at his own expense.

At first sight it is baffling to learn that Berlioz withdrew this astonishingly bold Opus 1 six months after publication. The performance of the Sylphs' scene at a Conservatoire concert and the lukewarm notices it provoked do not explain his precipitate action. The fact that the *Eight Scenes* are for diverse combinations of voices and instruments – and therefore unsuitable for concert performance – is unlikely to have discouraged him in the least. Had he not lived to rework these settings into the later masterpiece *The Damnation of Faust*, a question mark would remain. But we may surmise that he saw dimly how a different kind of work would be required to render musical justice to Goethe's *Faust*. The *Eight Scenes* are simply settings of the lyrical elements of the play; Faust himself does not feature at all, and there is little that even suggests the philosophical burden of Goethe's original.

Admiration as intense as Berlioz's for Goethe deserved to be expressed more fittingly. Writing from Italy in 1831, Mendelssohn reported that Berlioz dreamed of nothing but Shakespeare, Goethe and Schiller all day. How Berlioz must have envied his friend's intimacy with Goethe! It would have been helpful to him when he made a presentation of the score of the *Eight Scenes* to the poet, accompanied by a suitably flattering letter. Goethe, on the damning advice of his friend Zelter, failed even to acknowledge the offering.

The long gestation of *The Damnation of Faust* shows an interesting parallel with Goethe's own lifelong involvement with *Faust*, for when Berlioz returned to it in 1845 after a pause of fifteen years he was much nearer to the heart of his subject. *Romeo and Juliet*, in 1839, had opened up a rich new field of symphonic expression, and his decision to treat *Faust* on a large scale gave him the opportunity to attempt a more searching interpretation of the legend. Despite his admiration for Goethe he knew enough about earlier versions of the story to feel as free as Goethe himself in adapting it to his needs. Thus he returned to the old ending with Faust damned, not saved (as in Goethe), a revision embodied in the new work's title and chosen for its dramatic force, particularly in contrast with the scene of Marguerite's acceptance in Heaven; he also inserted his brilliant arrangement of the Rákóczy March by the simple expedient of naming Hungary as the locale of the first part of the drama.

German critics were outraged, but Berlioz knew clearly in his own mind what he was about. Untrue to the letter of Goethe he may have been, but not to the spirit. Working on the basic material of his *Eight Scenes*, Berlioz filled out the action, creating the entire part of Faust and most of that of Mephistopheles with music composed in a dozen towns of Europe during his tours of 1845 and 1846. 'Riding in my old German post-chaise,' he tells us in his *Memoirs*, 'I tried to write verses for my music. I began with Nature immense, neither trying to translate nor to imitate the original, but simply to extract the musical substance that it contained.' The opening pages were composed at an inn in Passau; Mephistopheles's 'Voici des roses' in Vienna; part of the 'Ronde des paysans' was written down by street gaslight in Pest; a column of infantry on the Boulevard Poissonnière, Paris, on a sunny August day, inspired the Latin chorus of students roaming the street, *sub ridente luna*. The original eight scenes ('Chant de la fête de Pâques', 'Ronde des paysans', 'Concert des Sylphes', 'Chanson de Brander', 'Chanson de Méphistophélès', 'Ballade du roi de Thulé', Marguerite's Air 'D'amour l'ardente flamme', 'Sérénade de Méphistophélès') were skilfully absorbed in the new design, as when, for example, a parody of fugal Amens (one of Berlioz's pet phobias) is inserted after Brander's song in the tavern scene.

Although Berlioz first described the work as an opera, he was soon calling it 'a kind of opera', and he finally gave it the heading 'Dramatic Legend' and placed it firmly in that flexible territory between symphony and opera of which he was such a master. We know from a correspondence with the librettist Eugène Scribe in 1847 that, if it had been staged, the work would have undergone considerable revision and adaptation. The score contains a number of stage directions which serve simply as aids to the imagination and as explanations of the sung text. Berlioz feels free to expand and compress his material without regard for the exigencies of the stage; he is pursuing the same formal freedom which had served him with such telling force in the 'dramatic symphony' *Romeo and Juliet*.

The first performance, at the Opéra-Comique, Paris, on 6 December 1846, conducted by Berlioz himself, was not a success, and a second performance a fortnight later drove home to him more forcibly than ever before the unbridgeable gap which existed between himself and his Paris audience. 'Nothing in my whole career as an artist wounded me so deeply as this unexpected indifference,' he wrote. He resolved at once to cultivate another patch, setting off to Russia to find the support and enthusiasm he longed all his life to receive at home. Many critics had in fact been impressed by the work, but a composer must have superhuman fortitude to read the following (by the influential critic Scudo) written about a work as deeply felt as this:

> Such is the composition in which M. Berlioz has disfigured one of the great conceptions of modern poetry. He has grasped neither the spirit nor the feeling of this drama . . . He has transformed Marguerite into a vulgar heroine who indulges in all the exaggerations of melodrama . . . Rarely has the alliance of drama and symphony been so unhappy. Not only is M. Berlioz incapable of writing for the human

voice, but even his orchestration is simply a string of curious sound effects without substance or development.

Yet Théophile Gautier boldly asserted that Goethe's conception of Faust had never been so clearly understood; he perceived the work's uncanny sense of mystery and profundity, its picture of human frailty in the face of the unknown, and its sharp portrayal of irony. Not until after Berlioz's death did the Paris public come to learn that Scudo was diametrically wrong on every point, and that *The Damnation of Faust* was a work to be admired and loved. By a strange twist of destiny it became the work through which Berlioz's name climbed back to posthumous acceptance and respectability.

Berlioz had performed it himself frequently outside France, and when the score was published in 1854 with a dedication to Liszt, it had the effect of releasing the torrential flood of inspiration that brought the *Faust Symphony* into being. This work was appropriately dedicated to Berlioz in turn, a felicitous exchange of compliments between two composers who shared a Faustian passion.

We must not look in *The Damnation of Faust* for a close reflection of Goethe's many philosophical themes; there is nothing, for example, about the regeneration of mankind. What we do have is a Marguerite of touching innocence, a Mephistopheles of rare conviction – he displays a real sense of irony – and a Faust who stands for a thousand Romantic aspirations. Goethe, with Shakespeare, satisfied Berlioz's requirement of a great poet: that he should be a mirror in which everything is reflected, whether graceful or ugly, brilliant or sombre, calm or agitated, intimate or grandiose. This far-ranging diversity, this universality, set up a stream of resonances in Berlioz's spirit, and when, in Part Four, Faust invokes Nature with the words:

> *Forêts, rochers, torrents, je vous adore!*
> *Mondes qui scintillez, vers vous s'élance le désir*
> *D'un cœur trop vaste et d'une âme altérée*
> *D'un bonheur qui la fuit*

(Forests, rocks, torrents, I worship you!
O worlds that sparkle above, towards you springs
the desire of a heart too large and a soul that thirsts
for a happiness which eludes it.)

Berlioz's music speaks to us not only with the voice of the Rousseauist cowering with wonder at the immeasurability of nature, but also with the supreme authority over his subject that he admired above all in Beethoven.

Part One

The Plains of Hungary. Faust, alone at daybreak, rejoices in the warmth of spring and the peace of a solitary life. But his soul is heavy, and the dancing and merriment of a group of peasants give him no cheer. He moves to another part of the plain where an army passes eager for battle and for victory (Rákóczy March). Not even this vision of glory can rouse Faust from his misery.

Part Two

Northern Germany. Faust, alone in his study, despairs of ever finding happiness. He has searched for it in vain, and now resolves to die. He takes a cup of poison and raises it to his lips. As he does so, he hears bells ringing and the Easter Hymn being sung in a nearby church. It reminds him of his childhood and the joyful faith of his youth. He draws back from his resolve.

Suddenly Mephistopheles appears, announcing himself as the Spirit of Life who can offer everything the heart can desire. Faust challenges him to show such marvels, upon which Mephistopheles briskly transports them both to Auerbach's cellar in Leipzig, where the company's carousing is in full swing. To the assembled drinkers Brander sings the 'Song of the Rat' and then calls for an Amen for the soul of the poor rat, which they sing in due ecclesiastical style. Mephistopheles in his turn sings the 'Song of the Flea'. Faust is disgusted with it all and begs to be led to calmer pleasures. Mephistopheles obliges, and they ride through the air to the bosky banks of the

Elbe, where Faust is laid to sleep on a bed of roses. A chorus of gnomes and sylphs provides enchantment. In his dreams he sees a vision of Marguerite and calls out her name in his sleep. The sylphs dance to complete the spell.

Faust awakes with a start and asks where he can find the angel of his dream. Mephistopheles agrees to lead him to her dwelling, and they join some students heading her way, their singing mingling with that of a troop of soldiers.

Part Three

Marguerite's room. The soldiers are heard in the distance as Faust enters the room and sings of his new-found happiness and his expectant delight. He is looking eagerly round the room when Mephistopheles enters, conceals Faust behind the curtains, and then leaves. Faust watches in ecstasy as Marguerite comes in. She has seen her lover in a dream and distracts herself by singing the 'Ballad of the King of Thule' as she plaits her hair. Meanwhile, in the street outside, Mephistopheles summons his Will-o'-the-Wisps to do his bidding. They dance and cast their spell on the lovers within. Mephistopheles sings a mocking Serenade, then dismisses the attendant spirits.

Back in Marguerite's room. Faust steps from his hiding place and Marguerite recognises him at once as the object of her dreams. They sing a rapturous duet and dissolve in each other's arms. But Mephistopheles breaks in to warn them that the neighbours have woken up and have sent for Marguerite's mother. Faust bids her an anguished farewell as Mephistopheles tears him away.

Part Four

Abandoned by Faust, Marguerite sings with despair of the love she has no sooner discovered than lost. As the soldiers and students are once more heard in the distance, her sorrow deepens.

Faust finds himself amid forests and caves, lost in admiration for the mighty works of nature which alone can soothe his broken heart. Mephistopheles appears once more and reports that Marguerite is now in prison, condemned to death for poisoning her mother: hoping that Faust would return, she had administered the sleeping draught, which he had given her to use on her mother, once too often. Faust is desperate to save Marguerite from the gallows. Mephistopheles offers to help if Faust will sign an ancient parchment agreeing to serve him in return. Faust does so, two black horses appear, and they set off, not, as Faust imagines, to Marguerite's rescue, but into the abyss of Hell. As they gallop headlong forward, grim visions beset them on either side, and when Faust finally falls into the pit, Mephistopheles roars in triumph at the capture of his soul.

In Pandemonium, a chorus of demons and the damned sings a strange syllabic language like that Swedenborg claimed to have heard in his vision of Hell. Faust is duly received into the 'infernal orgy'. In the epilogue, voices on Earth record the closing of Hell's gate and the accomplishment of an unnamed mystery, while, in Heaven, Seraphim bow before the Almighty and beg redemption for Marguerite. Pardoned, she rises to her apotheosis in Heaven.

∾ Requiem (*Grande messe des morts*), Op. 5 (1837)

1   Requiem and Kyrie: Introit
2   Dies irae: Sequence
3   Quid sum miser
4   Rex tremendae
5   Quaerens me
6   Lacrimosa
7   Offertorium
8   Hostias
9   Sanctus
10 Agnus Dei

The dramatic possibilities of the Requiem text had long interested Berlioz; and when, in March 1837, the French government commissioned him to write a Requiem Mass to commemorate King Louis-Philippe's escape from assassination on the anniversary of the July Revolution, he set to work with great enthusiasm and completed the score in three months.

In composing it, Berlioz set out to apply to church music the same principles of freedom and expressive truth – the watchwords of Romanticism – that inspired his secular works. Berlioz is first and always a dramatist, whatever the nature of the work in question and whether its scale is monumental or intimate. From his teacher Le Sueur he acquired a clear and consistent belief in the essentially dramatic character of religious music, of which the 'expression of feeling' is just as much the object as it is of opera. And rather as an opera composer considers himself quite free to alter even the most venerated play, he did not hesitate to modify the liturgical text – changing the order of phrases or sections or leaving them out altogether – if the music's dramatic structure or expressive purposes seemed to him to demand it.

In the 'Rex tremendae' of Berlioz's Requiem the chorus, awed by the terrible prospect of divine judgement, cannot complete the sentence 'Voca me [cum benedictis]' ('Call me [with the blessed]'): the voice-parts break off and fall silent before the vision of the bottomless pit (which in fact belongs to a different part of the Mass). In the 'Offertorium' the impression of the eternal supplication of souls in Purgatory is intensified by the disconnected fragments of text to which the chorus sings its sad, unvarying chant: 'de poenis . . . Domine . . . Domine . . . libera eas . . . de poenis . . . inferni' ('from the torment . . . Lord . . . Lord . . . deliver them . . . from the torment . . . of hell'). It is, as it were, all that we can hear of a plaint chanted unceasingly throughout the ages. Such changes have a structural as well as an expressive function: they reinforce the tripartite scheme of the work, in which Hell gives way to Purgatory and Purgatory to Heaven

('Sanctus'). But an orthodoxly devout composer would regard them as an unjustifiable liberty.

At the same time, Berlioz felt himself to be not destroying tradition but renewing and extending it. His Requiem belongs to the artistic heritage of late eighteenth- and early nineteenth-century France. Musical rites on a vast scale were an integral part of public life under the Revolution, the Consulate and the First Empire. The multiple orchestras and massed choruses for which Méhul, Gossec, Le Sueur and Cherubini wrote represented a grand idea: they symbolised the Nation, the People assembled for a communal act of worship. Indeed, the large forces required for Berlioz's *Requiem* are not peculiar to him. Le Sueur's *Chant du 1er Vendémiaire* of 1801 was performed by four separate orchestras, each one placed at a corner of Les Invalides – the same church in which, thirty-six years later, Berlioz's *Grande messe des morts* had its first performance. As a pupil of Le Sueur, Berlioz was the natural heir of that tradition. He did not invent it. But his imagination responded eagerly to it.

Hence the concept which the work embodies of music as the 'soul' of a great church, filling and animating the body of the building – a notion which came to Berlioz as he stood for the first time in the huge nave of St Peter's in Rome. Hence, too, the development of the Baroque idea – revived by the previous generation of French composers – of using space as an element in the composition itself. And hence the choice of a musical style characterised by broad tempos, simple, deliberate harmonic movement and massive, widely spaced sonorities: the style marks an attempt to produce a body of sound and a type of musical utterance commensurate with the scale and acoustics of a great church and with a solemn ceremonial occasion.

The massed drums and the four groups of brass instruments (which Berlioz directs to be placed at the four corners of the main body of performers) are the features for which the work is generally best known; but their effect is due precisely to the contrast they make with the predominantly austere texture of the rest of the score. For much of the time horns are the only brass to offset the bleak, mourning sound of the large woodwind choir. The apocalyptic armoury is reserved for special moments of colour and emphasis: its purpose is not merely spectacular but architectural, to clarify the musical structure and open up multiple perspectives. And it serves to underline a grandeur that is inherent in the style of the music as a whole, in its wide arcs of melody, its classically ordered cataclysms and its still small voice of humility. The Requiem transcends its local origins: the Revolutionary community has become the community of the human race throughout the ages.

Characteristic, too, is the systematic alternation of grand, powerfully scored movements with quiet, intimate ones. Each of the three numbers in which the brass choirs are used is followed by one that is devotional in mood; and the dynamic level is reduced at the end of the big movements in order to prepare for the contemplative music of the next number. The tumult of the 'Tuba mirum' sinks to a whisper which is continued in the 'Quid sum miser', scored for a handful of instruments and suggesting sinful man shivering in an empty universe. The splendour of the 'Rex tremendae' is subdued to a soft pleading – 'salva me' ('save me'), sung very quietly, emerging dramatically from the full orchestra in a succession of varied harmonisations – which leads to the gentle, unaccompanied 'Quaerens me'. The 'Lacrimosa' ends on a diminuendo as the procession of the lamenting dead sweeps onwards out of view, to be succeeded by the remote, ageless sadness of the Offertorium.

In two or three movements the music sets out to convey the grandeur of God in objective terms. In the 'Tuba mirum' the thunder of drums and the fanfares answering and overlapping one another from the four corners – a blaze of sound in E flat major, the antithesis of the austere texture and modally flavoured A minor of the 'Dies irae' – depict the awesome event itself, the universal upheaval of Judgement Day. The Sanctus – for solo tenor and women's voices accompanied by violins, violas and a single high flute – evokes a shimmering vision of the angelic host, while the long arches of phrase and static harmony of the fugal 'Hosanna' (directed to be sung 'smoothly, without emphasising the individual notes') suggest the unending chorus of praise round the throne of God. For the most part, however, the work is concerned with humanity and its weakness and vunerability: humanity on the edge of eternity ('Hostias'), humanity amid total desolation ('Quid sum miser'), humanity in the Dance of Death, the endless procession of the dead scourged towards judgement ('Lacrimosa'), pleading for salvation before the majesty of God ('Rex tremendae'), praying from one generation to another (Offertorium), hoping against hope (Introit) – humanity striving, out of its fear of extinction, to create a merciful God and a meaningful universe.

In this sense the Requiem is a profoundly religious work, notwithstanding Berlioz's confession of agnosticism. Religion, during his childhood and youth, had been (he wrote) 'the joy of my life'. The very loss of this joy left an imprint on his music. The work conveys a yearning for faith, an awareness of the need, the desperate need, to believe and worship; his own lack of faith, as it were, is used to evoke the eternal hopes and terrors of the human race. From time to time we get a glimpse of peace, as in the radiant stillness of the Sanctus and in the light that falls like a benediction on the closing page of the Offertorium. But the prevailing tone is tragic. Through all the music's contrasts of form and mood, the idea of humanity's wonder and bafflement before the enigma of death is central and constant, from the measured climb of the opening G minor phrases and the silences which surround them, to the acceptance of the final coda, where solemn Amens circled by luminous string arpeggios swing slowly in and out of G major, while the funeral drums beat out a long retreat.

© David Cairns

✺ *Romeo and Juliet*, dramatic symphony, Op. 17 (1839)

The choral symphony on *Romeo and Juliet* occupied Berlioz on and off for nearly twenty years. There is evidence that by 1829, if not earlier, he was thinking of writing a work based on Shakespeare's play, which he had seen for the first time two years before. The poet Émile Deschamps, translator of Shakespeare and author of the symphony's text, later recalled that Berlioz and he first discussed the project in 1829; and in the summer of that year, while composing the cantata *Cléopâtre* for the Prix de Rome competition, Berlioz inscribed at the head of Cleopatra's invocation to the spirits of the Pharaohs a line from the soliloquy spoken by Juliet before she drinks Friar Laurence's potion – a passage, he said, of which he had 'often imagined a musical setting'. The cantata of the following year, *Sardanapale*, with which he won the prize, included two themes later to appear in the 'Grande Fête chez Capulet'; they may well have been first conceived in connection with *Romeo and Juliet*.

A year later, in Rome, Berlioz mentioned to Mendelssohn the idea of a scherzo on Mercutio's 'Queen Mab' speech. And in an article on Italian music written at the end of the same year (1831), he gave a kind of ideal scenario for a *Romeo and Juliet* opera (stimulated by his disillusionment with Bellini's *I Capuleti e i Montecchi*) which foreshadows the symphony in several details. In particular, it emphasises the ritual act of reconciliation between the warring families. This idea is absent from Bellini's opera. In Shakespeare it is dealt with in a few concluding lines. Garrick's edition of the play, in the version of it that Berlioz saw in Paris in 1827 (and which in other respects he followed), ended with the death of the lovers, and therefore excluded it altogether. But it is a natural subject for a symphonic finale, and it eventually formed the climax and culmination of Berlioz's symphony.

In the event it was not until 1839 that – heartened by Paganini's public act of recognition after a performance of the *Symphonie fantastique* and *Harold in Italy*, and relieved of debts and financial anxieties by Paganini's cheque for twenty thousand francs – he felt free to compose the work so long projected. Its gestation had lasted more than ten years. Even after it had been performed three times at the Paris Conservatoire in November and December 1839, with the composer conducting, it went through a further seven years of revision before being published, with a dedication to Paganini, in 1847, twenty years after the momentous event that originated it.

Berlioz was not alone in feeling that that event, the performance of *Hamlet* and *Romeo and Juliet* by Kemble's English company at the Odéon Theatre in the autumn of 1827, changed his life. The entire French Romantic movement hailed the coming of Shakespeare as its long-awaited deliverance from the bonds of academic classicism. Berlioz's passion for Harriet Smithson, his identification of the ideal woman with the person of the actress who played Juliet and Ophelia, merely intensified the experience.

Like his contemporaries, the young French playwrights and poets, he found that his eyes had been opened to a new reality; in a flash he saw 'the whole heaven of art' and understood 'the true meaning of grandeur, beauty, dramatic truth'. The Romantics responded both to Shakespeare's marvellous richness of imagery – his boundlessly varied poetic invention, his vast range of feeling and mood – and to his formal freedom, his command of contrast and uninhibited mixing of genres. He confirmed their belief that since the subject of art is life and its limits those of existence itself, it followed that so far from conforming to established rules, form must be free, varying according to the demands of the particular material it embodies.

In the midst of heartbreak and the 'pangs of despis'd love' (for a long time Miss Smithson, his future wife, would have nothing to do with him), Berlioz too pondered the lessons of Shakespeare. If the Romantic playwrights seem sometimes to interpret liberty as licence, Berlioz, with his Classical upbringing, saw it somewhat differently. Freedom of form was essential, certainly: on it – he writes in 1848 in an open letter to 'Shakespeare's compatriots', the English critics – 'depends the entire development of the music of the future'; but it means not abandoning all rules but obeying the right rules, finding the form best suited to the content. As a musician, of course, he was concerned with problems different from those of the dramatists, and his solutions were necessarily his own. It is no accident that with the possible exception of the *Symphonie fantastique* – itself a highly innovative work – the Berlioz score that underwent the most thorough revision between first draft and publication was *Romeo and Juliet*, a work whose formal plan had no precedent, and which was by far the most ambitious of all his attempts to recreate a Shakespearean theme in music.

In any case such an attempt required a more developed and flexible musical style and technique than he possessed at the time of his discovery of Shakespeare. It required the complementary revelation of Beethoven. For that reason alone, the story of the young Berlioz coming away from the first night of *Romeo and Juliet* exclaiming, 'I shall marry Juliet and I shall write my biggest symphony on the play' – a remark he himself denied having made – cannot be true, at least so far as the symphony is concerned. It was the discovery of Beethoven's music six months later, in March 1828, that set his mind thinking along the lines that would lead eventually to the dramatic symphony. Once absorbed, the shock to his musical system of those first Conservatoire concerts brought about the final maturing of his style, and turned his art – reared on opera – in a new direction. Hence the *Symphonie fantastique* and, by extension and development of the methods and ideas pioneered in it, *Romeo and Juliet*. In both works Beethovenian principles of unification and thematic transformation are applied to a melodic style founded on French classical opera. *Romeo and Juliet*, impossible without Shakespeare, is unthinkable without Beethoven.

The lesson of Beethoven, like that of Shakespeare, was

both expressive and formal. In Beethoven's music, wrote Berlioz, 'one senses a poetic idea that is active at every moment'. It is realised by musical means; 'music is the be-all and end-all'. Beethoven revealed orchestral music's till then undreamed-of potential as a dramatic language, as an instrument for expressing human experience. The implications of a passage like the end of the slow movement of the 'Eroica', where the melody breaks into fragments like the last gasps of a dying man, were not lost on Berlioz. Music was free to do as it pleased. The symphonies – the overtures, too – were dramas, the 'Eroica' and the Fifth as much as, if not more than, the 'Pastoral': their dramatic content was no less evident for not being labelled. And they were dramas by virtue not only of their expressivity, but also of their form. The poetic idea of each was realised by the structure. The symphonic composer's responsibility was to find, each time afresh, the right form.

In his last symphony Beethoven had brought the drama into the open, making explicit in the choral finale the implicit meanings of the preceding movements. For the great nineteenth-century composers the Ninth was the fountainhead of modern music. But whereas for Wagner it led, inevitably, to music drama (since Beethoven, by calling on voices and words to resolve the mighty conflicts he had generated, had in effect acknowledged that the symphony as an art-form could go no further and must merge into a new kind of drama), for Berlioz it marked the final stage in the emancipation of the form from its eighteenth-century restrictions and the beginning of a new kind of symphony. The seven-movement 'dramatic symphony', *Romeo and Juliet*, was for him a natural consequence of Beethoven's Ninth, however unprecedented its scheme. Much later in his career he contemplated composing an opera on the play; but the work he wrote in 1839 was in no sense an expedient forced on him by his lack of commercial success in the opera house. It was conceived in symphonic terms, with the great celebration of all-embracing love, the heart of the work, cast in the form of a long orchestral Adagio (the language of instruments, as he said in his preface to the vocal score, being by its very indefiniteness better fitted than sung speech to express so sublime an emotion). The fundamental artistic choice was never in doubt.

The details, however, involved years of thought, experiment, revision. He was attempting to put so much, and so much that was central to his innermost experience and beliefs, into an entirely novel structural plan. The work was a repayment of debt and an act of homage to his god ('the English are quite right to call Shakespeare the supreme creator, after the Good Lord'). It was a distillation of the play – a play that had struck many deep chords in his imagination. He expressed some of them in words when, after a particularly satisfying performance of the symphony in St Petersburg, he spoke of 'that revelation of a love and a grief without limit, that vision of a Juliet ever dreamed of, ever sought, never attained'. Above all it was his tribute to the ideal of young love – complete and all-consuming, 'swift as thought, burning as lava', but tragic because the world can only destroy it.

Despite his long rumination of the problems and his careful calculation of ends and means, Berlioz was under no illusion as to the probable reaction to so unorthodox a solution. The formal plan of *Romeo and Juliet* has indeed been judged by some commentators an unsatisfactory compromise between symphony and oratorio (as has Beethoven's Ninth Symphony), and till recently the three central orchestral movements were often extracted and performed separately. Yet they are far more eloquent and meaningful when experienced in context. The different sections of the work are interdependent and illuminate one another. So far from being awkwardly devised, the scheme is logical, and the mixture of genres – the inheritance of Shakespeare and Beethoven – precisely gauged. The Introduction, depicting the feud of the two families, establishes the principle of dramatically explicit orchestral music. After that, the choral Prologue states the argument of the succeeding movements which the choral finale will later resolve. The Prologue, in chant-like three-part recitative suggestive of ancient tragedy, prepares us for the diverse themes, dramatic and musical, that the symphony will treat. In addition, the two least overtly dramatic movements, the Adagio and the Scherzo, are prefigured, the one in a contralto solo celebrating the ecstasies of first love, the other in a capering vocal Scherzetto which introduces the mischievous Mab. At the end the Finale brings the drama fully into the open, and evolves gradually from conflict to concord under the aegis of the priestly Friar Laurence; and it does so in the manner naturally suited to such an idea: an extended choral movement culminating in the solemn abjuring of the hatred depicted orchestrally at the outset of the work.

The main body of the symphony is given to the orchestra. But voices are not forgotten; they are used sparingly, but sufficiently to keep them before the listener's attention, in order to prepare for their full deployment in the Finale. At the beginning of the 'Love Scene', across the silence of the Capulets' garden float the songs of the distant revellers (tenors and basses) on their way home from the ball. Two movements further on, in the 'Funeral Cortège', voices – this time the whole Capulet chorus – sing a single-note chant against the orchestral fugato; furthermore, the musical roles are reversed halfway through the movement, which in consequence becomes choral. At the same time the two movements preceding the Finale take on an increasingly descriptive character. The funeral dirge develops into a repeated bell-like tone of hypnotic insistence; and the orchestral 'Tomb Scene' carries the work still nearer to narrative action. In this way, again, an abrupt transition is avoided; the quasi-operatic or oratorio-like Finale evolves from what has gone before.

Similarly, throughout the score thematic resemblances serve to link the different sections and to give unity to the diversity of musical imagery created in response to the play. The superimposing of the theme of the preceding Larghetto on the Allegro of the 'Ball Scene' (anticipated by the appear-

ance of its first six notes twice in the previous bars) is only the
most obvious example. The theme of the trombone recitative
which represents the Prince's rebuke to the warring families
(Introduction) is formed from the opening notes of their
angry fugato, which is mastered literally by being stretched
into notes three times as long. A transformation of the ball
music provides the departing guests with the material of their
lilting, dreamlike song. The trio in 'Queen Mab' is based on
the Scherzo theme, which itself recurs during the trio, on the
violas, as a buzzing counterpoint to its quivering stillness. In
the 'Tomb Scene' the clarinet's melodic line depicting Juliet
waking from her deathlike sleep uses note-for-note the rising
cor anglais phrase in bars 32 to 45 of the Adagio; and, as in
the Adagio, it is followed by the love theme, now feverish,
distorted, torn apart as the poison courses through Romeo's
body. And in the Finale, as the families' feud breaks out again
over the corpses of their children, the return of the opening
fugato in the same key, B minor, unites the extremes of the
vast score.

The work is also honeycombed with smaller thematic
cross-references. The solo oboe's last lingering notes which
follow Juliet's suicide echo a phrase from the funeral procession that bore her, supposedly dead, to the tomb. Many other
examples could be cited. The yearning, sighing phrases of
'Romeo Alone' recur in various guises in what follows, as sub-
sidiary figures or as elements of leading melodies. The principle is active to the end; for the theme of Friar Laurence's
oath of reconciliation, which closes the symphony, symboli-
cally takes as its point of departure the angry 'feud' theme in
B minor of the work's introduction, transformed into a broad
and magnanimous B major.

As so often with creative artists, the very difficulties that
Romeo and Juliet caused Berlioz helped to give it a special
place in his affections. Certainly no score of his is more abundant in lyric poetry, in a sense of the magic and brevity of
love, in 'sounds and sweet airs' of so many different kinds: the
flickering, fantastical Scherzo (which stands not only for

Mercutio's 'Queen Mab' speech but for the whole nimble-witted, comic-fantastical element in the play); the noble swell and curve of the great extended melody which grows out of the questioning phrases of 'Romeo Alone'; the cavernous sound of unison cor anglais, horn and four bassoons in the 'Invocation' in the 'Tomb Scene'; the sadness, the haunting beauty of the 'Funeral Cortège'; and the Adagio's deep-toned harmonies and spellbound melodic arcs, evoking the moon-lit night and the wonder and intensity of the passion that flowers beneath it.

© David Cairns

∾ *Te Deum*, Op. 22 (1855)

1   Te Deum laudamus
2   Tibi omnes
3   Dignare
4   Christe, rex gloriae
5   Te ergo quaesumus
6   Judex crederis

Berlioz passes for an agnostic, if not an atheist. That is how he usually spoke of himself. As a child, he had been a devout member of the Catholic Church; but, as he remarked in the opening chapter of his *Memoirs*, 'we have long since fallen out'. Yet paradoxically a large proportion of his music is concerned, one way or another, with religion – and this in a period when religious music was in decline in France.

Berlioz's first composition to be performed in public was a Mass. Three of his major works are religious works – the Requiem, the *Te Deum* and *The Childhood of Christ*. What is more, none of them owes its origins to external causes: the impulse came from the composer himself. Even in his secular works one is struck by the recurrence of religious imagery. This is more than simply a reflection of the contemporary Romantic vogue for religion as a picturesque detail of land-scape: it is a preoccupation.

'For seven whole years', Berlioz wrote of his childhood, religion was 'the joy of my life'. The very loss of this joy left a deep imprint. Certainly he was not a believer; but his music conveys an intense regret that he cannot be one, and a profound awareness of the need to believe. His own lack of faith is, as it were, used to evoke the eternal hopes and fears of the human race; his intuitive understanding of the religious instinct, his unsatisfied yearning for faith, enable him to respond to those immemorial feelings and express them in his art. The result, with all its unorthodox elements, is true religious music.

If the *Te Deum* and the Requiem seem to us unconventional works, this is partly because the tradition to which they belong has been forgotten. We would not think of their huge forces and grandiose, yet austere, style as peculiarly Berliozian if we knew the many similar works written a generation earlier in France by composers like Méhul, Gossec and Le Sueur. Musical rites on a gigantic scale were an important part of public life in the Revolutionary and Napoleonic eras in France; they represented a grand idea, the idea of the Nation, the People assembled for a solemn communal act of worship. As a student, Berlioz was taught by Le Sueur, and a close affinity grew up between the old man and his young disciple. From Le Sueur Berlioz learnt certain fundamental principles and practices: for example, the necessity for a special style of music for large, resonant buildings and ceremonial occasions, a style marked by broad tempos and simple, deliberate harmonic movement, and using space as an element of composition. The four choirs of brass in Berlioz's Requiem and the organ answering chorus and orchestra from (in Berlioz's own scheme) the opposite end of the nave in his *Te Deum* have an architectural function, being designed to clarify and emphasise the musical structure and open up multiple perspectives.

Above all, Berlioz acquired from Le Sueur a belief in the essentially dramatic character of religious music, of which the 'expression of feeling' is just as much the objective as it is of opera. Berlioz is first and always a dramatist, whatever the character of the work in question and whether its scale is monumental or intimate. The concept that lies behind both the *Te Deum* and the Requiem, of music as the 'soul' of a great sacred building, filling and animating the body (which came to him as he stood for the first time in the huge nave of St Peter's in Rome), is a dramatist's concept. Both works are conceived in consistently dramatic terms. There is a systematic use of contrast – contrast of scale, volume and density, contrast of texture – to emphasise a constant theme of the words, the majesty of God and the littleness of Man.

In pursuit of this idea the composer does not hesitate to change the order of the liturgical text, rather as an opera composer feels free to modify the most venerated stage play if the requirements of the music drama demand it. The first two movements of Berlioz's *Te Deum* observe the sequence of verses, but thereafter it is considerably altered. In order that the splendours of the 'Tibi omnes' and 'Christe, rex gloriae' shall be separated by a contrasting movement, subdued in character – the 'Dignare' – three verses are brought forward from later sections. The same principle is responsible for the 'Te ergo quaesumus' interposing its gentle prayer between the brilliant 'Christe, rex gloriae' and the monumental 'Judex crederis'. 'Judex crederis esse venturus' ('We believe that thou shalt come to be our judge') is actually only the nineteenth of the *Te Deum*'s twenty-eight verses, but here it is delayed until the end, so that the work can culminate in a movement which conveys in apocalyptic terms humanity's fear of divine judgement.

As in the Requiem, side by side with the feeling of personal awe and dread, here and now, there is an immense sense of antiquity, of unnumbered voices raised in prayer from age to age throughout time: for example, in the repeated cry of the woodwind at 'Have mercy upon us' in the 'Dignare' or the evocation of endless generations in the middle section of the 'Judex crederis'. The passages where the full forces are deployed suggest a God of truly 'infinite majesty', the music pealing out like a great bell, at once uplifting and terrifying.

While in Dresden in 1843, Berlioz was shown some scores by the eighteenth-century composer Hasse, and was struck by a *Te Deum* which he described as having 'the ceremonial brilliance of a great peal of bells'. Reading Hasse's score may well have been one of the stimuli that led him to conceive his own setting of the text a few years later. Another, perhaps, was the experience of conducting his own Requiem at St Eustache in Paris in 1846 – the first complete performance since the premiere in 1837. There is much in common between the two works. 'The Requiem has a brother,' he wrote to Liszt after the first performance of the *Te Deum*, also in St Eustache, and he described the 'Judex crederis' as 'first cousin' of the 'Lacrymosa' in the Requiem.

The *Te Deum* seems also to be related to a project which he had worked on in the 1830s, in honour of the great men of France's past, among whom Napoleon was to have had pride of place. This 'Fête musicale funèbre' was abandoned, but it is possible that the *Te Deum* owed some of its impulse, if not also some of its musical ideas, to it. There is a martial spirit in the work that is not present in the Requiem. Its most obvious expression is in the two instrumental movements, the 'Prelude' and the 'March for the Presentation of the Colours' (music designed to accompany the pageantry of military ceremonial, and thus having no place in a performance that doesn't include this element); but there are echoes of it elsewhere, for example in the timpani part in the opening movement and the sidedrums in the 'Judex crederis'. Yet the work transcends these local origins, expressing feelings common to all people. The Napoleonic tradition is universalised; the Revolutionary community becomes the community of humankind in all ages.

In 1851, while in London as a member of the jury on musical instruments at the Great Exhibition, Berlioz attended the annual Charity Children's service at St Paul's and was deeply impressed by the sound of the hymn 'All people that on earth do dwell' sung by thousands of young voices. By then the *Te*

Deum had been in existence for over a year and he had been trying to get it performed. Under the stimulus of the St Paul's service he added a third, unison children's chorus to the two three-part choruses which carry the main argument. The function of the third choir is to suggest the congregation – 'the People, from time to time taking part in the great religious concert'. As for the organ, its role is rarely to augment the sonority of the orchestra, but rather to contrast with it and complement it, and also to underline moments of particular formal or expressive significance. Organ and orchestra are independent powers: in the composer's words, they converse 'like Pope and Emperor'.

1 *Te Deum*

Massive chords, antiphonal on orchestra and organ and laid out with a long reverberation period in mind, set the scale and spatial character of the work. At their conclusion the organ proclaims a descending theme which will reappear at intervals during the movement, always to 'Te, aeternum Patrem' and associated with the third choir. The three-note falling phrase in the organ theme's fifth bar recurs during the work as a kind of motto, sometimes ringing out with bell-like splendour, sometimes as a soft, insistent prayer for mercy. It also forms part of the fugue subject which the sopranos announce immediately after the organ's statement, and which quickly builds up to a jubilant climax. 'Omnis terra' is sung quietly, in contrasting homophonic style, as though the whole earth were prostrating itself before the grandeur of God. Towards the end this more mysterious mood takes possession, and the movement comes to rest on a high pianissimo chord, in preparation for the 'Tibi omnes'.

2 *Tibi omnes*

An organ prelude introduces the movement (at the end it returns as orchestral epilogue). The sopranos of Choir 1 announce a short melody, modal in character. After several repetitions, each differently harmonised, it leads to a long crescendo on 'Sanctus', with an accompaniment suggestive of gathering multitudes, rising to a great shout on 'pleni sunt coeli', the cadence being marked by the reappearance of the organ. The process is repeated twice, each time with varied harmony and texture, the last time with an expanded conclusion of great pomp, before the quiet close.

3 *Dignare*

A subdued movement, after the powerful sonorities of the previous choruses. Over a series of pedal notes ascending and then descending by regular steps of a major or a minor third and supported by the basses in muttered unison, sopranos and tenors in free imitation repeat with a kind of gentle urgency the prayer for divine salvation from sin. Towards the middle of the movement the motto phrase appears again and again in the woodwind, like a timeless cry for mercy.

4 *Christe, rex gloriae*

A simple, brilliantly sonorous and rhythmically energetic movement, based on a descending theme for voices and a rising theme for orchestra. A short central section in slower time, dominated by the tenors, strikes a more contemplative note.

5 *Te ergo quaesumus*

As in the 'Agnus Dei' of the Mass of 1825, on which this movement is based, a solo tenor, above broken string phrases, unfolds a quiet but fervent prayer for Christ's compassion. The women's voices add a soft, faraway pleading, with the unusual but expressive accompaniment of cornets and trombones. Towards the end, at 'speravimus', G minor lightens to G major. The prayer closes with all voices unaccompanied and sotto voce, founded on the solo tenor's melody sung by the basses.

6 *Judex crederis*

The crowning chorus is based on a long modal theme, the rhythm of whose opening bars forms one of the gigantic ostinatos by which the music is controlled and propelled. There is no key signature; the theme is so constituted that each repetition of it begins a semitone higher than the one before, and for a long time the attempt to establish B flat as the principal key is in doubt. The metre, like that of the 'Lacrymosa', is a surging 9/8, majestic and menacing. A central section in 3/4 time asserts a calmer mood, and the prayer for salvation rises to a climax, with the motto theme ringing out confidently. Then, distant at first but growing in urgency (to which the baleful sound of trombone pedal notes contributes), the pounding rhythm returns and the theme of the 'Judex crederis' is developed at length, with constantly varied and increasingly grand sonorities; the writing for brass is as resplendent as anything by Berlioz. B flat, reiterated with implacable insistence, is finally revealed as the key-note. The choral part of the movement ends with repeated cries of 'non confundar in aeternum' ('let me not be confounded for all eternity'), the music swaying between terror and splendour like the swing of an enormous bell. There is a short but conclusive coda for orchestra and organ, this time united, as the prayer for salvation is lifted to the heights by the angelic trumpets.

© David Cairns

Leonard Bernstein (1918–90)

Bernstein's gifts were so wide-ranging, and his intellect so fired by curiosity, that his life was pitted with struggle and ambiguity: as well as his work as pianist, conductor and composer, he was a passionate educator and mentor. He was born in Massachusetts to Russian émigré parents and studied at Harvard, where he first met Copland, then at Tanglewood with Serge Koussevitzky. He became an overnight success in November 1943 having taken over at short notice a concert from the conductor Bruno Walter, which was broadcast across the States. Despite the demands of his burgeoning conducting career, he found time to compose, revealing Copland, Stravinsky, jazz and his Jewish faith as major influences. He balanced his extrovert stage works *On the Town*, *Wonderful Town*, *Candide* and *West Side Story* with three symphonies – 'Jeremiah', 'The Age of Anxiety' and 'Kaddish' – which touched upon religious themes. He reached a generation of young Americans with his fifty-three televised *Young People's Concerts*, broadcast between 1958 and 1972, and in 1973 gave a probing lecture series as Charles Eliot Norton visiting professor at Harvard.

∾ *Chichester Psalms* (1965)

1 Psalm 108, v.2; Psalm 100
2 Psalm 23; Psalm 2, vv.1–4
3 Psalm 131; Psalm 133, v.1

Bernstein's *Chichester Psalms* for treble solo, chorus and orchestra was commissioned by the Very Reverend Walter Hussey, Dean of Chichester Cathedral (and a noted patron of the contemporary arts), for the 1965 Chichester Festival. Bernstein first wrote it for a male chorus of boys and bass voices, and then prepared a second version for mixed chorus.

This latter version was actually premiered first, in New York on 15 July 1965, with the composer conducting the New York Philharmonic; the premiere of the original version for all-male voices followed a fortnight later in Chichester Cathedral, with the combined cathedral choirs of Winchester, Salisbury and Chichester. Bernstein originally scored the work for an orchestra of six brass (trumpets and trombones), two harps, a large body of percussion, and strings, but later produced an arrangement for organ, harp and percussion.

Dean Hussey had intimated that he personally would be 'very delighted if there was a hint of *West Side Story* about the music', and in fact much of the music of *Chichester Psalms* is based on Bernstein's drafts for a projected Broadway musical, *The Skin of Our Teeth*, which had been cancelled earlier in the year. The composer, reviewing his experiences of 1965 in humorous verse, wrote of the piece:

> These psalms are a simple and modest affair,
> Tonal and tuneful and somewhat square,
> Certain to sicken a stout John Cager
> With its tonics and triads in E-flat major.

Despite their English cathedral connection, he decided to set his Psalms in the original Hebrew. Each movement contains the full text of one Psalm and an extract from another, but the relationship between the two texts, both in their meaning and in their musical treatment, is different each time.

The work opens with an exhortation to praise the Lord: the mood is triumphal and authoritative, like a proclamation. This is the trigger for the main part of the movement, an ebulliently dancing (and in places jazzy) scherzo-like setting of Psalm 100, where the percussion is much to the fore in 'making a joyful noise'.

The second movement begins with the male alto soloist (boy or counter-tenor), accompanied by harp, serenely setting forth the opening lines of Psalm 23. As the psalm is taken up by female voices, however, Bernstein has the male part of the chorus sing verses from Psalm 2 ('Why do the nations rage' – a text familiar to British audiences through Handel's *Messiah*) to a much more angular and agitated music (based on a chorus cut from the Prologue to *West Side Story*), in which the noise of the percussion takes on a sinister meaning. These contrasted musics of peace and war proceed in uneasy counterpoint throughout the rest of the movement.

The final movement – which is also the longest – begins with a passionate and elegiac introduction for the organ. This leads into a warm, assuaging setting of Psalm 131, to a long and intensely memorable melody in 10/4 time which is first cousin to the love songs of Bernstein's stage shows. Finally the chorus, unaccompanied, intones a verse from Psalm 133 as a vision of peace before the closing Amen.

© Malcolm MacDonald

Johannes Brahms (1833–97)

Often seen as a classicist inhabiting the Romantic era, Brahms worked mainly in the established forms – concerto, sonata, symphony – rather than developing new ones, such as the tone poems of Liszt or the grandiose music dramas of Wagner. From an early age Brahms was forced to earn money for his family by playing the piano in Hamburg's seedy sailors' taverns. In 1853 a concert tour brought him famously into contact with Schumann, who publicly declared the young composer a genius. The *German Requiem* (1868) and *Hungarian Dances* (1868–80) advanced his reputation and his *Variations on the St Anthony Chorale* (1873) attracted attention ahead of his First Symphony (1876). He wrote much choral music (he conducted both the Singakademie and the Singverein in Vienna), and led a revival of interest in Renaissance and Baroque music. He also wrote over two hundred songs and much chamber and piano music, but no opera. Late in life he wrote a trio, a quintet and two sonatas inspired by the clarinettist Richard Mühlfeld, which are among his finest achievements in chamber music.

∾ *A German Requiem*, Op. 45 (1865–9)

When Robert Schumann, in November 1853, publicly hailed the twenty-year-old Johannes Brahms as 'someone . . . fated to give us the ideal expression of the times, one who would not gain his mastery by gradual stages, but rather spring fully armed, like Minerva from the head of Jove', he immediately made the painfully self-aware young composer the object of intense critical interest – and widespread scepticism. During the succeeding fifteen years, it was only a small circle of close friends who really felt that he was fulfilling Schumann's prophecy; his artistic progress was a difficult one, and some of his major works (such as the First Piano Concerto) had a very rough reception.

It was only towards the end of the 1860s, when he was in his mid-thirties, that the musical public at large came to accept that Brahms had, indeed, established himself as one of the contemporary masters. This shift in perception was essentially achieved by the performance and dissemination of one work, in forces and dimensions the largest he was ever to write: *Ein deutsches Requiem*. Schumann himself had foretold that 'when he waves his magic wand where the power of great orchestral and choral masses will aid him, then we shall be shown still more wonderful glimpses into the secrets of the spirit-world'.

Though most of its composition can be dated to the mid-1860s, in its ultimate origins the Requiem goes back to 1854, and to the terrible months that followed Schumann's suicide attempt and incarceration in a mental asylum, only a few months after he had become Brahms's friend, mentor and artistic father-figure. Just at that time Brahms, staying in the Schumann house in Düsseldorf to look after the older composer's wife and children, started work on a big, tragic symphony in D minor – an ambitious expression of *Sturm und Drang* which he was never able to finish. Eventually the symphony's first movement was reworked into that of the First Piano Concerto. But we have the testimony of Brahms's close friend Albert Dietrich that the material of the second movement, a 'slow scherzo in Sarabande tempo', became the basis of the second-movement march in the Requiem. And in the 1870s, in a letter to the violinist Joseph Joachim, the composer commented that the work 'completely and inevitably . . . belonged to Schumann'.

There was, however, a more recent and even closer inspiration for this profound expression of mourning. Brahms's mother, Christiane, to whom he had been particularly close, died in February 1865 from the effects of a stroke. Two months later, *A German Requiem* first began to emerge as a work in progress, when he sent drafts of two of the movements to Clara Schumann and mentioned other projected ones. 'I hope that a German text of this sort will please you as much as the usual Latin one,' he commented. 'I am hoping to produce a sort of whole out of the thing and trust I shall retain enough courage and zest to carry it through . . .'

Much of the composition was completed during the following year, and by 1867 it had stabilised into a large-scale work with six movements. Three of these were heard in Vienna that December at a concert of the Gesellschaft der Musikfreunde under Johann Herbeck, but the performance was seriously under-rehearsed and the music made if anything an unfavourable impression on the Viennese public. However, Albert Dietrich had managed to get the premiere of the complete work scheduled for Good Friday of the following year, at Bremen Cathedral – where the musical director, Karl Martin Reinthaler, had been much impressed with the score and was willing to spend all the time necessary to prepare the forces thoroughly, and where the North German Protestant ambience would be more sympathetic to it than Catholic Vienna. This Bremen performance, on 10 April 1868, aroused great interest and attracted an audience of over two thousand, including prominent musicians from all over Germany. Brahms conducted; his friend Julius Stockhausen was the baritone soloist; the solo soprano movement did not yet exist, but Amalie Joachim (Joseph's wife) sang 'I know that my Redeemer liveth' from Handel's *Messiah* as an integral part of the performance. The result was an artistic triumph; critical acclamation was almost universal, and three weeks later the Requiem was performed again under Reinthaler's baton.

During the summer Brahms came to feel that a soprano solo movement was required to balance those with baritone; he accordingly composed 'Ihr habt nun Traurigkeit', placed fifth in the overall scheme, and this final form of the *Requiem* was first performed in Leipzig under Carl Reinecke in February 1869. By the end of the year it had been given in over twenty German and Swiss cities; over the next five years it was heard in London, Vienna, Utrecht, Paris and St Petersburg, carrying Brahms's fame further afield than any previous work had managed to do. It should be noted that the Franco-Prussian War of 1870–1 also aided the dissemination of *A German Requiem*, as it proved a perfect contemporary work for services of commemoration of the war dead; transforming its highly personal inspiration into an expression of national mourning.

As the title implies, the work bears no relation to the Roman liturgy. It is 'a German Requiem' not in any nationalistic sense, but because it is rooted in the language of the Lutheran Bible; and it was almost unique among requiems in not being an enacted prayer for the dead (Schumann's *Requiem für Mignon*, to texts from Goethe's novel *Wilhelm Meister*, was perhaps a kind of modern precedent). Brahms, whose knowledge of scripture was subtle and profound, himself assembled the text out of diverse passages from the Old and New Testaments and the Apocrypha, and he essentially addresses the feelings of the bereaved in a consolatory meditation on the common destiny of the living and the dead. He here fully explores the poignant contrast, so central to his thought in almost all his choral works, between those already in a state of grace and those barred from it and afflicted with a sense of mortality. The progression of thought, like the overall form, is a grand arch, its keystone the central movement that evokes the bliss of those now 'in the dwellings of the House of the Lord'. Before that, movements 2 and 3 are expressions of mourning and exhortations to patience; after it, movement 5 promises comfort and future joy, and 6 expounds the mystery of the resurrection of the dead and the end of death itself. And these five movements are placed within 1 and 7, prologue and epilogue which unite the living and the dead in the grand, circular progression of ideas: for the first movement begins in F major with 'Blessed are they that mourn', and the seventh concludes – with the same music, eventually in the same key – with 'Blessed are the dead which die in the Lord from henceforth'.

The language is theistic, but at no point (any more than in Brahms's other works compiled from biblical texts) is it explicitly Christian. This fact disturbed Reinthaler as he was preparing the Bremen performance: he even suggested that Brahms should add a further movement of incontrovertibly Christian content. The letter Brahms wrote in reply to this suggestion is highly revealing as to his intentions and beliefs, for he is adamant that the omission of all Christian reference was entirely deliberate. It also includes a comment which leaves no doubt that Brahms intended the work to be of universal, and not national or sectarian, significance. 'As regards the title', he wrote, 'I will confess I should gladly have left out "German" and substituted "Human".' (It seems, in fact, that the inclusion of the extract from *Messiah* in the Bremen performance was a compromise in a Christian direction forced upon Reinthaler and Brahms by the cathedral authorities.)

A German Requiem was not, of course, the first requiem in German; precedents existed as far back as Schütz. But it was the first in which a composer had selected and shaped his text from sources quite other than the burial service in order to define essentially personal resonances and to speak to a contemporary audience in a shared tongue, transcending the constraints of ritual – the first requiem conceived as a prophetic sermon from individual experience, with universal application.

The Lutheran Bible remained the epicentre not just of religion but of general culture in Protestant-dominated nineteenth-century Germany, as it had been for Schütz and Bach in the seventeenth and eighteenth centuries. Almost inevitably, in *A German Requiem* Brahms was mindful of their example, turned to some of the words they had set in their religious choral works, and emulated some of their compositional responses. The complex and far-reaching nature of his feeling for early music almost certainly enhanced his chosen texts through a sense of partaking with these masters of the past in a shared tradition of sacred choral writing. Though he was perfectly confident about omitting all mention of Christ, he explained the archaic nature of much that he had retained to Reinthaler on grounds of precedent: 'I have no doubt included much because I am a musician, because I required it, because I can neither argue away nor strike out a "henceforth" from my venerable extracts. But I had better stop before I say too much.'

It seems likely that movement 4, 'Wie lieblich sind deine Wohnungen', was partly inspired by a setting of the same text in Book III of Schütz's *Symphoniae Sacrae*. Schütz also set portions of the texts used in Brahms's first and last movements, notably the verbal kernel of the entire work, 'Selig sind die Toten', in the 1636 *Musikalische Exequien*. Moreover, Brahms told the choral conductor Siegfried Ochs that he regarded the entire Requiem as founded on a Lutheran chorale, 'Wer nur den lieben Gott lässt walten', which is in fact especially closely related to the march theme in movement 2, 'Denn alles Fleisch es ist wie Gras', and whose presence may be detected by analysis in many other places, including the opening of the work. He may well have felt that in this use of a chorale he was emulating the practice of Bach's church cantatas.

It would certainly be a mistake, however, to search for a single model for Brahms's fundamentally original conception. *A German Requiem* is an inspired synthesis of archaic and modern – and one of the most seamless, the most infused with personal emotion, he ever achieved. The work's three great fugues (in movements 2, 3 and 6) are demonstrations of this: they are used to clinch the structures of entire movements in a much more dramatic fashion than anything in Bach or Schütz, owing more to the choral traditions of Handel and Beethoven. For all Brahms's love and mastery of strict Renaissance counterpoint, the grand fugue in movement 6, 'Herr, du bist würdig', is notably free, building upon the example of Handel (and indeed of the fugue in his own Handel Variations for piano); while that in movement 3 is a remarkable invention, entirely carried out over a sonorous pedal-point, no doubt to illustrate the idea of the Hand of God that supports the souls of the righteous.

Although, as noted above, the form of the work is in one sense circular or self-reflective, in another there is a clear emotional progression which makes a cathartic experience of any accurate performance. What Brahms has composed is the process of transcendence of grief: through human feelings of consolation, but also by the creation of a mystical sense of immortality as some kind of fact. As often in Brahms's officially religious or philosophical works, this immortality is a profoundly ambiguous phenomenon, inherent not so much in the individual soul as in the music which speaks to that soul; and yet inseparably bound up with human love, whose permanence he hymned in the setting of 1 Corinthians 13 which forms the last of his *Four Serious Songs*.

The first movement, 'Selig sind' ('Blessed are they that mourn'), establishes the Requiem's F major tonality and with it the atmosphere of calm resignation which is to be developed throughout the entire work. The writing for the chorus is austere and meditative, though the harmony is Romantic, mediated perhaps through Schumann. The crepuscular quality of sound is partly achieved by orchestration which entirely omits the violins. There follows the slow march, 'Denn alles Fleisch' ('For all flesh is as grass'). Despite a gentler and more hopeful episode at 'So seid nun geduldig' ('Be patient, therefore'), the march's baleful tread builds up in B flat minor, with a momentum of the utmost severity, to an overwhelming climax. But the trombones suddenly reinforce the chorus in a decisive 'aber . . .' ('but . . . '), with a switch to the major, and the accumulated dread is released in a fugue of solemn joy, 'die Erlöseten des Herrn' ('And the ransomed of the Lord shall return').

The third movement, beginning in D minor, introduces the baritone soloist with a necessary passage of teaching, 'Herr, lehre doch mich' ('Lord, make me to know mine end, and the measure of my days'). The music evolves freely, and once again a turn to the major precipitates a remarkable fugue: this, 'Der Gerechten Seelen' ('But the souls of the righteous'), is the one over the long tonic pedal, which enfolds the ecstatic variety of the polyphony in resonant splendour. 'Wie lieblich sind deine Wohnungen', the central lyric vision of the courts of the Lord, is in E flat, and stands as a mellifluous foil to the music that surrounds it. In essence this is a transfiguration of Brahms's song style; indeed, with its graceful 3/4 metre the movement almost resembles a celestial *Liebeslieder* waltz. The fifth movement, 'Ihr habt nun Traurigkeit', introduces the soprano soloist and, like the preceding movement, is a ternary form in a major key. Here the text is handled with especial intimacy and delicacy, played off against plangently pastoral wind writing. Towards the end the idea of comfort 'as one whom his mother comforteth' becomes intertwined with the repeated phrase 'I will see you again . . .' in the Requiem's supreme gesture of intimate tenderness, and Brahms's most personal avowal of feeling.

The sixth movement, which like movements 2 and 3 evolves from minor to major (of, in this case, the key of C), is the longest in the work, and its dramatic and philosophical core. The baritone soloist returns to expound a mystery (to a text already famous from *Messiah*), whose realisation is promised us first in an episode of stormy drama and painful triumph ('O death, where is thy sting?') and then in the most radiant and imposing of the work's fugues, whose subject is eventually developed into stupendous stepwise ascents, like ladders reaching from earth to heaven.

The last movement, 'Selig sind die Toten', returns to the style of the first, but the mood is radiantly transfigured; as before, the music rises from the depths, but now light, in the form of a high violin line, descends from the heights to infuse it with warmth and serenity. The finale evolves a broad ternary form at its own unhurried pace. Eventually the opening theme of the first movement returns, to the new text – at first in E flat, the key of the celestial dwellings of the fourth movement. At last this opening theme, the tonic F major, and the final message of hope coincide in peace. 'Selig' ('Blessed') is the last word we hear, as it was the first.

© Malcolm MacDonald

Benjamin Britten (1913–76)

Born in Suffolk on 22 November 1913 (propitiously, the feast day of St Cecilia, patron saint of music) Britten began piano lessons aged five, composing songs for his mother by the age of ten. At thirteen he began composition studies with Frank Bridge before entering the Royal College of Music in 1930. His documentary scores for the GPO (General Post Office) Film Unit brought him into collaboration with W. H. Auden, a liberating force; in 1937 he not only attracted international attention with his *Variations on a Theme of Frank Bridge* at the Salzburg Festival, but also met the tenor Peter Pears, who would become his lifelong partner and an influential interpreter of his work. Britten revitalised English opera with his first stage triumph *Peter Grimes* (1945), launching the Aldeburgh Festival three years later. He performed often as a conductor and pianist, and though he wrote a significant number of chamber and choral works (among them three string quartets and the *War Requiem*, 1961) it is principally for his vocal and especially operatic output that he is remembered.

❧ *Spring Symphony*, Op. 44 (1948–9)

Part One
 1 Introduction: Shine Out, Fair Sun
 2 The Merry Cuckoo
 3 Spring, the Sweet Spring
 4 The Driving Boy
 5 The Morning Star
Part Two
 6 Welcome, Maids of Honour
 7 Waters Above!
 8 Out on the Lawn I Lie in Bed

Britten's first meetings with the Russian émigré conductor Serge Koussevitzky, in New York and Boston early in 1942, resulted in the commissioning of his opera *Peter Grimes*. Their next encounter – at Tanglewood in 1946, at the American premiere of *Grimes* – earned Britten another commission from the Koussevitzky Music Foundation, this time for a large-scale choral and orchestral symphony. Although Koussevitzky wanted the work for the following season, Britten's involvement with the newly formed English Opera Group, for whom he was writing a new chamber opera (*Albert Herring*), compelled him to stall Koussevitzky's enquiries about the symphony's progress.

Writing on 12 January 1947, he declared:

> I am desperately keen to do it for you, & I have elaborate & exciting ideas for it! But all the same I am keen not to do it in a hurry; I want it to be my biggest & best piece so far . . . I am planning it for chorus & soloists, as I think you wanted; but it is a real symphony (the emphasis is on the orchestra) & consequently I am using Latin words.

A published note by the composer, dating from 1950, confirms his original intention of using a Latin text, but goes on to explain that 'a re-reading of much English lyric verse and a particularly lovely Spring day in East Suffolk, the Suffolk of Constable and Gainsborough, made me change my mind.'

Work on the symphony was postponed and it was not until August 1948 that Britten began shaping his new plan for the piece. By mid-October he was able to announce to Peter Pears, for whom the solo tenor part was conceived, that he was ready to start composition. A letter to the singer dated 22 October describes his progress:

The work started abysmally slowly & badly, & I got in a real state. But I think it's better now. I'm half way thro' the sketch of the first movement ['Shine out, fair sun'], deliberately not hurrying it, fighting every inch of the way. It is terribly hard to do, but I think shows signs of being a piece at last. It is such cold music that it is depressing to write, & I yearn for the Spring to begin.

By November Britten had sketched out six settings (the first four numbers, and the Herrick and Vaughan settings from Part Two) and confessed to Pears, 'It's coming out different, bigger (& I hope better!).'

The composer's optimism was short-lived: he showed symptoms of suffering from total physical and mental exhaustion and was ordered by his doctors to take complete rest for three months. Composition was not resumed on the symphony until the following year; the composition draft is dated 'March 15th 1949' on the final page, while the full score was completed in June.

With Koussevitzky's permission, the first performance of the *Spring Symphony* was given on 14 July 1949 in Amsterdam's Concertgebouw as part of the Holland Festival, with Jo Vincent (soprano), Kathleen Ferrier (contralto) and Peter Pears (tenor), the Dutch Radio Chorus and the Concertgebouw Orchestra conducted by Eduard van Beinum, who was an early post-war champion of Britten's music. The work's dedicatees – Koussevitzky and the Boston Symphony Orchestra – gave the US premiere at Tanglewood later that summer.

The *Spring Symphony* is divided into four sections broadly corresponding to the movements of the classical symphony, and owes some debt to the example of Mahler, particularly his 'song symphony' *Das Lied von der Erde*, a work much admired by Britten. The five numbers of Part One form an extended first movement; Parts Two and Three are shorter and provide a contemplative slow movement and a playful scherzo, respectively; Part Four is a rumbustious finale. Each of the work's twelve separate numbers reflects different aspects of spring, and is conceived for a different vocal and instrumental configuration.

Part One opens with a slow introduction, a setting for chorus of the anonymous sixteenth-century poem 'Shine Out, Fair Sun'. This prayer for spring's arrival is prefaced (and subsequently punctuated) by a refrain for percussion and harps. Between unaccompanied choral statements, whose mood reflects the barren wintry landscape, are interpolated interludes for strings, woodwind and muted brass, which powerfully combine at the climax. Spenser's 'The Merry Cuckoo' is heralded by a trio of fanfaring trumpets cascading around the solo tenor. Nashe's paean to spring in full bloom is entrusted to the solo vocalists, while the chorus echoes the opening phrase of the poem; each stanza is rounded off by a bird-call cadenza from the soloists. Britten's keen sensitivity to the dramatic possibilities of juxtaposing different texts is at work in the succeeding number, 'The Driving Boy', a setting of words by Peele and Clare. A carefree melody for boys' voices, accompanied by jaunty woodwinds, tuba and tambourine, is in perfect contrast to the poised grace of the soprano's description of the 'happy, dirty driving boy'. Part One closes with Milton's 'The Morning Star' (for chorus, brass and percussion), which includes nodding references to the heterophonic techniques of Far Eastern music that were so to preoccupy Britten from the mid-1950s.

Part Two begins with 'Welcome, Maids of Honour' (for contralto, single woodwind, harps and divided lower strings), devised as a theme and three variations. In 'Waters Above' Britten depicts Vaughan's description of a gentle evening shower of rain by directing the violins to play extremely quietly and close to the bridge. The final movement of Part Two, a setting of four stanzas from Auden's 'A Summer Night' (for contralto, wordless chorus and an orchestra devoid of strings), is one of the most highly developed in the symphony and stands at the work's centre. One of Britten's typically evocative nightscapes (alto flute and bass clarinet prominent), the setting develops towards a sudden outburst at the words 'Where Poland draws her Eastern bow'.

Part Three sees a return to the direct expression of the first part of the symphony. The impetuous 'When Will My May Come?' (for tenor, harps and strings) is a strophic setting. The graceful duet for soprano and tenor, Peele's 'Fair and Fair', toys with playful canons and syncopated rhythms. The brief 'Sound the Flute' unites the full chorus with the boys, but not before tenors and basses, sopranos and altos, and divided boys' voices have sung imitative duets.

Part Four is cast as a broad movement and comprises a setting of a single extended text from *The Knight of the Burning Pestle* by the Jacobean playwrights Beaumont and Fletcher. An attractive waltz is heard, as if from a distance, before a call from a cow horn and the tenor's declamation summon the populace to the festivities. Everyone joins in a boisterous and virtuosic Allegro pesante, at whose climax the cow horn once again rings out, and both chorus and orchestra take up the waltz. At the movement's height, the boys' chorus intones the thirteenth-century song 'Sumer is icumen in' as a cross-rhythm descant.

Philip Reed © BBC

∾ *War Requiem*, Op. 66 (1961)

1 Requiem aeternam
2 Dies irae
3 Offertorium
4 Sanctus
5 Agnus Dei
6 Libera me

In loving memory of Roger Burney (Sub-Lieutenant, RNVR); Piers Dunkerley (Captain, Royal Marines); David Gill (Ordinary Seaman, Royal Navy); Michael Halliday (Lieutenant, RNZNVR)

> My subject is War, and the pity of War,
> The Poetry is in the pity . . .
> All a poet can do today is warn.
>
> Wilfred Owen

From the early 1940s Britten had wanted to compose a significant, large-scale choral work that could take its place
among the monuments of the English choral tradition. With
W. H. Auden he planned a Christmas oratorio (Auden's *For
the Time Being*), begun in 1942 in the USA and continued
intermittently until 1946 when the scheme was finally abandoned owing to Auden's singular failure to prune the text to a
length reasonable for musical setting. In 1945, with Ronald
Duncan (librettist of *The Rape of Lucretia*), Britten considered
an oratorio entitled 'Mea culpa' which was designed as a
response to the dropping of the atomic bombs on Japan.
Three years later, following the assassination of Mahatma
Gandhi in 1948, Britten's unreserved admiration for the
Indian leader founded on a shared belief in the pacifist cause
– and thereby making a more direct link with the *War
Requiem* than any other of these unfulfilled projects – caused
him to ponder on the possibility of a requiem in Gandhi's
honour. Finally, in the mid-1950s, Britten and Duncan entertained the idea of a collaboration on another oratorio, this
time centred on the life of St Peter and intended for York
Minster.

While none of the foregoing was composed, one might
consider that the *Spring Symphony* (1948–9) fulfilled, at least in
part, Britten's need: scored for three soloists, large mixed
chorus with the addition of boys' choir (as in the *War
Requiem*), and large orchestra, and using a quintessentially
Brittenesque anthology of English lyrical verse, the *Spring
Symphony* has many of the hallmarks that would bring it within the choral tradition Britten wished to satisfy; yet its symphonic shape (a Mahlerian inspiration) and secular English
texts place it to one side of the tradition. When the invitation
from the Coventry Festival was made in the late 1950s, Britten
was ready and waiting to write the kind of work he had long
postponed: a large-scale setting of the Requiem Mass.

During the Battle of Britain, Coventry had been targeted
by the Luftwaffe for concentrated mass bombing. The city's
ancient cathedral was virtually destroyed and after the war, a

decision was made to rebuild the cathedral to a new design. An open competition was held, whose winner, Basil Spence, submitted an imaginative design for a building using modern materials which would be sited adjacent to the shell of the former cathedral. The spirit of the enterprise was one of reconciliation after conflict, reflected in the new cathedral's Chapel of Unity and in allowing the ruins of the former cathedral to remain as a stark reminder of the conflict. Spence wanted his building to be a showcase for the arts and crafts; his structure was enhanced by notable exponents of the arts: for example, Graham Sutherland was commissioned to design an imposing woven tapestry of Christ in Majesty to hang behind the high altar; John Piper (with Patrick Reyntiens) executed the vast Baptistry window, and Sir Jacob Epstein created the sculpture of St Michael defeating the Devil positioned on the wall outside the cathedral's main entrance. To celebrate the cathedral's consecration in May 1962, a showcase arts festival was planned by the local authority in association with the Arts Council. In keeping with the ideals behind the building itself, the Coventry Cathedral Festival was from the outset intended as an international symbolic act of reconciliation, as well as a national celebration.

The commission from the Coventry Festival for a work to celebrate the consecration of Spence's fine new cathedral building provided Britten with a twofold opportunity. On the one hand he was able to compose a large-scale choral work suitable for a reverberant acoustic and appropriate for such an important symbolic occasion, and on the other he seized the chance to make a private statement about his own long-held pacifist beliefs and to offer the work, in his own words, as 'an act of reparation'. Following the first performance on 30 May 1962 and the subsequent impact of the piece, particularly after the highly successful recording under the composer's direction, the *War Requiem* became rather more than its creator had originally bargained for: it was now regarded as a public statement of outrage against war, conflict and violence, sentiments that were intensified by the fiftieth anniversary of the outbreak of the First World War and the growing public awareness of and discomfort with atrocities in Vietnam.

For the *War Requiem* Britten recognised the possibility of setting the poetry of Wilfred Owen, whom he once described as 'by far our greatest war poet, and one of the most original poets of the century', within the seemingly unlikely context of the Latin Mass for the Dead. (He had already set Owen's 'The Kind Ghosts' in his *Nocturne*, Op. 60, as a trial run for the *War Requiem* settings.) The combination of these disparate elements, which under Britten's guiding hand became one of the work's strengths, is played out on a distinctly triplanar level. Nearest to the audience are two soldiers, one British (tenor), the other German (baritone), who are accompanied by the chamber orchestra and operate very much at a human level. They sing the Owen poems. The soprano soloist, large chorus and full symphony orchestra represent formal grief, and are confined to the 'official', liturgical text. Lastly, sited away from the other performers, come the boys' voices accompanied by the neutral-sounding chamber organ, whose innocent, pure sounds keep them divorced from the human experience. Within this framework Britten explores and exploits the inherent contrasts and ironies. By writing the *War Requiem* for three specific solo singers – Peter Pears, Dietrich Fischer-Dieskau and Galina Vishnevskaya (who at the premiere was substituted at the last moment by Heather Harper, because the Soviet authorities refused Vishnevskaya permission to sing) – Britten neatly embraced three of the national protagonists of the Second World War. Each of these singers had lived through the conflict and experienced the public and private torments and difficulties that only such a conflict can bring: Pears, like Britten, as a pacifist and conscientious objector in England; Fischer-Dieskau as a young soldier in Germany and later as a prisoner of war; and Vishnevskaya as a civilian caught up in the horrific deprivations of besieged Leningrad.

At a private level, the work is dedicated to the memory of four of the composer's schoolboy friends, all of whom, with the exception of Piers Dunkerley, perished in the 1939–45 conflict. Dunkerley, a professional soldier, lived beyond the war years, remaining a close friend of the composer and occasionally meeting up with Britten and Pears in Aldeburgh or London. He left the Royal Marines in the late 1950s and tried to make his way in civilian life, but alas committed suicide in 1959, around the period when Britten was beginning to turn over the *War Requiem* in his mind. Britten's inclusion of Dunkerley among the dedicatees can be interpreted as a private gesture of reparation, as he felt that somehow the war and military life had been responsible for Dunkerley's sad demise.

Because Britten was here deliberately concerned with communicating to a mass audience, the musical language of the *War Requiem* is, at a basic level, straightforward to comprehend. At the same time, however, it avoids the merely commonplace or banal. Much of the tonal outline of the work can be attributed to Verdi and – to a lesser degree – Mozart's supreme examples in the same genre. It is a curious irony that the image of rest in the *War Requiem* is accompanied by the traditional musical image of unrest, the tritone (C–F sharp) heard on the bells at the outset of the opening 'Requiem aeternam'. The only occasion this tension is fully resolved occurs at the end of the Agnus Dei, the Requiem's basic moment of truth when Owen's 'At a Calvary near the Ancre' and the words of the Agnus Dei run concurrently. That we might feel uneasy in our seats at the end of the piece is because of the reappearance of the hollow tritone, once again intoned by the bells. As Peter Pears once said: 'It isn't the end, we haven't escaped, we must still think about it, we are not allowed to end in a peaceful dream.' A sobering thought in a world that evidently still needs its war requiems as we are faced, virtually on a daily basis, with the horrors of man's inhumanity to man. We evidently still need our poets to warn us, to make us aware.

© Philip Reed

Anton Bruckner (1824–96)

Bruckner's path to recognition was a slow and arduous one. Born in Upper Austria in 1824, he began his career as a teacher at the Church of St Florian, where he had earlier been a choral scholar. In 1856 he became organist at nearby Linz Cathedral, and seven years later was deeply and lastingly affected by Wagner's *Tannhäuser*. Until this time his compositions centred on sacred music – he was devoutly religious throughout his life – but in 1866 he produced his First Symphony. It was only with the premiere of his Seventh (1884), by which time he had reached sixty, that Bruckner first gained public recognition. In 1891, to his great delight, he became the first musician to be honoured with a doctorate from the University of Vienna.

❧ Mass No. 2 in E minor (1866; rev. 1876, 1882)

1 Kyrie
2 Gloria
3 Credo
4 Sanctus
5 Benedictus
6 Agnus Dei

That Bruckner self-confessedly strove to convey something of the grandeur of God in all his music up to the *Te Deum* and Ninth Symphony of his last years is a fact well known to any student of the man and his work. Thus it is unsurprising to find among his earliest output three Masses: the first for contralto, two horns and organ (*c.*1842), the last a Missa solemnis for soloists, chorus and orchestra (1854). But his three masterpieces of the genre date from 1864–8. Of these the orchestral Masses in D minor and F minor continue the tradition of the classical Viennese festive Mass as perfected by Haydn, Mozart, Schubert and Beethoven.

The E minor Mass, the second of these three great settings, stands apart from the others, and indeed almost all other contemporary liturgical works, because of the forces used (no soloists, organ, timpani or strings) and because of its intense expressiveness, its uniquely personal harmonic language, boldness of texture, subtlety of counterpoint and, above all, its apparent simplicity of language.

The simplicity is deceptive. Bruckner, in his peculiarly rigorous forging of technique, had for long years applied himself to the refiner's fire of contrapuntal study. The result was that, when he finally closed his exercise books, he had transcended mere technique and gained the ability to speak intimately in a confident, personal language. The roots of that language can be found in the Renaissance masters Bruckner studied and revered, and this Mass springs from those historical forebears. Yet no work of the 1860s reveals his musical personality so vividly, and (with the exception of some of Liszt's most striking liturgical works) no Catholic church music of the later Romantic era approaches this Mass in the effective combination of simple, direct utterance and inward, profoundly felt spiritual power. Its instrumentation, harmony and style of motivic development are uniquely Brucknerian (and thus of the later nineteenth century), but its restraint, devoutness and austere power recall the highest era of Italian Renaissance polyphony.

The Mass was completed in Linz in November 1866 and first performed there, outside the new cathedral, in September 1869. Bruckner revised the work for the premiere and again in 1876 and 1882. Comprising oboes, clarinets, bassoons, horns, trumpets and trombones, the orchestra is employed discreetly but by no means as mere background accompaniment. It weaves unbroken links between vocal phrases; it sets in motion motivic figures that propel whole sections; it reinforces and highlights moments of vocal declamation; and it is used to create constant variety of sound and contrast of texture.

The Kyrie opens in the Phrygian mode, its unhurried pace creating a sense of dignity and awe. The characteristic poignancy of the harmony of this Mass makes itself felt at the outset with a dissonance as the fourth strand of the women's voices enters. The male voices then sing the Kyrie, the rich strand of eight-part polyphony only unfolding in the more intense 'Christe' section.

The first phrases of both the Gloria and Credo are intoned in plainsong (as Bruckner intended this Mass for liturgical use). The bassoon figures at the start of the Gloria provide the rhythmic impetus for the first section which is freely reprised at 'Quoniam'. In between comes a new idea in slower tempo at 'Qui tollis'. In the Classical manner, the Amen is fugal: in this case a double fugue of forthright virility. C major is the 'key' of both Gloria and Credo, although the rich procession of dramatic key changes that heighten the meaning of the words is of the greatest importance. The busy, jubilant outer sections of the Credo flank a slow movement ('Et incarnatus est') of exquisite tenderness.

The Sanctus begins with an eight-part canonic structure based on a phrase from Palestrina's *Missa brevis*, majestically crowned with the brass at 'Dominus Deus sabaoth'. The final climb to the G major cadence for 'in excelsis' is made truly powerful through a sonorous use of dissonance. The Benedictus, a sonata-form structure, is rich in chromatic colouring, every verbal context winning an apt emotional response from Bruckner within his formal concept. In the Agnus Dei the repeated cries of 'miserere' rise like huge Gothic arches, and at the final plea for peace ('dona nobis pacem') the Phrygian cadence of the Kyrie reappears in transfigured form.

© Derek Watson

↜ Mass No. 3 in F minor (1867–8)

1   Kyrie
2   Gloria
3   Credo
4   Sanctus
5   Benedictus
6   Agnus Dei

This Mass was composed between September 1867 and September 1868, during the last year of Bruckner's tenure as organist of Linz Cathedral and immediately before his move to Vienna. It is therefore roughly contemporary with the First Symphony and the D minor Symphony which Bruckner later called 'Die Nullte' (no. 0). There is nothing at all immature in the language and structure of Bruckner's three great Masses (of which this is the last and grandest), and the fact that they precede by some years his full maturity as a symphonist tells us a great deal about his musical character.

The uncompromising time-scale of the later symphonies shows a musical mind which naturally thinks in terms of subjugating the momentary sensation to the permanent vision. The vision in this instance is a religious one, and while any number of inferior nineteenth-century composers might express a mood of faith by writing the word 'religioso' at the head of their scores and then reaching for the harps and the syrup, Bruckner is made of tougher stuff. He was drawn to express himself through abstract symphonic argument, never opting for easy solutions to the constructional problems he set himself, with the result that the triumphs are not rhetorical gestures but the product of an exploring mind well aware that the more intense the faith, the greater the doubts to be overcome (how could Bruckner's faith possibly have been as simple and naive as some of his biographers have suggested?). The musical structure of a mass setting, as opposed to that of an abstract instrumental work, however, will always be determined to a great extent by its need to illuminate the text. It would be quite untrue to suggest that Bruckner fretted at such a restriction – his devotion to the text makes such an idea absurd – but after the huge achievement of this F minor Mass he may well have felt that his further development lay in exploring forms less dependent on traditional models.

The F minor Mass clearly belongs to the hundred-year-old tradition of the Austrian symphonic Mass exemplified by the works of Haydn, Mozart, Schubert and Beethoven, although certain aspects of its language look back even further – the themes formed from the contours of plainsong, for example, or passages of choral writing which have more in common with the polyphony of the sixteenth century than with the harmonic style of Bruckner's own period. Tradition and nineteenth-century modernity are blended and contrasted in a way that inevitably recalls the *Missa solemnis* of Beethoven, whose Ninth Symphony (which was to have so profound an effect on his musical thinking) Bruckner had heard for the first time only a year before beginning this Mass.

All considerations of its background and origin, however, inevitably take second place to the actual experience of the work's deep emotional and spiritual strength. Every detail of the vast design contributes to the power of this 'choral symphony', not least those intensely personal moments that stand out from the rest and remain in the memory long after the performance is over: the rock-like interpolations of 'Credo, credo' in the 'Et vitam venturi' fugue, for instance, or the huge span of the cello melody in the Benedictus (sketched, appropriately, on Christmas Eve 1867), or the final section of the Agnus Dei, whose prayer for peace echoes the Mass's dark minor-key opening, but at the same time transfigures it into a radiantly calm F major.

© Andrew Huth

William Byrd (*c.*1540–1623)

Byrd was born in London and sang as a chorister in the Chapel Royal before being appointed organist of Lincoln Cathedral in 1563. He returned to the Chapel Royal as a Gentleman in 1570, becoming joint organist in 1575 with Tallis, his former teacher. Together, Byrd and Tallis were granted an exclusive publishing licence by Elizabeth I, allowing rapid dissemination of their music. Their first printed volume was of *Cantiones sacrae* ('Sacred Songs', 1575; motets for five to eight voices), of which Byrd published two further volumes on his own by 1591. In addition to his contribution to the development of the Anglican anthem, Byrd also wrote for the Catholic liturgy, including three Latin Masses, one each in three, four and five voices. He also joined clandestine celebrations of the Catholic Mass and was fined for recusancy (refusal to attend Church of England services). Vocal works form the principal part of his output, though he also composed secular motets and was one of the earliest composers to establish a body of music for keyboard.

⁓ Mass for Five Voices (*c.*1595)

1   Kyrie
2   Gloria
3   Credo
4   Sanctus
5   Benedictus
6   Agnus Dei

It was politically expedient for Thomas Cromwell to make claims for England's ancient independence when overseeing the draft of his Act in Restraint of Appeals of 1533, one of several legislative manoeuvres intended to ease Henry VIII's marital difficulties. While Cromwell's efforts to deny the historical relationship between the English state and the Roman Church eased his monarch's progress towards divorce, they also caused a seismic shift in the country's religious status quo, leaving many conservative-minded worshippers in fear of eternal damnation or earthly persecution. Public unrest over the king's 'Protestant Reformation' was brutally repressed under Henry; old religious traditions and sentiments, however, survived the sword and even the theological revolution of Edward VI's brief reign. The Marian reaction restored papal authority over a country by now divided in its religious allegiances, delivering committed Protestants to the stake as heretics and forcing thousands more to seek sanctuary abroad. Order and tolerance were finally added to the Reformation scene by Elizabeth I, whose accession prepared the way for a shrewd settlement of religious conflict: regular attendance at Anglican church services was declared compulsory and religious dissent outlawed.

Musicians who had trimmed their sails to catch changing ideological winds – Thomas Tallis prominent among them – enjoyed greater tolerance under Elizabeth's rule. Those like William Byrd, who continued to follow the Roman Catholic faith, were periodically fined for recusancy, or failing to attend church, and watched by Elizabeth's network of security agents. In fact, Byrd's Catholic convictions appear to have strengthened in the early 1580s, not long after the brutal public executions of the Jesuit missionaries Robert Parsons and Edmund Campion on Tyburn Hill. In 1585 Byrd was himself fined as a recusant and again bound to pay the enormous sum of £200 two years later. The authorities must have known that he periodically met with prominent Catholic missionaries and other high-profile supporters of the Roman Church; he was even accused of 'seducing' neighbours and servants to become converts. Yet Byrd managed to survive and prosper at first under the direct patronage of Elizabeth I and in later years under that of Sir John Petre, son of the queen's former secretary of state and himself a discreet Catholic.

Byrd moved with his family to the village of Stondon Massey in Essex in the early 1590s, a few miles from the Petres's manor house at Ingatestone. Like many other members of the gentry, the Petres supported regular undercover Catholic services, for which Byrd supplied settings of texts from the Latin liturgy. His three settings of the Ordinary of the Mass were published defiantly in the composer's name between 1592 and 1595, no doubt intended for use at other secret centres of Catholic observance. 'The clandestine Masses at Ingatestone, always in danger of exposure by spies,' Joseph Kerman has observed, 'had no leisure for the grandiose, drawn-out, florid music of Tallis and his generation.'

The Mass for Five Voices, printed in London by Thomas East and issued around 1595, employs a polyphonic style of remarkable, pristine austerity. The work stands among the composer's best-known pieces, routinely cited by music historians as comparable with the finest mass settings of Palestrina, Victoria and Lassus. The movements of the Mass are linked not by the conventional use of plainchant cantus firmi but by Byrd's choice of common themes, albeit modified, particularly establishing clear melodic connections between the Kyrie, Gloria, Credo and Agnus Dei. The similarity of many of Byrd's contrapuntal themes, whether intended or coincidental, adds a powerful sense of unity to the third of his Mass settings. More immediately recognisable, however, is the composer's intensely reverential response to the Latin text, which dispenses with florid ornamentation and the type of note-spinning commonly employed by his famous continental contemporaries to prolong parts of the Mass.

Andrew Stewart © BBC

Frederick Delius (1862–1934)

Born in Bradford, Delius rejected a role in his father's wool-trade business, and ran an orange plantation in Florida before studying at the Leipzig Conservatory (1886-8). He moved first to Paris, then, in 1897, to nearby Fontainebleau – after which he wrote his fourth and most successful opera, *A Village Romeo and Juliet* (1900–1), the Walt Whitman setting *Sea Drift* (1903–4) and his Nietzsche-inspired *A Mass of Life* (1904–5). He also wrote a series of evocative tone-poems – including *Brigg Fair* (1907), *Summer Night on the River* (1911) and *On Hearing the First Cuckoo in Spring* (1912). His pantheism fuelled an impressionistic flair for orchestration, and he drew regular inspiration from the black American music which he heard on his plantation, and from Scandinavia (he had befriended Grieg in Leipzig, and he spent many holidays in Norway). In 1907 Thomas Beecham began an unswerving championship of Delius's works (he regarded the composer as 'the last great apostle in our time of romance, beauty and emotion in music'). By 1925 syphilis had blinded Delius, and his last works were dictated to his amanuensis, the composer Eric Fenby.

∾ *Sea Drift* (1903–4)

It is striking how much English music during the first half of the twentieth century was inspired by the sea. Between Elgar's *Sea Pictures* (1899) and Britten's *Four Sea Interludes* from *Peter Grimes* (1945) fall Stanford's *Songs of the Sea* and *Songs of the Fleet*, Delius's *Sea Drift*, Henry Wood's *Fantasia on British Sea-Songs*, Vaughan Williams's *A Sea Symphony*, Bridge's *The Sea*, Ireland's *Sea Fever*. Natural enough, perhaps, for an island race to consider the sea (it is convenient at the moment to overlook Debussy's *La mer*). But there was more to it than that. A plane flight may be swift and exhilarating, but the sheer length of a sea voyage promotes reflection. The sea presents a challenge, an adventure, a symbol of infinity: a sea voyage is a metaphor for a life's journey. At the same time the sea can be a soothing comforter, as the opening lines of the poem from which Delius took his text suggest: 'Out of the Cradle Endlessly Rocking'. It is just this surface tranquillity with an undertow of power and menace that Delius so disturbingly caught in his orchestral introduction to *Sea Drift*.

That so many composers of this island turned to the poetry of Walt Whitman (1819–92) is equally striking. 'Darest thou now, O Soul' was a call that found a ready response. Radical minds were eager to push back frontiers, to seek freedom from orthodoxy, to be elevated by democratic and humanistic ideals; and composers enjoyed the free verse. Vaughan Williams and Holst were sketching music to Whitman's words as early as 1903; the *Sea Symphony* itself came to performance in 1910. Both Holst and Harty listened to the Wild Trumpeter. Bliss sought a parallel for the spirit of the 1914 volunteers, and found it in the outbreak of the American Civil War, for his *Morning Heroes* (1930). Vaughan Williams also went to *Drum-Taps* in 1936 in his song of warning, *Dona nobis pacem*, for the war to come.

For Delius, a long sea voyage and a sojourn in Whitman's native land came together in 1884, when he sailed to Florida to manage an orange plantation. The exotic beauty and the solitude furthered his introspective, egocentric bent. What he admired in Whitman was close to his own creed: 'Whitman spent his whole life writing *Leaves of Grass*. It is his individual contribution to art. Nobody else could have written it. So with my own work.' (The influence of that foreign environment on Delius can be heard directly in his *Florida Suite*, in *Appalachia*, and in his operas *Koanga* and *The Magic Fountain*.) Study in Leipzig followed, and the lively, vigorous Paris years; then he settled in the idyllic village of Grez. There, in 1903–4, he composed *Sea Drift*. To Eric Fenby, years later, he described it as 'one of my best works', and told how the music came to him:

The shape of it was taken out of my hands, so to speak, as I worked, and was bred easily and effortlessly of the nature and sequence of my particular musical ideas, and the nature and sequence of the particular poetical ideas of Whitman that appealed to me.

At the time Delius was better known in Germany than in England, and the first performance was at Essen, under Georg Witte, on 24 May 1906. (The first English performance was in 1908, at Sheffield, under Henry Wood.) *Sea Drift* was dedicated to the conductor Max Schillings, published as *In Meerestreiben*, and sung to German words. However, in a letter to Ernest Newman of 19 August 1929, Delius made it plain that 'I composed *Sea-Drift* in English and could not have done otherwise, as the lovely poem inspired my music.'

'Once Paumanok . . .' Paumanok was the Indian name for Long Island, 'over a hundred miles long; shaped like a fish – plenty of sea shore, sandy, stormy, uninviting, the horizon boundless . . . a wonderful resort of aquatic birds' – so runs an old guidebook. Whitman, in his essay on his life as a child and young man on the 'island' where he was born, says he 'always liked the bare sea-beach, south side, and have some of the happiest hours on it to this day. As I write, the whole experience comes back to me after the lapse of forty and more years – the soothing rustle of the waves, and the saline smell – boyhood's times.' (The poem was first published in 1859 as *A Child's Reminiscence*.) In that 'lapse of forty and more years' lies the quality of Whitman's and Delius's great work: by the pressure of time on memory, the child's intense emotion is deepened through the man's experience. The truth is laid bare in the baritone's anguished cry that the bird's call to his lost mate has 'meanings which I of all men know'.

For this music, with all its sea and sea-bird imagery, is about human love and loss. 'We two together' forms the ecstatic, fulfilled opening. The baritone enters unobtrusively over the chorus, in a seamless binding of voices and instruments. The melody of the 'curious' boy watching, absorbing, swells nobly at 'translating' – a very Whitmanesque word, suggesting a move from the plane of narrative to that of metaphor. The harmonic tension is high: grief ('con dolore e passione') brings Elgarian suspensions (but this was composed before the Second Symphony, which it recalls). Delius professed disdain of traditional formal procedures; but there are, of course, thematic allusions, key and rhythmic relationships, and carefully controlled densities to be discovered in what sounds like a continuous flow of sensation. The joyous choral outburst at 'Shine! Shine!' is balanced later by the lonely desire of 'O rising stars'. The swinging passages at 'Singing all time' and 'Blow! blow!' act as refrains. Delius's final evocation of 'O past! O happy life!' is heart-breaking for being in the major key of the opening. The final bars, 'We two together no more', hold the ache of lovers torn apart by elements too strong for them, made the more poignant by the symbol of the frail sea-bird.

© Diana McVeagh

Maurice Duruflé (1902–86)

Duruflé followed in the tradition of the French Romantic organist-composers at a time when Stravinsky and others were embracing twentieth-century modernism. He was born in Louviers, Normandy, and joined the choir school of Rouen Cathedral aged ten. At seventeen he moved to Paris, studying with Tournemire and Vierne before entering the Paris Conservatoire in 1920. Here he was a pupil alongside Messiaen in Dukas's composition class, and he left with a handful of *premiers prix*. He assisted Vierne at Notre-Dame from 1929 to 1931 and became organist at St Étienne-du-Mont in 1930. He published few works, but they are finely crafted and often incorporate harmonisations of Gregorian chant. Among such works are his Requiem (1947) and the *Quatre Motets sur des thèmes grégoriens* (1960). His organ music, especially the Suite, Op. 5 (1933), is regularly performed, though his two orchestral works are forgotten. An active performer, he premiered Poulenc's Organ Concerto in 1939 and gave recital tours of the USA in 1964 and 1966, but was forced to stop playing in 1975 when injuries following a car accident largely confined him to his bed.

❧ Requiem, Op. 9 (1947)

1 Introit
2 Kyrie
3 Domine Jesu Christe
4 Sanctus
5 Pie Jesu
6 Agnus Dei
7 Lux aeterna
8 Libera me
9 In paradisum

Maurice Duruflé's musical language and aesthetic sensibilities, unlike those of his friend and near-contemporary Olivier Messiaen, were rooted securely in the past, both recent and distant. He had joined the choir school at Rouen Cathedral as a ten-year-old, imbibing the daily office of Gregorian chant and other liturgical music every day of the school week and performing the same at High Mass and Vespers on Sundays. During his time studying at the Paris Conservatoire, Duruflé drew inspiration from composers such as Debussy, Fauré, Ravel and his composition teacher, Paul Dukas, great figures of French musical life whose mature works were revered by the gifted young organist-composer from Louviers. Modal harmonies, Gregorian melodic nuances and subtle, impressionistic instrumental colours were to distinguish the small number of works that Duruflé completed or considered worthy of publication during his creative life.

In 1947 Duruflé was approached by his publisher, the Paris-based firm of Durand & Cie, with a commission for a setting of the Latin Requiem for choir and orchestra. The obsessively self-critical composer was at that time drafting a suite for organ based on plainsong themes; this project was abandoned and its Gregorian tunes recycled to supply the substance of the new Requiem. Critics have noted the apparent similarities between Duruflé's treatment of the Requiem text and that of Fauré, whose work was widely respected and often performed by the late 1940s. The two works are at their closest in terms of atmosphere, with Duruflé clearly affected and influenced by the peaceful, reverential nature of Fauré's vision of the Requiem. He also followed the older composer's omission of the hell-fire sentiments of the 'Dies irae' sequence, and likewise introduced baritone solos into the Offertory prayer and 'Libera me'. Any further comparisons, however, appear irrelevant given the sheer quality and expressive range of Duruflé's work, its lyrical outer movements especially presenting the listener with a message of optimistic faith in the after-life.

Duruflé himself wrote that:

This Requiem is entirely composed on the Gregorian themes of the Mass for the Dead. Sometimes the musical text was completely respected, the orchestral part intervening only to support or comment on it; sometimes I was simply inspired by it or left it completely, for example in certain developments suggested by the Latin text, notably in the Domine Jesu Christe, the Sanctus, and the Libera. As a general rule, I have above all sought to enter into the particular style of the Gregorian themes.

The last observation can be positively tested in each movement, for example, in the flowing accompaniment and opening melody of the Introit, the drawn-out suspensions of the final 'Christe', the robust declamation of 'libera eas de ore leonis' ('deliver them from the lion's mouth') in the 'Domine Jesu Christe' and the majestic Sanctus.

Duruflé makes a dramatic virtue of rare outbursts from full orchestra and choir, set in relief against a tranquil background of economic instrumentation and prayer-like melodies. According to the composer, 'This Requiem is not an ethereal work which sings detached from worldly anxiety. It reflects, in the unchangeable form of the Christian prayer, the anguish of man facing the mystery of his last ending.' Such was the strength of this reflection that Duruflé was called upon to oversee two further versions of the work – one for choir with reduced orchestral forces, the other for choir and organ – testimony to the communicative power of his response to the traditional Requiem text.

Andrew Stewart © BBC

Antonín Dvořák (1841–1904)

It was Brahms who recognised Dvořák's talent when, around 1875, he recommended the Czech composer to his own publisher, Simrock. Born in a village north of Prague in 1841, Dvořák worked as a viola player at the Provisional Theatre, then as an organist. The success of tours in the 1880s led to wider recognition, and his appointment in 1891 as director of the newly founded National Conservatory of Music in New York. During his three years in America he was influenced by Negro and indigenous music, composing the 'New World' Symphony and the 'American' Quartet, Op. 96. But the pull of his homeland, whose folk music and pastoral beauty were reflected strongly in his music, was great: he returned to a post at the Prague National Conservatory, later becoming director. He never achieved the success of his older compatriot Smetana in the field of opera, but wrote three concertos (for violin, cello and piano), some fine string quartets, and established the Czech oratorio with his *Stabat mater*. He is best known for his symphonies and his sets of *Slavonic Dances*, originally written for piano duet, then arranged for orchestra.

∾ *Stabat mater*, Op. 58 (1876–7)

Dvořák was a man of strong and simple Catholic belief. He told his friend and mentor Brahms that he read the Bible every day; Brahms later commented that 'a man so industrious as Dvořák by no means has time to get stuck on doubts; rather all his life he stands by what he was taught in his childhood.' In turn, Dvořák was astonished by Brahms's atheism: 'Such a great man! Such a great soul! And he believes in nothing!' Dvořák's first setting of a sacred text (apart from a lost student Mass) was his *Stabat mater*, a prayer to the bereaved mother of the crucified Christ. It was drafted between

February and May 1876, apparently as a delayed reaction to the death of the Dvořáks' daughter Josefa the previous September, two days after her birth. Several other projects intervened before he got down to the task of orchestrating the work, in October and November 1877 – by which time the couple had lost their second daughter, Růžena, who had died aged less than a year in August, and a month later their only son, the three-year-old Otakar.

Having been written out of personal impulse rather than to a commission, the *Stabat mater* had to wait some time for its first performance. It was eventually performed, rather unseasonably, two days before Christmas 1880, by the opera company of the Czech Provisional Theatre in Prague. But subsequently the *Stabat mater* became the work which introduced Dvořák to amateur choral societies all over the world – just as the first set of *Slavonic Dances* made his name known to orchestras and their audiences, and to domestic piano duettists. For example, the *Stabat mater* was given its first British performance in March 1883 in the Royal Albert Hall; and it was repeated there a year later, with Dvořák himself, on the first of his many visits to England, conducting a choir numbering over 800 and an orchestra to match.

For a work with no precedent in Dvořák's output, and indeed no significant precursor in nineteenth-century Czech music, the *Stabat mater* is remarkably assured in establishing its own style, without undue recourse to past models. It is surprisingly free in its handling of tonality; and it dispenses with the extended fugal movements which had previously been virtually obligatory in large-scale sacred works. There is certainly counterpoint, notably in the extended 'Amen' – but even there it is noticeable that it does not end the work, instead giving way to a chordal double coda. However, academicism is not replaced by nationalism: there are no more than a few traces of Czech or Slavonic colouring, in modal touches in the melody and harmony rather than in rhythm. Dvořák's personal voice is chiefly in evidence in some highly individual turns of phrase, and in his handling of the orchestra, with its characteristically generous writing for woodwind and brass.

As for influences, that of Brahms's *A German Requiem*, published and first performed at the end of the 1860s, crops up from time to time, most obviously in the introduction to 'Fac me vere' over a sustained bass note. But the vocal writing seems to owe most to the example of Verdi, many of whose operas Dvořák had played as a member of the Provisional Theatre orchestra, and whose Requiem had been published and first performed in 1874. When Dvořák was awarded an honorary Cambridge degree in 1891, and conducted a performance of the *Stabat mater* on the eve of the ceremony, he surprised his host, Charles Villiers Stanford, by his lack of enthusiasm for any living composer other than Verdi. Incidentally, at the degree ceremony itself Dvořák was embarrassed to find himself being praised in Latin, a language he did not understand; but he later consoled himself with the thought that, 'after all, it is better to have composed the *Stabat mater* than to know Latin'.

The sequence *Stabat mater*, of thirteenth-century Franciscan origin and long attributed to Jacopone da Todi (d. 1306), begins as a description of the Virgin Mary at the foot of the cross, and turns into a prayer to her for her intercession. Dvořák set it in its entirety, grouping varying numbers of its three-line stanzas together to form substantial self-contained movements.

By some way the longest movement is the first, a setting of the first four stanzas for chorus and all four soloists, with an extended orchestral introduction and an overall A–B–A shape; in B minor, it begins with bare octave F sharps, perhaps symbolising the cross itself – the German word for a sharp is *Kreuz* ('cross') – and continues with a sorrowing descending chromatic phrase which is to dominate the outer sections of the movement, usually associated with the opening words, 'Stabat mater dolorosa'. 'Quis est homo', for all four soloists, similarly gathers four stanzas into a substantial A–B–A structure; it is in E minor, and its outer sections are again dominated by the short, expressive phrase to which the opening words are set.

The stanza in which description turns to prayer, 'Eja, mater', is set as a short, solemn chorus in C minor. The following movement, in B flat minor, alternates between the bass soloist's 'Fac, ut ardeat cor meum', declamatory and then lyrical, and the chorus's devotional 'Sancta mater'; the choral episodes have a part for organ (originally harmonium) – an instrument which is otherwise absent from the score, but which Dvořák perhaps expected to be in use throughout to support the chorus. 'Tui nati', in E flat major (the first major-key movement in the work), is set for chorus in a gently flowing 6/8 time, with a more agitated, and more contrapuntal, middle section. 'Fac me vere', in B major, after its Brahmsian introduction, is set for solo tenor and male chorus, in alternation and then in combination; the stanza 'Juxta crucem' appears twice for brief, urgent contrast.

'Virgo virginum praeclara', in A major, is a predominantly quiet movement for chorus alone, for much of the time unaccompanied or discreetly supported by the orchestra. After this, Dvořák rings the changes on his vocal scoring: 'Fac, ut portem', in D major, is a lyrical duet for soprano and tenor; 'Inflammatus', in D minor, is an alto solo, beginning with the Handelian colouring of oboes, bassoons and strings and with a trudging Handelian bass line. The setting of the final stanza reunites all four soloists with the chorus: it begins in B minor with the octave F sharps of the opening of the whole work, but turns decisively to D major at the first choral climax; in this key, the descending motive of the first movement reappears, now consoling rather than sorrowing, and is even incorporated into the contrapuntal fabric of the exuberant 'Amen'. After a blazing chordal passage for unaccompanied chorus, the descending motive makes its last appearances in the D major coda, a final calm affirmation of Dvořák's abiding faith.

© Anthony Burton

Edward Elgar (1857–1934)

Elgar rose from humble beginnings (his father was a piano tuner and organist) to become Britain's leading composer: he was knighted in 1904, awarded the Order of Merit in 1911 and became Master of the King's Musick in 1924. Born in Worcester, he failed in his early attempt to establish himself in London, though his reputation grew steadily during the 1890s. The *Enigma Variations* of 1899 first brought him to national attention, followed closely by his darkly imaginative *The Dream of Gerontius* (1900). He wrote two further works of a planned trilogy, *The Apostles* and *The Kingdom* but *The Last Judgement* remained unrealised. He was over fifty when he produced his First Symphony, the first of his large-scale orchestral works, which was followed by the Violin Concerto, the Second Symphony and the Cello Concerto. After the death of his wife in 1920 he lost his will to compose, though in 1932 the BBC commissioned his Third Symphony. Elgar left 130 pages of sketches for the symphony at his death, which were elaborated by the British composer Anthony Payne. Fittingly, the completed work was finally premiered by the BBC Symphony Orchestra in 1998.

❧ *The Apostles*, Op. 49 (1902–3)

Pinpointing the exact moment of conception of a work of art is rarely easy. But for Elgar, there was a clearly defined event that set his creative imagination working on the subject of the Apostles. It came during his time as a pupil at Littleton House School, Worcester. His teacher, Francis Reeve, remarked that 'The Apostles were young men and very poor. Perhaps, before the descent of the Holy Ghost, they were no cleverer than some of you here.' The idea of writing a religious work that would centre on the ordinary men called to lay the foundation of Christianity stayed with Elgar into his adult life. The first sketches appear to date from the early 1880s – when the summit of Elgar's musical activity was conducting a band at a local lunatic asylum. When the commission came to write a work for the 1900 Birmingham Festival, he thought hard about tackling the Apostles project then. In the end, it wasn't to be; instead, Birmingham was given *The Dream of Gerontius*, in which a dark-hued theme originally intended for Judas now appears accompanying the Angel of the Agony.

When *The Apostles* was finally completed, in 1903, Judas had acquired other music, and a prominent dramatic role. Well, the betrayer of Jesus was one of the original twelve Apostles chosen by Jesus, so his place in the work was more or less assured. But Elgar had been fascinated by some remarks in a book by Archbishop Whately of Dublin. Judas, Whately had said, was a thinker, a man a cut above the others, perhaps with even a touch of the aristocrat. His intention in betraying Jesus was not to bring about his death, but to force his hand – to compel him to show his power by saving himself, so that the Jews (and perhaps the Romans, too) would have had to acknowledge him as King. Judas's despair and agonising guilt when he realises that his plot has failed, and that Jesus has been brutally executed, is central to the drama of *The Apostles*. It drew some particularly fine music from Elgar, especially Judas's confession of guilt before the indifferent priests in the Temple (choral psalm-singing in the background only emphasising his aloneness), or again at the very end of the 'Betrayal' section, where a rapid crescendo is suddenly cut off, leaving the chorus to comment quietly, almost unemotionally: 'He shall bring upon them their own iniquity.'

At this point, the Scriptures tell us, Judas kills himself. Elgar omits any reference to that desperate act. We are left to imagine it – an effective device, all the more effective after music of such power. But there was probably another reason. In a sense, Elgar hadn't finished with Judas. There were plans for him to turn up in another human guise as Simon Magus, the magician who tries to buy spiritual power, in *The Kingdom*, the work Elgar intended as the second part of a projected biblical trilogy, following on from *The Apostles*. The third part, 'The Last Judgement', was never written, but Elgar's sketches and letters make it clear that the character of Antichrist was to have been another manifestation of the Judas type, the despairing thinker who tries to force God's hand. Did Elgar identify with Judas? He certainly understood what Whately had called 'the sin of despair'. After the failure of *Gerontius* at its Birmingham first performance, Elgar had written to his close friend August Jaeger, 'I always said God was against art and I still believe it . . . I have allowed my heart to open once – it is now shut against every religious impulse and every soft, gentle impulse for ever.' The mood hadn't lasted, but that is not to say that the confession was anything other than deeply felt.

The prominence of Mary Magdalene in *The Apostles* is more surprising. She was not one of the chosen twelve (these were unambiguously patriarchal times), and in the Bible she is dealt with in a few verses. But in this work she plays a larger part than any of the disciples other than Judas. This is partly because Elgar wanted to show how Christ speaks to human beings in their weakness, their sinfulness. In the Bible we learn that Mary was a poor prostitute. The self-righteous condemn Jesus for mixing with such a disreputable creature. But Jesus's response marks the doctrinal climax of *The Apostles'* first part: 'Thy sins are forgiven; thy faith has saved thee: Go in peace.'

A few critics have doubted the success of Mary Magdalene's music. One may feel that Elgar is not as involved personally in her scenes as he is in those of Judas; but that's not to say that the musical invention is weaker. A more serious charge has been levelled against *The Apostles* as a whole – that it lacks the dramatic pace and unity of purpose of *The Dream of Gerontius*. This, it is often argued, goes a long way towards explaining the success of the latter work and the failure of the former (*The Apostles* remains one of the most neglected of all Elgar's major works). In that sense, *The Apostles* is bound to suffer by comparison with *Gerontius*. But if one can shed oneself of such expectations, it is possible to accept *The Apostles* simply as a work that contains plenty of good music – and to enjoy those moments where music and text are in harmony as a luxurious bonus.

And *The Apostles* is full of good music. The Prologue is recognisably by the Elgar of *Gerontius* and the First Symphony (with which it shares its key, A flat major). The 'Dawn' section, on the other hand, is like nothing else in Elgar: we hear the characteristic upward-sixth call of the Hebrew *shofar* (ram's horn), combining with the ancient Hebrew chant in 'Morning Psalm' and building to an overwhelming climax. Judas's music has already been mentioned. It is matched in intensity by the opening of the 'Golgotha' section, in which muted violins and violas wordlessly intone the Biblical line 'Eli, Eli, lama sabachthani?' ('My God, My God, why hast thou forsaken me?'). The Passion and Crucifixion of Christ are not directly depicted by Elgar; we see only their effects on the bystanders. 'My wish was to look at things more from the poor man's (fisherfolk etc.) point of view than from our more fully informed standing place,' he wrote. It is that intention – combined with Elgar's natural brilliance of musical invention – which raises *The Apostles* head and shoulders above the overwhelming majority of pious English choral works of his day.

© Stephen Johnson

∾ *The Dream of Gerontius*, Op. 38
(1899–1900)

Today, Elgar's *The Dream of Gerontius* is a national monument. But at its first performance, a century ago, the music was thought daring, even difficult, while the subject-matter was viewed in some quarters with intense suspicion. One of Elgar's problems is neatly, if unintentionally, illustrated on the reverse side of the Bank of England £20 note. The composer is portrayed against a background which includes the cathedral of his native city, Worcester. But Worcester Cathedral is Anglican, Protestant; Elgar was a Roman Catholic.

The text of *The Dream of Gerontius* – by the Victorian Catholic convert, Cardinal John Henry Newman – is rich in doctrine that had been emphatically rejected by the Protestant Church since the time of the Reformation. The central character, Gerontius (the name derives from the Ancient Greek geron, meaning simply 'old man'), prays for assistance to the Blessed Virgin Mary and to other saints, and after his soul-searing first sight of God, he doesn't go straight to Heaven, but is committed to Purgatory for purification. For some Protestants in Elgar's day, all this would have been pure heresy. When a performance of *Gerontius* was proposed for the 1902 Three Choirs Festival, the Bishop of Worcester objected. Performance in the Cathedral was only permitted once the text had been modified: the words 'Jesus', 'Lord' or 'Saviour' were substituted for 'Mary'; 'souls' for 'souls in Purgatory'; 'prayers' for 'Masses'; and so on. It may seem petty now, but in early twentieth-century England these were acutely sensitive issues.

As for the music, let us not forget that Elgar was a Wagnerian, and that for many English music-lovers in 1900, Wagner was still very difficult modern music. The modernity of Elgar's writing was too much even for the experienced Birmingham Festival Choir: the Demons' Chorus and much of the semi-chorus writing came over poorly at the Birmingham premiere.

Elgar's debt to Wagner was recognised at an early stage of the work's composition by his close friend August Jaeger (the 'Nimrod' of the *Enigma Variations*):

> Since *Parsifal* nothing of this mystic, religious kind of music has appeared to my knowledge that displays the same power and beauty as yours. Like Wagner you seem to grow with your greater, more difficult subject and I am now most curious and anxious to know how you will deal

with that part of the poem where the Soul goes within the presence of the Almighty. There is a subject for you!

But it was at that very point in the story that Elgar's Wagnerian nerve temporarily failed him. 'Please remember that none of the "action" takes place in the presence of God,' he replied to Jaeger. 'I would not have tried that, neither did Newman. The Soul says "I go before my God" – but we don't – we stand outside.'

Fortunately for us, Jaeger was underwhelmed by Elgar's first, over-cautious musical setting of this passage and bullied the composer repeatedly: 'I have tried and tried and tried, but it seems to me the weakest page of the work! Do re-write it! . . . It seems mere whining to me and not at all impressive.' Eventually Elgar gave in and complied – and the result is possibly the most original moment in the whole score. As *Gerontius* goes to be 'consumed, yet quicken'd, by the glance of God', there is an awe-inspiring crescendo; then the full orchestra, with organ and four percussionists, delivers a lacerating *Parsifal*-like discord – but only for a split second: Elgar marks it *fffz-p*. The effect is like a blinding flash of light, infinitesimally brief, but one which leaves the eyes and brain reeling. Even the supremely egotistic Wagner would have had to acknowledge Elgar's mastery here.

There was something else Elgar learnt from Wagner – though, as with every influence on *Gerontius*, he digested it so thoroughly that the listener hears only authentic Elgar. Before Wagner, operas and oratorios tended to be arranged in numbers: arias, duets, ensembles, choruses – all more or less detachable from the larger dramatic argument. In his music dramas Wagner found a way of making dramatic works evolve continuously, seamlessly, like huge symphonies. Elgar achieves something very similar in *The Dream of Gerontius*. Some sections – like the Angel's beautiful lullaby 'Softly and gently' from the end of Part Two – can be extracted, with the help of a little surgery; but even then there are details (recollections of earlier themes, for instance) which only make

sense if heard in context. And the sense of symphonic current
– steadily, if at times slowly, unfolding – is essential to the
work's message. Early in Part Two, Gerontius's disembodied
soul describes how 'a uniform and gentle pressure tells me
that I am not self-moving, but borne forward on my way'.
Elgar's music registers the sense of that 'uniform and gentle
pressure' with subtle power. In a good performance, we can
feel that we too are 'borne forward', through the Demons'
Chorus, through the angelic hymn 'Praise to the Holiest in
the height', to the final, agonising yet transfiguring
encounter with God.

The sense of symphonic current is audible right from the
start. Clarinets, bassoons and violas introduce a quiet,
lamenting theme, at first unaccompanied, then continuing
against a slow, heavy tread from double basses and low woodwind. Slow as it is, it moves; there is a sense – as in all great
symphonies – that something could grow from this. The
theme doesn't merely provide the impetus; it is also a melodic seed. The shape created by the first four notes (A–G
sharp–A–G natural) has an influence on almost all the important motifs in *Gerontius*. These thematic inter-relations are so
ingenious and far-reaching that one can imagine Elgar
spending hours of concentrated mental effort on them. But
Elgar insisted that it all came about by instinct – none of it
was consciously contrived.

The orchestral Prelude leads without a break into
Gerontius's first words, 'Jesu, Maria . . .' The music keenly
registers the dying man's hope and dread. Other voices join
with him: souls on Earth and in Heaven, praying for his
deliverance. There is a magnificent, impassioned declaration
of faith ('Sanctus fortis'), more choral prayers, then the
moment of death ('and I fain would sleep, the pain has wea-
ried me'). The almost heart-breaking sadness of this passage
may derive, not so much from Elgar's faith, as from his
doubts, and from the dark, depressive side of his character.
The critic Ernest Newman remembered an occasion, not
long after the premiere of *Gerontius*, when Elgar's wife 'tact-

fully steered the conversation away from the topic of suicide that had suddenly arisen; she whispered to me that Edward was always talking of making an end of himself.' But this is not the end of Gerontius's adventures. The words of the Priest ('Go forth upon thy journey, Christian soul') send him on his way to the next world.

Then in Part Two comes the meeting with the Angel, the encounter with demons, the angelic hymn, and the spiritual thunderbolt when Gerontius glimpses God for the first time. Elgar reserves one of the most beautiful of all the melodies in *Gerontius* for the end: the Angel's consoling 'Softly and gently'. Nearly a century after *Gerontius* was almost denied entry to Worcester Cathedral, this music is now cherished by believers of many denominations, as well as by countless agnostic music-lovers. It is no longer the doctrine that matters, but the heartfelt expression of loss and hope in the face of death: 'Farewell, but not for ever!'

Stephen Johnson © BBC

∾ *The Kingdom*, Op. 51 (1901–6)

It was to have been one of the grandest things in English music – if not the grandest of them all: a trilogy of oratorios, dealing, not with selected events from Christian or Old Testament history, but with the foundation and ultimate purpose of the Church. As mentioned in the note on *The Apostles*, it was a teacher at Elgar's Worcester school, Francis Reeve, who first set the composer's imagination working towards this exalted goal. The idea stayed with him into adulthood – the first sketches date from the early 1880s – but by the time he sat down to compose in earnest, it had become clear that one work, however ambitious, could hardly contain all he wanted to say. And so Elgar arrived at the idea of the trilogy: three full-length oratorios depicting the calling of the twelve lowly, uneducated young men (*The Apostles*), the beginning of their evangelical mission on earth (*The Kingdom*) and – most ambitious of all – the outcome at the end of time ('The Last

Judgement'). Wagner's monumental operatic *Ring* cycle would at last have found its religious counterpart.

But Elgar only managed to get two thirds of the way through his trilogy. *The Apostles* was finished in 1903, *The Kingdom* in 1906; but although he continued sketching out 'The Last Judgement' almost up to his death in 1934, the music remained fragmentary. In the end, a few of the more striking ideas were commandeered for the Third Symphony, which Elgar began in 1933, but never finished. The austerely powerful idea associated with 'Antichrist' in the 'Last Judgement' sketches can now be heard in the opening bars of Anthony Payne's magnificent reconstruction of the unfinished symphony.

Why was the trilogy never completed? For one thing, the experience of writing *The Kingdom* was unusually draining. Elgar's physical health declined, and towards the end he began to suffer seriously from anxiety and depression. The first performance seems to have been a success with the audience, and critical reaction was far from damning; one reviewer even ranked *The Kingdom* with Bach's *St Matthew Passion*. But several critics were politely dubious – and gently expressed doubt can be far more dangerous to an artist's self-confidence than outright abuse. One article, by the influential critic Ernest Newman, seems to have left a deep imprint:

> He has seen fit to fasten upon his own back the burden of an unwieldy, impossible scheme for three oratorios on the subject of the founding of the Church; and until that scheme is done with, and Elgar seeks inspiration in a subject of another type, the most sanguine of us cannot expect much from him in the way of fresh or really vital music . . . At present he is simply riding post-haste along the road that leads to nowhere.

It may be pure coincidence – or it may be that Newman had instinctively fastened onto something that Elgar was beginning to feel himself; but about the time that article appeared, Elgar began work on his First Symphony, which –

at its premiere in 1908 – was to prove one of the greatest successes in the history of British music. It was followed by more great symphonic works: the Symphony No. 2, the violin and cello concertos, and the 'symphonic study' *Falstaff*. Elgar had found his true métier. He may have gone on tinkering with 'The Last Judgement', but it seems that, at heart, he knew the trilogy idea was dead in the water.

Still, *The Kingdom* itself survives, and it has had some distinguished admirers, among them the conductors Hans Richter and Adrian Boult (who rated it above *The Dream of Gerontius*). So why isn't it widely appreciated as the thing of beauty it undoubtedly is? Well, dramatically speaking, Elgar did set himself a few problems. The character of Judas, who inspired such memorable, dark music in *The Apostles*, is absent (his suicide takes place before the action of *The Kingdom* begins), and Elgar doesn't seem to have been in a hurry to find a substitute for him. As a result, the Good–Evil contrast of the first oratorio is nowhere near as pronounced in the second. Opposition to the early Church is portrayed in *The Kingdom*, but with nothing like comparable force. The Apostles are arrested and brought before the Jewish authorities; but the latter are incapable of finding anything serious to charge the young evangelists with, and so they let them go. Also, it has to be admitted that Peter the preacher – as depicted in the biblical Acts of the Apostles – is far less sympathetic a figure than the fearful, ultimately remorse-racked human being of the Passion narrative.

But if one tries for a moment to imagine how *The Kingdom* might have worked in its originally intended context – as the second part of a huge trilogy (possibly performed, like Wagner's *Ring*, on successive evenings) – these objections begin to sound like accusing the Devil of not being a Christian. Within that grand scheme, *The Kingdom* can be understood as a kind of symphonic 'slow movement'. Granted, the opening of the orchestral Prelude may not initially suggest slowness, but this ardent, confident music soon settles down into something more typical of *The Kingdom* as a whole: a splendid slow march tune, quietly dignified at first, but growing to a rapturous climax. Elgar called this theme 'New Faith', and if it doesn't actually carry his favourite marking, 'nobilmente' (nobly), that's probably because it goes without saying.

In terms of story, the emphasis in *The Kingdom* is not so much on the vigorous action of the young Church as it sets out to convert the world, but on its spiritual consolidation. Some of the most wonderful moments in the work are those that depict the Apostles together: celebrating Mass in the first and final scenes, and receiving the Holy Spirit at Pentecost. Nevertheless, there are moments where the emphasis is on individuals. Peter's condemnation of the 'men of Israel' for crucifying Christ is given much space – too much, perhaps, for modern ears; though it may well be that Elgar chose this scene to show how those who rejected Christ could also repent and be accepted into his Church, rather than for any specifically anti-Semitic reasons. Less controversial – and musically much more memorable – is Mary's solo 'The sun goeth down' after the arrest of the Apostles. It is simply one of the most haunting, touching things Elgar ever wrote, and during the composer's lifetime it became popular as a separate concert piece. It is much better, though, to hear it as Elgar intended it: as the culminating point of this radiant, serene confession of faith.

© Stephen Johnson

Gabriel Fauré (1845–1924)

Fauré received his early training at the École Niedermeyer, where he had a thorough grounding in counterpoint and church music. He worked at a number of churches, with both Widor and Saint-Saëns, before becoming assistant organist and choirmaster at La Madeleine in 1877. Though his earlier music, such as the *Cantique de Jean Racine* (1865) and the *Requiem* (1887–94), was written in a conservative Romantic style, his works of later years – including the lyric drama *Prométhée* (1900), the Piano Trio (1923) and the String Quartet (1924) – were of bolder expression. Notable in his output of over fifty songs are the cycle of Verlaine settings, *La bonne chanson* (1892–4). In 1896 he became a professor at the Paris Conservatoire, where he taught Ravel, Koechlin and Nadia Boulanger. He acted as director from 1905 until 1920, when a hearing impediment forced him to retire. Aside from his body of song repertoire he had a fondness for the piano, writing thirteen each of Nocturnes and Barcarolles, five Impromptus and a Ballade.

❧ Requiem, Op. 48 (1877; rev. 1887–1894; orch. 1900)

1 Introit and Kyrie
2 Offertory
3 Sanctus
4 Pie Jesu
5 Agnus Dei
6 Libera me
7 In paradisum

Until recently the genesis of Fauré's *Messe de Requiem* was unclear, obscured in part by the composer's own hazy rec-ollection of its creation and the assumption of early biographers that it was written at some point between the death of Fauré's father in July 1885 and that of his mother in December 1887. In March 1910, however, Fauré wrote to the musicologist and composer Maurice Emmanuel to confirm that his Requiem setting was performed for the first time in 1890. 'My Requiem was composed for nothing ... for fun, if I may be permitted to say so! ... If my memory serves me right, the deceased of 1890 was a M. Le Soufaché, which is not exactly an ordinary name!' The register of deaths at the Parisian church of La Madeleine, where Fauré served as *maître de chapelle* for almost thirty years, shows that the funeral service held for the architect Joseph Le Soufaché on 16 January 1888 (not 1890, as Fauré misremembered) did involve the participation of a choir and orchestra. A telegram from the composer sent the previous day confirms that the earliest version of his Requiem was indeed first performed for the sake of Le Soufaché's soul.

Fauré worked on the Requiem's original form from the autumn of 1887 to early January 1888, setting five sections of the Latin Mass for the Dead. He first composed the 'Pie Jesu' before completing the Introit and Kyrie, 'In paradisum', Agnus Dei and Sanctus, scoring what he described as his 'little Requiem' for the unusual but highly effective combination of violas, cellos, organ, harp and timpani. In May 1888 he added parts for two trumpets and two horns for another performance at the Madeleine. Although the Offertory had been sketched in 1887, the 'Hostias' setting for solo baritone remained incomplete until the spring of 1889. The 'Libera me', composed for solo voice and organ in 1877, was revised and added to the Requiem in 1891, while the opening and closing choral sections appear to date from 1894.

Fauré's publishers, Hamelle, were reluctant to issue so potentially popular a work in its original, idiosyncratic scoring. The composer eventually responded to their requests for a version of the Requiem for symphony orchestra with additional parts for violins and woodwinds. This revision was performed in concert on 17 May 1894 but only given its 'official' premiere as part of the Universal Exhibition at the Trocadéro in Paris on 12 July 1900. Published by Hamelle the following year, its orchestration has recently been attributed by the French musicologist Jean-Michel Nectoux either in part or whole to Fauré's pupil, Jean Roger-Ducasse.

Fauré explained in 1902 that he had intended to 'do something different' with his Requiem. 'Perhaps my instinct led me to stray from the established path after all those years accompanying funerals.' The tender, intimate style of expression adopted by the composer for the 'Pie Jesu' and 'In paradisum', the heartfelt qualities of the 'Libera me', and the prevailing lyricism certainly set his work apart from the grand Requiem settings by Berlioz and Verdi, with their tumultuous treatments of the Day of Judgement. One critic described Fauré's Requiem setting as 'a lullaby of death', a view welcomed by the composer, who saw death as 'a joyful deliverance, an aspiration towards a happiness beyond the grave, rather than a painful experience'. The composer Charles Koechlin later observed, 'We need not regret that [Fauré's] art could not tackle a detailed and minute picture of a hell which his heart could not desire when, thanks to the overflowing of that heart, the *aeterna requies* ['eternal rest'] is of such serene gentleness and consoling hope.'

© Andrew Stewart

George Frideric Handel (1685–1759)

Even before he had left his Saxon home town of Halle, Handel began to absorb musical influences from France and Italy, while exploring the library of music at St Michael's church. He became organist at Halle Cathedral and worked at the Hamburg Opera House, composing his first opera, *Almira*, in 1705. He then spent more than three years in Italy, during which time he set Latin religious texts, including his *Dixit Dominus* and, it is believed, the *Gloria in excelsis Deo*, rediscovered in 2001. The oratorio *La resurrezione* was performed in Rome on Easter Day 1708 and the opera *Agrippina* in Venice in 1709. The next year he was appointed Kapellmeister to the court of Hanover, but promptly took leave to visit England, where he was based until his death. Among the first of his productions in London was *Rinaldo*, prompting a string of over thirty Italian-style operas, though the success of *Messiah* in 1742 persuaded him to concentrate on oratorios. Among his instrumental works are the *Water Music* and *Music for the Royal Fireworks*, as well as sets of *concerti grossi* and organ concertos.

∾ *Dixit Dominus* (1707)

1   Dixit Dominus Domino meo
2   Virgam virtutis tuae
3   Tecum principium
4   Juravit Dominus
5   Tu es sacerdos
6   Dominus a dextris tuis
7   De torrente in via bibet
8   Gloria Patri et Filio

The years Handel spent as a young man in Italy, from 1706 to 1710, were formative ones in his development as a composer. It was there, in the land of opera and of the latest developments in vocal and instrumental music, that he met and engaged with famous musicians such as Corelli, Pasquini and the Scarlattis Alessandro and Domenico, attended the latest operas (including some to librettos he would later set himself), composed two operas of his own as well as church music and numerous secular cantatas, and established links with some of the star singers who would later perform in his operas in London. Above all, it was in the compositions he produced in Italy that he perfected his own musical language, adding to his native gifts a melodic fluency, vocal lustre and natural elegance that were to remain characteristic of his work for the rest of his life.

If this sounds as if Handel was on a learning curve while in Italy, it should not obscure the fact that much of the music he produced there was of startling and lasting quality. Perhaps the most striking of all his Italian works, and today one of his most popular choral pieces, is *Dixit Dominus*, written in Rome in April 1707. The exact occasion for which this ebullient psalm-setting for soloists, chorus and string orchestra was written is not known, but likely candidates include a private Vespers service sponsored by one or other of Handel's wealthy patrons, perhaps in one of their palaces, or alternatively the elaborate Vespers service mounted by Cardinal Carlo Colonna for the feast of Our Lady of Mount Carmel at the Carmelite Order's Roman church, Santa Maria di Monte Santo, on 16 July. That it fulfilled both functions is, of course, another distinct possibility.

Like many of Handel's Italian works, *Dixit Dominus* simply bursts with ideas, as if it were concerned above all with proclaiming its composer's youthful quality and promise to the world in the strongest terms. The vocal writing may not have the idiomatic fluency of later years – indeed it is often distinctly instrumental in cast – but the sheer range and power of its choral textures make it a work of almost visceral excitement. The twenty-two-year-old Handel had written little or no choral music up to this point; here he seems keen to try everything almost at once.

The opening chorus alone makes use of a vocal version of the concertino–ripieno contrasts of the *concerto grosso* style (it is possible that Corelli himself, the most celebrated exponent of this style, was involved in performances of the work) before cranking up the tension by setting stern plainchant melodies in long notes for one voice part against punctuating figures from the rest of the choir, in a manner that can only remind today's hindsight-blessed listeners of the 'Hallelujah Chorus' from *Messiah*.

The other choruses, too, show Handel already at home with other devices that would later be a regular part of his choral armoury, including the imitative textures of 'Judicabit in nationibus'; the busy and intricate counterpoint of 'Tu es sacerdos'; imposing chordal utterances in 'Juravit Dominus', answered by thrown-around phrases at 'Et non poenitebit'; and pure free-ranging choral imagination in 'Dominus a dextris tuis', culminating, at the pile-driving repeated chords of 'conquassabit capita in terra multorum', in one of the most extraordinary passages he ever wrote.

Three solo numbers bring some respite from this choral tidal wave, with the soprano duet 'De torrente in via bibet' (gently accompanied by men's voices) providing the work's most beautiful and restful music. But the concluding chorus returns us to the driving choral energy that makes this piece such a gripping one. As all five choral parts run up and down scales and leap octaves with scarcely a pause for breath, it is not hard to imagine the impression this onslaught must have made on its first, bedazzled listeners – or to recognise, as they must have done, the arrival of a genius among us.

© Lindsay Kemp

∾ *Israel in Egypt* (1737–8)

Part 1: The Lamentations of the Israelites for the Death of Joseph – Overture
Part 2: Exodus
Part 3: Moses' Song

Israel in Egypt is a unique work in Handel's output. While most of his oratorios set librettos which dramatise their subject with named characters and dialogue, *Israel in Egypt* uses a narrative text drawn directly from the scriptures. And whereas the usual format consisted of a more-or-less even mix of choruses and solo numbers, *Israel in Egypt* is dominated by choruses to a striking degree. *Messiah*, composed three years later, comes nearest to this style among the other oratorios, but it was *Israel in Egypt* which tried the idea out first, even if its conception was partly the result of an act of opportunism.

In 1737 Handel had composed an anthem for the funeral of George II's consort, Queen Caroline. Entitled *The Ways of Zion Do Mourn*, it was a lengthy and dignified piece, but its provenance meant that it would have reached only a small audience, and Handel must have been keen to use it again. His solution was to make a few textual alterations and turn it into 'The Lamentations of the Israelites for the Death of Joseph', the first section of a three-part oratorio about Moses leading the Israelites out of Egyptian bondage. The other two parts – using texts probably compiled by Charles Jennens, who would later do the same job for *Messiah* – were then composed in reverse order during October 1738. Part Three was 'Moses' Song', the Israelites' extended celebratory hymn of praise, set up as a counterbalance to the recycled anthem, while Part Two linked these outer panels with a slightly more active description of the events leading from one to the other, namely those of the Exodus itself, from the misery of the captive Israelites to the torments visited upon the Egyptians to the parting of the Red Sea.

The subject was a resonant one. Growing self-confidence and sense of identity, together with a bit of Protestant siege mentality, had encouraged the British in the eighteenth century to see parallels between themselves and the Chosen People of Israel, a view of things that could only have been more sharply focused by ongoing hostilities with the Spanish in the West Indies in which, it was said, captured British mariners were suffering numerous atrocities.

Even so, *Israel in Egypt* was not a great success when it was first performed at the King's Theatre, Haymarket, in April 1739. For many members of the public who stayed away, the exposure of a biblical subject in a public theatre was more than they were prepared to tolerate. For some of those who did attend, the nature of the music itself was unsatisfactory. Oratorio in English was still a relatively new type of entertainment in the 1730s, and for Handel and his audiences alike this was a period of experimentation. With Italian opera's popularity in London flagging, lovers of the genre were looking to oratorio to provide the kind of soloistic vocal writing and dramatic situations they craved. Three months earlier Handel's previous oratorio, *Saul*, had given them that, compared to which the numerous choruses and thinly spaced solo arias and duets of *Israel in Egypt* must have sounded a little too churchy – 'too solemn for common ears', as one later observer put it. Handel hastily tried to salvage things by bringing in arias from other works for the second night, but it was not enough and the work received only one further performance that season, and was only intermittently revived in later years.

Yet it was precisely this choral emphasis and churchiness that would later contribute to the work's popularity. Within a few years of Handel's death his oratorios were being performed by ever more grandiose forces, and in the nineteenth century *Israel in Egypt* and *Messiah* – both notably chorus-heavy – became easily the most commonly performed among them, favourites above all with the growing number of large amateur choral societies. (The irony is that these two oratorios, the least typical in the composer's output, should have ended up being most people's idea of what a Handel oratorio is.)

The mark of *Israel in Egypt*'s cool initial reception was not entirely erased, however. For a London revival in 1756, Part One was removed and a new one substituted, fashioned from movements of other works. This hotchpotch did not survive long, but somehow the original Part One failed to make it back into the score, with the result that for the next two centuries the oratorio was familiar in a truncated version comprising Parts Two and Three only. Beautiful though Part One is, its dramatic stasis means that it can struggle to get the oratorio off the ground; this note relates to the work in its two-part guise, prefaced by the Overture from Part One.

One reason for the strong choral bias in *Israel in Egypt* may be that Handel was deliberately trying to attract audiences by plugging into the English choral tradition, which even in those days was much cherished. The four magnificent anthems which he composed for George II's coronation in 1727 had made a huge impression on the public, and his first English oratorios of the early 1730s had capitalised on that success by advertising 'Musick to be disposed after the manner of the Coronation Service'. The sonorous choral utterances of *Israel in Egypt* – not to mention its opulent orchestral scoring of strings, oboes, bassoons, trumpets, drums, trombones and continuo – can be seen as extensions of this approach. This little look backwards may also explain why Handel made even more extensive use than usual of pre-existing material, not all of it by himself. Of the thirty numbers of the two-part version, ten were based on music from a Magnificat by Dionigio Erba and five borrowed from a cantata by Alessandro Stradella, while other composers who contributed unwittingly to the work included Giovanni Gabrieli, Francesco Urio and Johann Kaspar Kerll. These models all date from the seventeenth century, and most of them are contrapuntal in texture, suggesting that Handel was finding a convenient way to lend the music a genuinely archaic air.

This is a moot point, perhaps. What is certain is that the result is a work of thoroughly Handelian cast. Recycling a little bit of ready-made counterpoint is one thing, but turning it into something vital is another, and few could deny that Handel achieves that many times over in this oratorio. The most striking moments are all his, even in the 'borrowed' movements, to which he adds telling touches such as the upper strings' simulation of buzzing flies in 'He spake the word', the cries of 'fire' and thundery brass and timpani of 'He gave them hailstones for rain', or the orchestral hammerblows of 'He smote all the first-born of Egypt'. Other vivid (even humorous) descriptive passages include the leaping violins of 'Their land brought forth frogs', and suitably pictorial music for 'But the waters overwhelmed their enemies' and 'Thou didst blow with the wind'.

Elsewhere, however, Handel's genius as a truly original master of choral texture shines out, as much in small moments such as the soft music which accompanies the words 'he led them forth like sheep' or the precipitous bass-line plunge at the last appearance of 'sank into the bottom as a stone', as in the two finest choruses in the work: the recitative-like 'He sent a thick darkness over all the land', with its groping harmonies; and 'The people shall hear, and be afraid', a monumental, almost chilling testament to divine authority.

We may regret that among the collective utterances of *Israel in Egypt* Handel does not have the chance to reveal his skill in depicting individual human characters and emotions, as he did in his operas and 'dramatic' oratorios, yet his equal ability to encapsulate the sentiments of whole nations – be they Israelite, Egyptian or British – is never better shown than here. In its finest moments, *Israel in Egypt* is a reminder that this is a composer who can make a chorus express things that no one else can.

© Lindsay Kemp

↭ *Messiah* (1741; rev. 1743–50)

Messiah may be the closest Handel ever came to writing autobiography. The idea of doing so in musical terms was completely foreign to the early eighteenth century during which he lived and worked. Egotism of the kind which so enthrals us in music of the Romantic era, such as Berlioz's *Symphonie fantastique* or Wagner's *Die Meistersinger*, would have seemed impertinent or else positively grotesque to the audiences of Georgian London, for whom artists held no glamour whatsoever. Handel's most loyal friends, however admiring of his indomitable single-mindedness and independence, would have found any large-scale work based on his private life or developing his aesthetic credo totally alien and mystifying. To suggest that, as a sincere Christian engaged on a composition affirming the Saviour's victory over death, Handel might also have been writing about himself is of course outrageous. Yet the context of *Messiah* in his artistic career gave it a greater personal significance than anything he had written before or was to compose in the years which followed. When he began work on the oratorio during the late summer of 1741, his stock with London audiences was at its lowest. His last ever opera season had folded ingloriously a few months earlier and his enemies sabotaged subsequent concerts by trashing the posters. The capital had turned its back on him, but there was a world elsewhere. Taking up an invitation from the Duke of Devonshire, Lord Lieutenant of Ireland, to visit Dublin, he arrived there on 18 November, bringing *Messiah* with him.

It was an oratorio unusual in the comparatively brief history of the genre for being based, like the earlier *Israel in Egypt* (1737–8), exclusively on passages from scripture; its text had been compiled by the wealthy dilettante Charles Jennens, who had already collaborated with Handel on *Saul* and an adaptation of Milton's poems 'L'Allegro' and 'Il Penseroso'. In theory, this was not a partnership made in heaven. Handel was bound to England's Hanoverian royal family not just through his German origins or his role as music master to two of the princesses, but because King George II had always been among his most loyal supporters. Jennens's sympathies, on the other hand, lay with the Jacobites, faithful to the exiled house of Stuart, currently intriguing to regain the throne. He was never satisfied with Handel's treatment of his texts and his own social insecurity as the son of a self-made industrialist, conscious of the deference due to him from a mere musician, made friendship between them impossible. Yet this edgy collaboration was to result in two of Handel's greatest music dramas, *Saul* and *Belshazzar*, and in the invincible, ageless impact of *Messiah*.

Jennens's 'scriptural collection' divides into the three acts to which contemporary audiences, whether for opera or oratorio, were accustomed. We begin with the good news of Christ's birth, foretold by the Jewish prophets and buoyantly translated into reality as witnessed by the shepherds at Bethlehem. The central section deals with the Passion story and the emotions it arouses, ranging from impotent grief to scornful rage, while the ending sublimely elaborates on the mysteries of the Resurrection, the soul's victory over death, and Christ's Second Coming.

Almost every oratorio written so far, whether in Italy, Germany or England, where Handel introduced the form, had told a story conceived in dramatic terms, with characters, dialogue and action. Even *Israel in Egypt*, Handel's most recent essay in the genre, was essentially a narrative work, though giving unusual prominence to the chorus in recounting events. For *Messiah*, Handel grafted onto this concept of massed voices as articulate participants in the drama an obvious scattering of allusions to the world of Italian opera he had left behind. An air like 'Rejoice greatly' has diva bravura written all over it, while we can smell the greasepaint and catch the flicker of theatrical candles in the bass rage aria 'Why do the nations'. The siciliana 'How beautiful are the feet' recalls Handel's use of the same rhythm for amorous or sorrowful outpourings in works like *Julius Caesar* or *Rodelinda*. As for the placing of 'Oh death, where is thy sting?' in its duet form shortly before the work's close, this seems like an echo of comparable third-act movements in the operas, celebrating the triumph of earthly rather than divine love.

In the score of *Messiah*, we hear Handel, most cosmopolitan of masters, taking stock of his international inheritance. Besides a French-style overture and the Italian-accented Pifa, recalling the bagpipe music of mountain shepherds he had heard in Rome at Christmas years before, there are reminders of his native German chorale tradition in the 'Hallelujah Chorus', where snatches of 'Wachet auf, ruft uns die Stimme' trigger the melodic inspiration for 'The kingdom of this world' or 'And he shall reign for ever and ever'. Enriching the discourse yet further is that new, more flexible style in the setting of English words he had evolved in *L'Allegro, il Penseroso ed il Moderato*, another of his works to find favour in Ireland, following an unsuccessful London premiere.

The first night of Handel's *Messiah* took place at the Music Hall in Dublin's Fishamble Street on 13 April 1742. The month, by the way, is significant, since this is an Easter, not a Christmas, oratorio. 'Words are wanting', ran an ecstatic review, 'to express the exquisite Delight it afforded to the admiring crouded Audience. The Sublime, the Grand and the Tender, adapted to the most elevated, majestick and moving Words, conspired to transport and charm the ravished Heart and Ear'. No wonder Handel himself, writing to Jennens about his Irish triumph, extolled 'the Politeness of this generous Nation'. The English would take a good deal longer to accept the oratorio for the unique concept it embodied of making Holy Writ the material of an evening's entertainment.

Everything Handel wrote was, in some sense, work in progress, susceptible to his later adaptations, and he never produced a definitive version of *Messiah*, trusting in the resilience at its spiritual core to endure all the amazing metamorphoses which have since been imposed on the score. The libretto's Christian parabola doubtless satisfied the penchant of Baroque audiences for a happy ending. In focusing on the Second Coming, was Jennens even hinting at Jacobite hopes for the Stuart Pretender's return? For Handel himself, the text's affirmative outline must have held a more profound significance. In 'I know that my Redeemer liveth' and 'The trumpet shall sound' the music's note of confidence, serene and authoritative, is for the composer's benefit as much as ours. His Christian conviction had been all too recently tested by personal experience in a London which had despised and rejected him. Something of his own capacity for survival and self-renewal surely clinches the incorruptible beauty and power of this great work.

Jonathan Keates © BBC

❧ *Zadok the Priest* (1727)

The image of Handel's music that many people have today – that of mighty choral utterances resounding around large public spaces – undoubtedly owes much to later performances of *Messiah* and the grandiose nineteenth-century oratorio tradition it helped inspire. Its first prominent manifestation, however, came with the four anthems which Handel wrote for the coronation of George II in Westminster Abbey in 1727. Of these, the best known and most striking is undoubtedly the one he provided to accompany the Anointing that preceded the Crowning, *Zadok the Priest*. This is a work whose monumentalism has ensured it a place at every British coronation service since, and whose identification with the growingly confident nation that was Georgian England is shown by the fact that nearly twenty years later Handel used it again, with new words, at the end of the jingoistic *Occasional Oratorio* he composed to raise morale during the darkest months of the Jacobite Rebellion. For English eighteenth-century audiences, this work was quite simply 'the Grand Coronation Anthem'.

The power of *Zadok the Priest* to thrill lies mainly in its opening – a supremely Handelian moment in which the tension builds inexorably through a stealthy introduction to be released in a grandiose and neck-tingling choral eruption. But there is scarcely less to marvel at in its subsequent intensifications of joy, from the dance-like setting of 'and all the people rejoiced' to the jubilant shouts of 'God save the King!' and the resplendent concluding 'Amen, Alleluia'.

© Lindsay Kemp

Joseph Haydn (1732–1809)

Haydn trained in the choir of St Stephen's Cathedral in Vienna, and in 1757 became Kapellmeister to the Morzin family. In 1761 he landed a position at the court of the wealthy Esterházy family. During his many years in the family's employment, Haydn claimed he was exposed to little external musical influence, but the position allowed him scope to write anything from dances to full-scale operas, and 'forced me to become original'. One of the first composers to develop the string quartet (of which he produced sixty-eight), he also extended the form and expressive range of the symphony – writing no fewer than 106. He composed a number of dramatic works and was released from the Esterházy court – in 1790, in his late fifties – in order to visit London. He enjoyed two highly successful visits, composing his twelve 'London' symphonies, and produced two great oratorios – *The Creation* (1798) and *The Seasons* (1801) – as well as his six late masses for the Esterházy family.

∾ *The Creation* (1796–8)

The Creation (*Die Schöpfung*) was not Haydn's first oratorio, but it has no real precedent in his work. Completed in 1798, when the composer was in his mid-sixties, it was an inspired response to the stimulus of Handelian oratorio, which he had encountered for the first time during his two visits to London earlier in the decade. Triumphant though those visits had been, and notwithstanding the fact that his symphonies and chamber music had excited almost universal admiration, the large-scale biblical oratorio was one genre in which the English public remained confident that they were already well enough served; it had, after all, been practically invented in England by Handel himself six decades earlier, succeeding where rarefied Italian opera had failed thanks to its broad appeal to middle-class audiences and its sympathy with the increasing assurance and sense of identity of a growing empire. After Handel's death in 1759, his oratorios continued to be performed throughout the country, embedding themselves in the national consciousness and increasingly acquiring the air of ritual celebration. In 1784, the (erroneously calculated) centenary of the composer's birth was marked in London by a festival of his music, including some of the oratorios performed by over five hundred people in Westminster Abbey. The success of the occasion was followed up in subsequent years by further massive Handel festivals, and it was at one of these, in 1791, when performances of *Israel in Egypt* and *Messiah* were given by over a thousand singers and players, that Haydn first heard them.

Their impact was immense: one of Haydn's early biographers recalls that 'he was struck as if he had been put back to the beginning of his studies and had known nothing up to that moment'. Another report tells us of a remark to a friend that he would like to compose something similar, but was stuck for a subject, whereupon the friend took up a Bible and said, 'There, take that and begin at the beginning!' No doubt there was a little more to it than that, but it is certainly true that by the time Haydn left for Vienna after his second London visit in 1794–5, he had an English libretto in his hands, and the subject of that libretto was the Creation.

The origins of the text are obscure. It has not survived in its original form, nor is it known who its author was, but it does seem reasonable to accept the commonly made assertion that it was first intended for Handel. It derives from two sources: the Bible (Genesis of course, but also the Psalms) and Milton's *Paradise Lost*, whose style and imagery are reworked and imitated by the unknown librettist. When Haydn got back to Vienna he showed it to the court librarian, Baron Gottfried van Swieten, an amateur music enthusiast who through his aristocratic concert society, the Gesellschaft der Assoziierten, had himself sponsored private performances of Handel oratorios during the 1780s.

Swieten tells us that, when he saw the *Creation* libretto, he 'recognised at once that such an exalted subject would give Haydn the opportunity I had long desired, to show the whole compass of his profound accomplishments and to express the full power of his inexhaustible genius: I therefore encouraged him to take the work in hand.' But Swieten's encouragement did not end there. At Haydn's request, he translated the text into German (though from the start Haydn ensured that the work existed in parallel German and English versions), as well as revising it and making a number of suggestions as to how certain passages could be treated musically. And, for good measure, it was the Gesellschaft der Assoziierten who formally commissioned *The Creation* and mounted its first private performance at the Schwarzenberg Palace in Vienna on 30 April 1798.

Its success was immediate. Further private performances were arranged, and in March 1799 *The Creation* had its first, keenly anticipated public airing, given by about 180 singers and players in the Burgtheater in Vienna. One member of the tightly packed audience was overwhelmed:

> In my whole life I will not hear another piece of music as beautiful; and even if it had lasted three hours longer, and even if the stink and sweat-bath had been much worse, I would not have minded. For the life of me I would not have believed that human lungs and sheep gut and calf's skin could create such miracles. The music all by itself described thunder and lightning, and then you would have heard the rain falling and the water rushing and the birds really singing and the lion roaring, and you could even hear the worms crawling along the ground. In short, I never left a theatre more contented, and all night I dreamed of the creation of the world.

Large-scale performances of *The Creation* soon followed in London, Paris, St Petersburg, Stockholm and Budapest, while smaller ones took place in cities all over Europe. In Vienna it was heard over forty times in the next decade alone, and indeed the work seems never to have lost its special place of affection among German-speaking audiences. If Haydn's intention had been to appeal to as wide and as receptive a national public as Handel had done with *Messiah*, he could hardly have succeeded better.

The Creation is divided, *à la* Handel, into three parts. Parts One and Two present, through the narrations of the archangels Gabriel, Uriel and Raphael, an account of the six days of the Creation itself: the first four days, in which heaven, earth, land, sea, plant life and the celestial bodies are made, are described in Part One, while Part Two witnesses the appearance on the fifth and sixth days of birds, beasts, fish and, finally, man and woman. The end of each day is marked by a climactic chorus of praise, music which provides the most exalted and overtly Handelian moments in the score. The shorter Part Three introduces us to Adam and Eve as they enjoy the delights of Eden. Here the musical style is deliberately less high-flown; these are not angels singing but a mortal man and woman, and Haydn provides them with music which is more popular, more *Magic Flute*-like in style. The final chorus, however, as befits the climax of the entire work, is an even more splendid exultation of praise.

Except in the fugal choruses, Haydn's music for *The Creation* does not actually sound like Handel, of course. After more than sixty years on this earth, the composer was picturing the world as he had seen it and, in doing so, used the musical language of classicism that he himself had done so much to forge. It is one he found particularly congenial to his descriptive purpose, and the vivid way in which, in Part Two, the various beasts are brought to life and the birds given voice are among the work's most immediate charms. Here, in Raphael's accompanied recitative for the sixth day, we hear the roaring lion evoked by blaring brass; the leaping tiger, light-footed stag and prancing horse, each depicted in an appropriate string figure; docile cattle and sheep represented by music in traditional pastoral mode; swarms of insects in fidgety string tremolandos; and the slow-creeping worm in music suitably low-to-the-ground. In each case, in defiance of expectation, Haydn places his musical description *before* the verbal one. Similar resourcefulness colours Raphael's account of the storms of the second day, with its succession of wind, thunder, rain, hail and snow.

But it is not just in the recitatives that Haydn shows off his descriptive skill: Gabriel's Part One aria 'With verdure clad the fields appear' ('Nun beut die Flur das frische Grün') is luxuriant with evocative pastoralisms, from the lilting rhythms to the clarinet ornaments like wisps of birdsong. Birds feature in more concrete musical imagery in Gabriel's aria in Part Two, 'On mighty pens uplifted soars' ('Auf starkem Fittiche schwinget sich'); initially it is the eagle who soars aloft, but soon we are also introduced to the respective vocal qualities of the lark, dove and nightingale.

Perhaps the most memorable passages of all, however, are the mysterious, harmonically daring 'Representation of Chaos' which opens the oratorio, the superb orchestral sunrise of the fourth day, and the awe-inspiring depiction of the creation of light which bursts in on the work's very first chorus. According to one contemporary report, the composer kept this passage back at the work's first rehearsals in order to make a bigger impact: 'Haydn had the expression of someone who is thinking of biting his lip, either to conceal embarrassment or to conceal a secret. And in that moment when light broke out for the first time, one would have to say that rays darted from the composer's burning eyes.'

In the end, though, the most lasting impression left by *The Creation* is of its composer's uncomplicated joy in the world. Even at sixty-six, Haydn shows a wide-eyed wonder at the beauties and variety of creation, and a straightforward belief in the God who lay behind it, which inspire only the warmest affection for the man. Today, we may be more ready to acknowledge this great composer's towering musical intellect than our predecessors were, but it is not hard to see what the great Romantic songwriter Hugo Wolf was responding to when he exclaimed, 'What a spirit of childlike faith speaks from the heavenly pure tones of Haydn's music! Sheer nature, artlessness, perception and sensitivity!'

© Lindsay Kemp

ᔌ Mass in B flat major, 'Creation' Mass (1801)

1 Kyrie
2 Gloria
3 Credo
4 Sanctus
5 Benedictus
6 Agnus Dei

In the years around 1800, Haydn was basking in the esteem and recognition he enjoyed as Europe's most famous and venerable composer. His duties as Kapellmeister to the latest of the princely Esterházys, Prince Nikolaus II, were light; he was a relatively wealthy man from his two recent, highly successful visits to London; and he had taken a town house in Vienna for the first time since the 1750s. In the light of all this, he could have been forgiven if in his final years he had contented himself with composing a few trifles, happy to live off the reputation he had made for himself in an astonishingly vast and varied corpus of works. Yet, in his late sixties, Haydn was still full of adventure. In London he had heard Handel's oratorios performed on a giant scale in Westminster Abbey, and had drawn from them the inspiration to come home and compose two rich and uplifting oratorios of his own, *The Creation* and *The Seasons*. And in his principal remaining duty for the Esterházys – the unpromising one of composing a mass to mark the name-day each September of the Prince's wife – he found a new vehicle for his boundless creative energy and produced between 1796 and 1802 six choral masterpieces of truly symphonic breadth and vigour.

The work known as the 'Creation' Mass dates from the summer of 1801, just after the completion of *The Seasons*. In that oratorio, Haydn had cheekily alluded to his new-found fame by putting the theme from the slow movement of his 'Surprise' Symphony on the lips of a whistling ploughboy. For the listener, it is a charming moment of surprise and recognition, and in his new Mass Haydn repeated the self-referential trick by including in the Gloria a short melodic quotation from *The Creation*, a work which had already been performed many times in Vienna by 1801. The quotation comes from the third part of the oratorio, where it had jauntily set the words 'The dew-dropping morn, O how she quickens all!' in a duet depicting the pre-Fall happiness of Adam and Eve. In the Mass, however, it is used for the words 'qui tollis peccata mundi' ('who takes away the sins of the world'), a portion of text normally set to sombre music. According to Haydn's first biographer, Griesinger, the composer had been struck by the idea 'that weak mortals sinned mostly against moderation and chastity only . . . In order that this profane thought should not be too conspicuous, however, he let the "Miserere" enter straight afterwards with the full chorus. In the copy of the Mass that he made for the Empress, he had to change this passage at her request.' Not everyone, it seems, found Haydn's latest joke so very amusing. Nevertheless, such a bold move suggests a measure of confidence on Haydn's part, a confidence which turns out to be one of the dominating characteristics of the music itself.

The 'Creation' Mass shows us a composer at the height of his powers, completely in control of his resources and not afraid to do his own thing. His handling of a variety of choral textures is masterful, seamlessly moving from intricate counterpoint (including a superbly vital fugue to end the Gloria) to disarmingly simple, almost song-like writing for choir and soloists, while his approach to orchestral sound is as questing as ever, evincing some real Beethovenian dash in the work's final section.

Word-painting of typically Haydnesque frankness also abounds: in the Credo, a tootling organ signifies the presence of the Holy Spirit at 'Et incarnatus est', the name of Pontius

Pilate breaks forth in a loud accusatory outburst, and a clarinet tolls quietly on 'et mortuos'; in the Agnus Dei, dramatic unisons on 'miserere nobis' offer a chilling glimpse of the abyss. With any other composer this might seem like showing off; for Haydn the devout and grateful believer, however, one suspects that he simply saw such awe-inspiring demonstrations of his talents as the most fitting way to express his faith.

Lindsay Kemp © BBC

∽ Mass in B flat major, 'Harmoniemesse' (1802)

1 Kyrie
2 Gloria
3 Credo
4 Sanctus
5 Benedictus
6 Agnus Dei

Haydn's 'Harmoniemesse' was the composer's last major work, written at the age of seventy in 1802. Although Haydn was to live for a further seven years and was able to invent promising musical ideas, the increasingly frail old man lacked the physical stamina to attend to their potential. The 'Harmoniemesse', however, is certainly not the work of a weary composer, neither is it an introverted, spiritually reclusive work. There is no such thing as 'third period' Haydn: the enquiring and confident optimism that had sustained him in over half a century of composition are as keenly felt here as in any of his output.

By 1802 Haydn had served the Esterházy court for forty-one years, and the reigning prince, Nikolaus II, was his fourth master. During the previous decade, because of the diminished interest of his employers and the pervasive effects of taxation and inflation in late eighteenth-century Austria, the court had lost its position as a leading cultural centre. Haydn was retained as Kapellmeister, mainly out of loyalty, but also because the Esterházy family could rightly claim some of the glory that this world-famous figure had earned. In this late period Haydn's principal duty as Kapellmeister was the direction of an annual mass to celebrate the name-day of Nikolaus's wife, the Princess Marie Hermenegild (1768–1845). Haydn was happy to accept this duty, and between 1796 and 1802 composed six masses, the 'Harmoniemesse' being the last. For Haydn, a devout and unquestioning Catholic who once said that whenever he thought of God it made him feel cheerful, it meant that for the first time since the late 1760s and early 1770s he could consistently devote his energies to sacred composition; the results were six unique masterpieces composed by an artist who had returned to his roots but who at the same time was communicating a lifetime of musical and personal experience.

The performing resources of the Esterházy court fluctuated from year to year, and each one of the masses is differently scored. From 1800 onwards a full complement of wind players – a 'Harmonie' – was available to Haydn, and so this last Mass was scored for one flute, two oboes, two clarinets, two bassoons, two horns, two trumpets, timpani, strings and continuo; the vocal forces were the customary choir of sopranos, altos, tenors and basses, plus soloists (the latter augmented by an extra soprano and tenor for a few bars near the end of the Credo). One of the special features of this Mass (and its companions) is the integration of these forces into one seamless texture: the instruments are as much vocalists declaiming the text as the singers are instrumentalists projecting a complementary musical argument.

In the opening Kyrie, the typical frankness of the main melodic statement is undermined by the chromatic note that begins the second phrase, and throughout the movement soloists and choir enhance this feeling of a supplication made in the hopeful knowledge of a response; the literal meaning of Haydn's tempo marking 'Poco adagio' seems very appropriate here – 'a little at ease'. Carefully wrought musical argument is typical of much of the Mass, allowing those passages of routine texture of theme and accompaniment, such as the 'Gratias' (in the Gloria) and the 'Et incarnatus est' (in the Credo), to yield a touching simplicity.

As well as unselfconscious manipulation of forces, Haydn shows, too, how easily his mature language can move between the two extremes of melody with accompaniment and the most intricate fugal writing. The final clauses of the two largest movements, the Gloria and the Credo, are set, as tradition required, as fugues; Haydn's two fugues are not staid set pieces that impart a spurious authority, but contrapuntal finales of tremendous energy and commitment. Perhaps the least expected movement in tone is the Benedictus which, rather than being an expansive lyrical movement for soloists, is a brisk Molto allegro featuring, for the most part, the chorus and a principal melody sung and played in pianissimo octaves over a restless accompaniment.

The home key of the Mass is B flat major, asserted and reasserted with great dignity and aplomb in the first four movements. For the beginning of the Agnus Dei Haydn turns to a bright G major, emphasised by extended solo writing for the vocal quartet and members of the Harmonie, creating an optimistic mood that is crucially tempered by chromatic harmony and, later, by a single ominous timpani roll. Of his feelings when setting this portion of the liturgy, Haydn once said:

> I prayed to God not like a miserable sinner in despair but calmly, slowly. In this I felt that an infinite God would surely have mercy on his finite creature, pardoning dust for being dust. These thoughts cheered me up. I experienced a sure joy so confident that as I wished to express the words of the prayer, I could not suppress my joy, but gave vent to my happy spirits.

'Happy spirits' are signalled by a brisk fanfare heralding the 'Dona nobis pacem', a section of increasing joy, both exhilarating and, typically, unflinchingly secure.

© David Wyn Jones

∾ Mass in B flat major, 'Theresienmesse' (1799)

1 Kyrie
2 Gloria
3 Credo
4 Sanctus
5 Benedictus
6 Agnus Dei

In his late sixties Haydn was at the height of his international fame and, following two overwhelmingly successful visits to London, he had returned to Vienna fully conscious of this stature. He composed two oratorios (*The Creation* and *The Seasons*) that soon dominated musical life in the Austrian capital and further enhanced his reputation abroad, and as Austria's favourite son he was more than willing to accept the challenge to compose a national anthem, the *Volkslied* 'Gott erhalte Franz den Kaiser', to rouse national pride in the face of the threat posed by Napoleon's France.

But there was another side to Haydn's life at this time: he was still the Kapellmeister to the Esterházy court. He was both successful enough and rich enough to have given up this post, and he was certainly better known than his employer, but a typical combination of old-fashioned duty and a desire never to sever connection with his roots meant that Haydn was perfectly happy – perhaps even relieved – to continue as court Kapellmeister. There were occasional frictions – as when Prince Nikolaus II addressed him in the customary manner for servants, in the third person singular ('He must . . .') prompting a reminder from Haydn that 'he' was a Doctor of Music from Oxford University – but by and large it was a fruitful continuation of a patronage that had already lasted over thirty years. The court's musical activities were not nearly so numerous and demanding as they had been in the 1770s and 1780s. The summer palace at Eszterháza, with its two opera houses, was no longer in use, and 'academies' (concerts) of symphonies, concertos and vocal items no longer took place on a regular basis because there was no permanently constituted court orchestra. However, Prince Nikolaus II, who had held the title since 1794, was interested in church music, and began the practice of celebrating the name-day of his wife, Princess Marie Hermenegild, with a church service featuring a newly composed mass in September of each year. Between 1796 and 1802 six new masses by Haydn were performed, including the *Missa in tempore belli*, the 'Nelson' Mass and the present work; the task was then taken over by Johann Nepomuk Hummel (two, perhaps more, masses) and, in 1807, by Haydn's former pupil Beethoven (his Mass in C, Op. 86).

It might well be thought that composing a Mass for local consumption in a small town twenty miles south-east of Vienna where it was performed by ad hoc forces would have had limited appeal for Europe's leading composer. On the contrary, it was an opportunity that Haydn welcomed. It allowed him to reassert his deeply held religious convictions, using half a century of experience of composition, so that the music has the same commitment and flair as the contemporary oratorio, *The Creation*. Whereas Haydn had composed symphonies consistently throughout his life, his output of masses was more intermittent, and they are consequently fewer in number (thirteen complete settings as opposed to 106 symphonies). Before the six late masses there had been a period of fourteen years during which no masses – indeed no significant items of Catholic liturgical music at all – had been composed. The enthusiasm with which Haydn returned to sacred composition is evident.

Princess Marie Hermenegild's name-day was 8 September, the Feast of the Nativity of Our Lady, and the service was usually held in the small (and very resonant) Bergkirche, in Eisenstadt, on the nearest convenient Sunday to that date. The 'Theresienmesse' was the fourth in the series, composed in 1799, and, though absolute proof is not available, it is assumed that it was performed on 8 September (a Sunday).

The Empress Marie Therese subsequently acquired a copy of the Mass from Haydn, and it is this copy that gave rise to the view that the Mass had been composed for her; hence the misleading nickname 'Theresienmesse'.

Though the 'Theresienmesse', like its companions, is firmly rooted in the traditions of eighteenth-century Austrian church music, it builds and extends these traditions in a resourceful yet considered way. Perhaps the most striking aspect of the Masses is that only one of them, the *Missa in tempore belli*, is in C major – the standard key for the Austrian mass of the time. Four of them, including the 'Theresienmesse', are in B flat major, but with trumpets and drums – a new sonority for that key, which Haydn had first exploited in three orchestral works composed for London, the *Sinfonia concertante* and Symphonies Nos 98 and 102, and later in many numbers in *The Creation*. That it was recognised as a novel sonority in settings of the mass is attested by a review by the writer Johann Friedrich Rochlitz in the journal *Allgemeine musikalische Zeitung* (July 1802). The work in question is the first of the six late Masses, the *Missa Sancti Bernardi de Offida*, but Rochlitz's words could equally well apply to the 'Theresienmesse':

> . . . the composer has understood how to achieve the most shining effects through a great deal of reflection and long experience; the nobility and pious attributes of the work are effected by devices not apparent at first glance – of which we would draw attention to only one feature, namely that in those movements of the Mass in B flat, the trumpets and drums (not used exactly sparingly) are, because of their low pitch, of the greatest strength, dignity and gravity.

Exclusive to the 'Theresienmesse', however, is the replacing of the customary oboes with clarinets, providing a pervasive warmth to the music. These varied orchestral hues are immediately apparent in the slow introduction, where they are supported by an appealing lyricism. This gentle, formal introduction to the ensuing Allegro also unostentatiously hints at the shape of the themes that are to be used in the Allegro, the fugue subject associated with the text 'Kyrie eleison' and the secondary, more lightly scored idea associated with the text 'Christe eleison'. This kind of thematic cross-reference between slow introduction and fast section is directly influenced by the composer's symphonies. In broader matters, too, there is the same love of vivid drama; instead of reaching a climactic ending in a fast tempo, the first movement returns quite unexpectedly to the opening material, providing a neat frame to the movement.

While the emotional response of the Kyrie (and the Mass as a whole) is typical of Austrian church music of the time – the aural equivalent to the stunningly decorated Baroque and Rococo churches of the area – what is unique is the desire to reinforce this tradition with a powerful sense of musical argument that is modern rather than backward-looking.

Two further instances will have to suffice. At the end of the Credo Haydn has a fugue, as was the norm, to draw the lengthy movement to a climactic conclusion. But Haydn's fugue is not a dry-as-dust, dutiful conclusion; it is founded on an infectiously jaunty subject that proclaims the joy as well as the certainty of eternal life. The Benedictus always constituted a musical and spiritual highlight in settings of the text in the classical period. The Benedictus movement in the 'Theresienmesse' is one of Haydn's most captivating. After four movements in B flat major – some twenty-five minutes of music – the Benedictus switches magically to a luminous G major; the delightfully tuneful orchestral introduction leads to an extended setting of the text, culminating in the central climax when the music swings round to B flat major, the home key, so that the composer can feature trumpets and timpani to punctuate a martial declamation of the text.

The traditional three statements of 'Agnus Dei, qui tollis peccata mundi' are set in an Adagio tempo and in G minor. This mood of severity is swept away by the return to B flat major and a fast tempo for the final section, 'Dona nobis pacem'. As always, Haydn is not merely asking for peace and deliverance, but also rejoicing in the fact that they are to be granted. There is no anguish or doubt, just a wonderful certainty.

© David Wyn Jones

∾ *The Seasons* (1799–1801)

Haydn had just celebrated his sixty-ninth birthday when the first performance of *The Seasons* took place in Vienna in April 1801. One of the people present in the audience was Georg August Griesinger, tutor, part-time journalist and unofficial representative for the publishing firm of Breitkopf and Härtel. He knew Haydn well, had already acted as an intermediary between the composer and Breitkopf and Härtel, and within the decade was to provide the first authorised biography of the composer. For the Leipzig journal *Allgemeine musikalische Zeitung* he wrote an enthusiastic account of the composer's latest work:

> *The Seasons*, after Thomson, arranged by Baron Swieten and set to music by J. Haydn, was performed in the rooms of Prince Schwarzenberg on 24 and 27 April and on 1 May. Silent devotion, astonishment and loud enthusiasm relieved one another with the listeners; for the most powerful penetration of colossal ideas, the immeasurable quantity of happy thoughts surprised and overpowered even the most daring of imaginations.
>
> The very subject of this poem invites everyone to participate. Who does not long for a return of spring? Who is not oppressed by the heat of summer? Who does not rejoice over the fruits of autumn? To whom is the numbing frost of winter not tiresome? The wealth of such a subject makes great demands on the poetry, but even if all are fulfilled, a special talent is required for judging musical effects . . . That he [Haydn] did all this to perfection, however, is the unanimous opinion of the

public here. Every word, under the hands of this musical Prometheus, is full of life and perception.

The idea of an oratorio on the timeless subject of the procession of the seasons had been conceived two years earlier, in 1799, when Haydn's *The Creation* was given its first public performances. The enthusiasm with which that work was greeted encouraged Baron Gottfried van Swieten (1734–1803), the editor of the text, to think of a sequel. *The Creation* had been born out of Haydn's and Swieten's shared enthusiasm for the oratorios of Handel, and the Austrian composer's chance acquisition of an English-language libretto during his second visit to London in 1794–5, enabling the two to demonstrate their admiration and to realise their desire of producing a modern equivalent.

For the follow-up oratorio Swieten, rather than Haydn, took the initiative, and turned once more to the English tradition for a subject, to James Thomson's epic poem *The Seasons*. This had been issued in instalments between 1726 and 1728, its success prompting the poet to increasingly extravagant flights of lyrical imagination. The final poem consisted of over five thousand lines – far too long for any musical setting. Out of the poem Swieten cleverly culled a text for Haydn of some 650 lines, concentrating on the passages of narrative and description and omitting the many digressions and passages of moralising. He drew extensively on a German translation of the poem by Barthold Heinrich Brockes. Swieten rightly saw that the last part of Thomson's epic, 'Winter', with its repeated descriptions of a bleak landscape, was incapable of providing the expected uplifting conclusion to an oratorio. He therefore included two items in lighter vein which drew on other sources, the first a spinning song (poetry by Gottfried August Bürger), the second a 'Lied mit Chor' ('Song with Chorus', on a text derived from Charles Simon Favart), telling a story about a saucy girl outwitting a dirty old nobleman. In addition, to end the section and the entire oratorio, Swieten provided the text for a chorus of praise and thanks, explicit Christian sentiments largely absent from Thomson's original.

Apart from the easy appeal of the subject-matter – the measureless tread of the seasons – what specifically attracted Swieten to Thomson's poetry were the numerous descriptions of natural life: the weather and climate, sunrise, birdsong, hunting, harvesting and so on. For nearly fifty years Haydn's music had shown a penchant for descriptive writing, and precedents for many of the illustrative passages in *The Seasons* abound in his earlier music. Though these earlier passages are always charming, they are often gratuitous too. In *The Seasons* (as in *The Creation*) Haydn was presented with a context in which the pictorial was a persistent and governing element, in turn delighting and enthralling the listener. Indeed, Haydn remarked on more than one occasion during the composition of *The Seasons* that there was too much word-painting. In 'Autumn' there is a chorus extolling the work ethic of the peasant. Haydn, in the autumn of his days and remembering his many years of hard work, wrily remarked that it had never occurred to him to set the word *Fleiss* ('diligence') to music; equally wryly he responded with a learned fugue. In the concluding movement of 'Summer', Haydn, within a space of thirty-eight bars and always in advance of the words, evokes cattle (loud 'moos' in wind and low strings), a quail (oboes), a cricket (flutes), a frog (woodwind) and the tolling of the evening bell (horns). The composer complained about the frog, perhaps because for once his aural imagination was not equal to the task. Haydn's resourcefulness, nevertheless, is remarkable, as is his ability to contain such detail within the flow of the music.

When Haydn attended a performance of Handel's *Messiah* in London, he was overwhelmed by the power of the choral writing but was indifferent to the arias; as he told Griesinger, 'Handel was great in his choruses but mediocre in his song.' In *The Creation* the chorus had played the distinctive role of offering praise and thanks at cumulative moments in the narrative. In *The Seasons* the chorus plays a more central role, the choral writing showing more variety and demanding great technical resource and stamina. There are moments in the narrative, such as the ends of 'Spring' and 'Winter', when the chorus stands back from the action, summarises and offers praise, but the chorus members are also active participants, peasants who respond with the full gamut of emotions, from enthusiasm to fear, to the year's events. We first hear them welcoming the onset of spring, the whole village together and then separately as womenfolk and menfolk. Later in the oratorio they are heard in prayer, witnessing the sunrise and a storm, resting at the end of a hot summer's day, singing while spinning and reacting readily to Hannah's saucy tale.

Two numbers in 'Autumn' provide a particularly prominent role for the chorus, and constitute a tour de force in any performance. The first describes a hunt and the second is in praise of wine, both numbers being as graphic as anything in nineteenth-century opera. The hunt for the stag is recounted stage by stage by the onlookers, their commentary punctuated by a series of actual hunting horn calls, taking the listener from the 'search' (the very opening) to the 'kill'; in an extravagantly colourful score, Haydn even notates *forte* grace notes for trombones (effectively short glissandi) to suggest the exhausted stag. Following the excitement of the hunt comes the equally extensive chorus in praise of wine. It features a recurring cadential phrase, characterised by a leap to an emphasised sforzando note which, in any stage presentation, would no doubt be accompanied by a clash of mugs. The middle section of the chorus is an increasingly confused dance, the orchestra providing onomatopoeic representation of the fife, the drum, the fiddle, the hurdy-gurdy and the bagpipes. More wine is called for and the participants attempt a fugue to the words 'Jauchzet, lärmet' ('Be joyful and noisy', the perfect antidote to the earlier fugue on *Fleiss!*), only to take refuge in a 6/8 harmonic rendering of the theme; the babble increases as triangle and tambourine join in and the movement moves to a boisterous close. Haydn's 'Autumn' is clearly not for the faint-hearted.

The oratorio has parts for three soloists, their names allotted by Swieten rather than taken from Thomson: Simon (a farmer, bass), his daughter Hannah (soprano) and Lucas (a young peasant, tenor). They are not fully rounded characters in the manner of individuals in a Mozart opera or, indeed, in many Handel oratorios. Rather they are representatives of their fellow peasants, as much part of the landscape as the storm, the hunt, the brook and even the despised frogs. They are recognisably human, however, because Haydn gives them music strongly redolent of contemporary German opera (*Singspiel*). Simon's first aria is typical of many solo numbers in the oratorio. Set as an Allegretto in 2/4, the vocal line is predominantly syllabic and folk-song-like, reminding modern listeners of Papageno's music in Mozart's *The Magic Flute*. Simon ploughs the land and sows the seed, joyfully whistling a theme from Haydn's own 'Surprise' Symphony. (Haydn's self-quotation is a perfectly just reflection of his popularity as well as being nonchalantly amusing. Over a century later Schoenberg expressed the forlorn hope that the ploughman would be singing his melodies in years to come.)

There are more ambitious arias to set alongside these homely numbers, such as the accompanied recitative and aria for Hannah, welcoming the shade in the heat of midsummer. In the recitative the orchestra illustrates successively a brook, swarming bees and a shepherd's pipe. The shepherd's pipe, in the form of a solo oboe, then provides an intermittent obbligato in the following aria, an appropriate response to the burgeoning coloratura of the soprano line. The final aria in the oratorio introduces a rare moment of melancholy and introspection as it compares the progress of *The Seasons* with the course of human life. In two parts, a 3/4 Largo and a 2/4 Allegro molto, it is a moving portrayal of resignation tinged with resentment at the passing of time, a virtual self-portrait of Haydn in his old age. There is also a reference to the untimely death ten years earlier, in 1791, of Mozart, as the music quotes the distinctive descending phrase from the slow movement of the G minor symphony (No. 40, K550) and, less obviously, in bass instruments, the beginning of the main theme of the first movement of the E flat major symphony (No. 39, K543).

That Haydn thought of his soloists as archetypes rather than individuals is further suggested by the ready interaction that occurs between them and the chorus. Each season contains one example, sometimes more, of a trio with chorus in which the three peasants first represent their community and then easily withdraw into it. The concluding number of 'Summer' begins as another 2/4 Allegretto, with the three soloists commenting on the appearance of the countryside after the storm. Following the sound of the evening bell, they lead the singing of a hymn to the evening – the simple measured style, the key of E flat major and, not least, the prominence of the clarinet in the orchestral accompaniment providing another aural reminiscence of *The Magic Flute*.

The orchestral forces required by Haydn for the oratorio are the largest in his output: one piccolo, two flutes, two oboes, two clarinets, two bassoons, contra-bassoon, four horns, three trumpets, three trombones, timpani, tambourine, triangle, strings and continuo (fortepiano). Many felicities of orchestral scoring have already been mentioned and certainly few oratorios since Haydn have managed to demonstrate a massiveness of sonority as well as local individual, sometimes idiosyncratic colouring; not for nothing was Rimsky-Korsakov an admirer of Haydn's powers of orchestration. The introductions to 'Summer' and 'Winter' are miniature tone poems, the first evoking the half-light that precedes dawn, the second the thick fogs that herald winter.

That Haydn was able to indulge his creative imagination to the full, knowing that the project would be realised in performance, is also due to Gottfried van Swieten. For fifteen years he had been the driving force behind an informal committee of aristocrats, the Gesellschaft der Assoziierten, who shared his enthusiasm for oratorio, principally the works of Handel and latterly of his modern counterpart, as they saw it,

Haydn himself. In the 1780s it was this body that sponsored Viennese performances of Handel's *Messiah*, *Ode to St Cecilia* and *Alexander's Feast*, all newly orchestrated by Mozart, and, in the 1790s, the choral version of Haydn's *Seven Last Words from the Cross* and the first performance of *The Creation*. It was Swieten and the Gesellschaft der Assoziierten who again underwrote the costs of the first performance of *The Seasons*. The first performance was to have taken place on 21 April in the Schwarzenberg Palace, but a death in the aristocratic family meant that it had to be postponed until 24 April. It was to be the last oratorio performance sponsored by the Gesellschaft. There were rumours that Haydn was working on a further oratorio, 'The Last Judgement', but nothing came of the scheme. Swieten himself died in 1803, the Gesellschaft disbanded, and Haydn – after the exertions of composing two large-scale oratorios in five years – had suddenly become an old man.

The Seasons draws on a rich variety of artistic stimuli: the English tradition of the Sublime and the Beautiful, Handelian oratorio, Austrian Catholicism and German opera. These are fused together by the intellectual control of Europe's leading composer, one who had unrivalled experience of composition but who – crucially in this work – still saw himself as a gifted peasant. This balance of intuition and reason was very much a product of the eighteenth century and was replicated in many areas of intellectual activity. Particularly appropriate to *The Seasons* is the life work of the French natural historian, George-Louis Leclerc, Comte de Buffon, his *Histoire naturelle, générale et particulère, avec description du cabinet du roi*, published between 1749 and 1767. This huge work begins with an essay entitled 'How to Study Natural History'. The awe, reverence and humility of the author as he contemplates his subject are qualities found in Haydn's oratorio too:

> Nature's mechanism, art, resources, even its confusion,
> fill us with admiration. Dwarfed before that immensity,

overwhelmed by the number of wonders, the human mind staggers. It appears that all that might be, actually is. The hand of the Creator does not appear to be opened in order to give existence to a certain limited number of species. Rather, it appears as if it might have cast into existence all at once a world of beings some of whom are related to each other, and some not: a world of infinite combinations, some harmonious and some opposed: a world of perpetual destruction and renewal. What an impression of power this spectacle offers us! What sentiments of respect this view of the universe inspires in us for its Author!

© David Wyn Jones

Gustav Holst (1874–1934)

Holst was born in Cheltenham and studied under Stanford at the Royal College of Music, where he befriended his contemporary Vaughan Williams. He began his professional career as a trombonist, but later became a committed teacher, his principal positions being at St Paul's Girls' School (1905–34) and at Morley College (1907–24) in London. He keenly encouraged community and non-professional music-making in such works as his *St Paul's Suite* for strings. Like Vaughan Williams he was inspired by folk music, which he used to great effect in his *Somerset Rhapsody* (1907); but an interest in Eastern mysticism also fed into many of his works, among them the early opera *Savitri* (1908) and the four groups of *Choral Hymns from the Rig Veda* (1908–12). An interest in astrology bore fruit in his orchestral suite *The Planets* (1914–17), a work whose unique and fascinating sound-world has been widely copied by film-music composers. Ten years later he wrote his own favourite among his works, the tone poem *Egdon Heath* (1927).

∾ *The Hymn of Jesus*, Op. 37 (1917)

'Ye who dance not, know not what we are knowing.' The idea of dancing as a route to mystic enlightenment is found in many Eastern religions; less often in European Christianity. Holst, who was familiar with the concept through his studies of Sanskrit texts, must have been thrilled to discover it in the traditional English carol 'This have I done for my true love' (beginning 'Tomorrow shall be my dancing day'), which he set to his own music in 1916. His search for other 'dancing hymns' led to the Hymn of Jesus in the Apocryphal Acts of St John – Jesus's song with his disciples, gathered round him in a ring, before he was captured, tried and crucified.

Holst made his own English version of the original Greek text of the Hymn, and devised the plan of prefacing it with an introduction based on two Latin plainsong hymns, describing Christ's suffering on the Cross and rejoicing in his victory over death. He composed most of *The Hymn of Jesus* in the summer of 1917, in his soundproof room at St Paul's Girls' School in Hammersmith. The score was published (in the prestigious Carnegie Collection of British Music) in 1919. The first performance, conducted by Holst himself, took place at the Queen's Hall in London in March 1920. It was the biggest success of his career.

The work is laid out for two choruses, equal in size and as widely separated as possible, together with a semi-chorus of female voices, to be placed 'above them and well apart'. (The score also asks for 'a few tenors and high baritones in the distance' to sing the *Pange lingua* chant.) The choral writing is laid out with all Holst's customary practicality, to ensure in particular that complex harmonies can be built up by simple means. The same practicality led him to indicate various options for dispensing with some of the orchestral instruments. But the full scoring is hardly excessive in its demands (despite Holst's reference to the orchestra in a letter as 'a damned big one'): the principal luxuries are a third flute and a cor anglais in the woodwind, and three keyboard players, on celesta, piano and organ.

The fascination of the Prelude lies in the way it reconciles the free time of the two plainchant melodies with conventional metre. *Pange lingua* is played freely by two trombones in unison, repeated by cor anglais over shifting string harmonies in *senza misura* bars of changing length, and later sung freely by the distant men over a single sustained string chord. *Vexilla regis* is sung in free time by the female semi-chorus, while high strings, celesta and piano maintain an alternation between two chords in strict rhythm. In the short passages linking the statements of the chants, triadic undulations in the flutes are pierced by sharp dissonances. A coda grows out of the Amen of *Pange lingua*, and dies away to silence.

The Hymn itself opens with the electrifying first entry of the main choruses, bursting out from octave Cs to a blazing chord of E major. The tramping ostinato bass bridges the gap between the two tonalities; the semi-chorus adds Amens in what is to prove a familiar rising-and-falling pattern, largely in triads. An extra dimension is given to this passage by the choruses' 'Glory to Thee, Holy Spirit!' in quiet, measured speech. The separation of the two choruses is put to full effect in the sequence of antiphonal exchanges beginning 'Fain would I be saved: And fain would I save.'

Then the dance begins – in E major, and in a fast 5/4 tempo. The rising and falling Amens are still present, alongside initially fragmented and later more unified contributions from the main choruses, incisive rhythmic patterns in the orchestra, an exultant melodic figure heralding the line 'The Heavenly spheres make music for us', and brilliant orchestral interjections – like the descending scale at 'Fain would I flee'. The pace of the dance slackens, with bars of 5/2 alongside the 5/4; then the tempo broadens to a 5/2 Lento for the words 'To you who gaze, a lamp am I'. Here, in a series of suitably luminous chord-progressions, the two choruses each time begin on the same chord, slide a semitone apart, then reach a resolution of the discord.

The passage which follows is in the nature of an interlude, recalling ideas from the Prelude. The Pange lingua melody is chanted by altos and basses to the words 'Give ye heed unto my dancing', and by the whole choir to 'For yours is the passion', accompanied by the alternating chords. The Vexilla regis melody is turned into a flowing 12/8 tune on the bassoons, then into a wordless cry of exultation in all the sopranos, accompanied by martial drumming and fanfares. The undulating triads and stabbing dissonances also return – now confirmed as a representation of the physical ordeal of the Crucifixion.

In the next section, indeed, they accompany an expressive phrase to the words 'Beholding what I suffer'. A crescendo leads to a return of the 'sliding' discord and resolution at

'Behold in me a couch'. At 'Rest on me', the tramping ostinato and the radiant Amens of the first part of the Hymn return (along with its C major tonality). 'Fain would I move to the music of holy souls!' prompts a momentary, distant echo of the 'heavenly spheres' melody of the dance section. 'Know in me the word of wisdom!' ends on a whole-tone cluster, with closed lips on the 'm' of wisdom. After a pause, 'Glory to Thee' bursts out once more, to launch a reprise of the opening of the Hymn; but this time a succession of rising (and not falling) Amens leads to a quietly ecstatic conclusion.

The Hymn of Jesus is undoubtedly one of Holst's masterpieces. In its musical language it occupies much the same world as his previous major work, *The Planets* – with the addition of some still bolder strokes, like the combination of free and strict tempo, and the semitonal dissonances. But here the vast expressive range of *The Planets* is compressed into a span of not much more than twenty minutes; and its application to a religious subject carries it onto a different plane. Most striking of all is the sense that the work triumphantly embraces and reconciles apparent opposites: Christian theology and Eastern mysticism; ageless plainchant and modern harmonies; earthy dance metres and heavenly floating Amens. Holst would surely have approved of Wallace Stevens's description, in his poem 'Life is Motion', of a dancing couple:

> Celebrating the marriage:
> Of flesh and air.

© Anthony Burton

Leoš Janáček (1854–1928)

Born in the northern Moravian village of Hukvaldy, Janáček trained as a teacher and organist, and was choirmaster at an Augustinian monastery before becoming choirmaster of the Brno Philharmonic Society. He achieved wide recognition late in life with the first Prague performance of his opera *Jenůfa* (1894–1903) in 1916, when he was sixty-two. His new-found success, and his intense infatuation with Kamila Stösslová, a married woman thirty-eight years his junior, resulted in a highly productive dozen years before his death, during which he wrote his operas *Katya Kabanova* (1919–21), *The Cunning Little Vixen* (1921–3) and *The Makropulos Case* (1923–5), two string quartets (1923 and 1928), and the blazing *Sinfonietta* and *Glagolitic Mass* (both 1926). He was a passionate Czech nationalist and collected Moravian folk songs earlier in his career, but worked in a more modern idiom than his compatriots Smetana and Dvořák. He was intrigued by everyday sounds and by nature, and made a particular study of Czech speech-rhythms, which characterised his vocal and non-vocal writing.

∾ *Glagolitic Mass* (1926)

1 Introduction
2 Gospodi pomiluj [Kyrie eleison]
3 Slava [Gloria]
4 Veruju [Credo]
5 Svet; Blagoslovl'en gredyj [Sanctus; Benedictus]
6 Agnece bozij [Agnus Dei]
7 Organ solo
8 Intrada

Late one night in November 1927, ten days before the first performance of his *Glagolitic Mass* in Brno, Janáček wrote to his friend Mrs Kamila Stösslová, the young Jewish woman (thirty-eight years his junior) whom he had first met in the Moravian spa town of Luhačovice in 1917 and with whom he had been conducting a largely one-sided and imaginary affair ever since:

> In this work, which will be given on 5 December, I try a little to depict the tale that when Christ was crucified on the cross, the heavens were rent. Well now, I do the noise and lightning flashes, but what if in the heavens, in the portal, Kamila were to appear – I would portray that even better! . . .

> Today I wrote a few lines [for *Lidové noviny*, the Brno daily newspaper] about how I see my cathedral. I have set it in Luhačovice. Not bad, eh? Where else could it stand than there, where we were so happy! And the cathedral is so tall that it reaches the vault of the sky. And the candles that burn there, they are the tall pine trees, and at the top they have lighted stars. And the bells in the cathedral, they're from the flock of sheep. The cathedral is the subject of my work for 5 December.

> But now. Into that cathedral two people enter, they walk ceremonially as if along the highway, one long carpet – that's the green lawn.

> And these two want to be married. And it's strange that all the time there are just these two. So, priest, come at last! Nightingales, thrushes, ducks, geese make music! For their general wants to marry that dark girl, that small, tender, that dear Kamila. End of dream. You are already sleeping and I daydream about you.

Some of the images with which Janáček here described his 'cathedral' are common to the more familiar 'few lines' he'd written earlier that day for his local newspaper:

> I felt a cathedral grow out of the giant expanse of the woods . . . A flock of little sheep were ringing the bells . . . The tall firs, their tips lit up by stars, were the candles . . . I see the vision of St Wenceslas and I hear the language of the missionaries Cyril and Methodius.

Not, however, the music-making birds and especially not the concept of the two people – Janáček and Kamila – processing ceremonially into the cathedral to be married. Was this, perhaps, a flight of fancy imposed on an already-written score, and one that says more about Janáček's increasingly intense attitude towards Kamila in the last year of his life than about the *Glagolitic Mass*?

In July 1926, at the unveiling of a memorial plaque to Janáček in his native village of Hukvaldy, the Archbishop of Olomouc (the ecclesiastical capital of Moravia) had suggested to the composer that he write a mass. Janáček began work almost at once, it seems, and took the sketches on holiday with him to Luhačovice, where he spent a few weeks each year. He didn't usually compose in Luhačovice, but in 1926 the unusually wet weather confined him indoors.

Frantisek Kolár, an old acquaintance from Brno, was now a clerk at the local savings bank, and during his stay Janáček often dropped in at closing time to take him off for a walk. Not having seen Janáček for several days, Kolár got anxious, and with his wife called on the composer at his rooms in the Augustinian House. He greeted them in his dressing-gown and in a state of elation: he had been composing the Mass that he had promised to the Archbishop. And despite the Kolárs' protests that there were sick people in the building, Janáček dragged them off to the chapel for the first 'performance' of the work, which took place, very energetically, on the chapel harmonium with Janáček barking out the voice parts in a hoarse baritone.

A mass by the non-believer Janáček is not quite so extraordinary as it sounds. Janáček had had a thorough church upbringing as a schoolboy in the Augustinian Monastery in Brno, and (for all his professed atheism) this left traces in many of his works. Most of his operas include some type of religious reference, all of a sympathetic nature. Furthermore, Janáček had written three movements of a mass in 1907–8 as a demonstration piece for his pupils at the Brno Organ School (parts of this early mass seem to have been pressed into service in the first draft of the *Glagolitic Mass*).

Nor was his new Mass a liturgical vehicle. As can be seen from Janáček's description, with all its nature imagery, it was conceived more broadly, in virtually pantheistic terms. And also in nationalist terms. It was a 'Slavonic' mass, the 'Glagolitic' of the title referring to an early form of the Cyrillic alphabet which the missionaries, St Cyril and St Methodius, had brought with them to aid them in their efforts to convert Moravia in the ninth century. After their deaths, the territory became subject to the Bishop of Bavaria, and Moravia and Bohemia were drawn permanently into the sphere of Western, rather than Eastern, Christianity. But the Moravians were proud of their history and the millennium of the start of the saints' mission in 862 was celebrated with fervour. This had an effect on the young Leoš Janáček. Thereafter, he was temperamentally attuned to the Slavonic world, especially Russia, which he visited in 1896 and from where he sought inspiration for many of his works. Turning to a Slavonic text was simply a late manifestation of this pan-Slavonicism.

The text of the Slavonic mass, transliterated into Roman script, had been printed in the Czech church-music journal *Cyril* in 1920, and had already attracted the attention of Janáček's contemporary Josef Bohuslav Foerster, whose own *Glagolitic Mass* was written in 1923. The Cyril text was a hybrid, as Janáček was later to discover: a form suitable for the Western rite, but in an anachronistic version whose pronunciation caused many problems. This 'Catholic' version did, however, allow the mass, for all its Glagolitic trimmings, to be liturgically exchangeable with the Catholic mass, and its movements will be familiar to all those who know the Latin version.

As an opera composer with lively dramatic instincts, Janáček naturally conceived his *Glagolitic Mass* in dramatic terms. In the letter to Kamila quoted above, he mentions 'the noise and lightning flashes' when the heavens are rent. This is a reference to a striking instrumental passage in the middle of the fourth ('Vcruju') movement: a quiet interlude provides a meditation on the Incarnation; this gradually develops into a violent climax, when (after a furious organ solo) the choral voices come thundering in with the words 'Raspetze zany' ('Crucified for us'). Equally distinctive are the frequent, unifying references to the haunting opening of the movement, the repeated 'Veruju' ('I believe') set for full, though pianissimo, chorus against a trilling orchestra. And towards the end of the movement, after a general pause and the choral words 'I jedinu svetuju', comes one of Janáček's most thrilling moments. Against the surging figure in the orchestra that forms the accompaniment for the rest of the movement, the solo tenor, very high and exposed, declares his belief in the one, Catholic, apostolic church. The movement ends, as does the 'Slava' (Gloria), in a peal of distinctive short Amens for full chorus.

The *Glagolitic Mass* belongs to Janáček's final creative period and was one of the last works whose premiere he supervised. This was not without its problems. The original version had a number of passages, such as the polyrhythmic opening movement, or the extremely high choral writing, which had to be hurriedly simplified during rehearsals. Moreover, the Kamila affair seemed to be coming to a head. Janáček began talking of leaving his wife and changed his will partly in Kamila's favour. Perhaps, after all, Janáček's letter to Kamila about their appearances in his new Mass was not so fanciful. To the standard mass movements Janáček had added an orchestral introduction and two closing instrumental movements, an organ solo, followed by an orchestral 'Intrada' – a jaunty little march with astonishing whoops on the trumpets bringing the work to a festive close. Perhaps Janáček, who saw so much of his music in concrete, programmatic terms, could imagine himself walking solemnly with Kamila into his 'cathedral' in the hieratic, brass-heavy introduction, and then, the nuptial mass over, stepping out at the end, firmly united with his Kamila, to some of the most joyfully exuberant music he ever wrote.

© John Tyrrell, 1989

Constant Lambert (1905–51)

Lambert's fertile life was short (he died just before reaching forty-six) but filled with activity as composer, conductor and writer. He entered the Royal College of Music aged seventeen, studying with Vaughan Williams, and completed his first ballet, *Prize Fight*, in 1924. *Romeo and Juliet* soon followed (1926) for Diaghilev's Ballets Russes, and with *Pomona*, first danced in 1930, and broadcast by the BBC in 1929, he set up a long-standing working relationship with Frederick Ashton. Like Walton, Lambert aligned himself with the urbane piquancy of Les Six, fashionable jazz idioms, and the rhythmic vitality of Stravinsky's early ballets. He worked tirelessly for the Vic-Wells ballet company, and from 1946 to 1951 conducted nearly seventy concerts for the BBC's Third Programme, as well as appearing regularly at the Proms. Aside from his jazzy *Rio Grande*, he wrote a concerto for piano and ensemble (1931) and the large-scale cantata *Summer's Last Will and Testament* (1935). He died soon after the poorly received first performances of his final ballet *Tirésias*, and is known today principally for *The Rio Grande* and for his highly personal book on the 1930s musical scene, *Music Ho! A Study of Music in Decline*.

◈ *The Rio Grande* (1927)

Lambert composed *The Rio Grande* in 1927 and conducted its first performance at the BBC's Savoy Hill studios in February 1928. Its first concert performances, in 1929, catapulted the twenty-four-year-old Lambert to celebrity as a composer who had produced a genuinely creative response to the idioms of jazz. A setting of a poem by Sacheverell Sitwell more remarkable for its associative word-music than its precise meaning, the work is scored for brass, strings, a large percussion section, and a brilliant obbligato piano part (taken at the premiere by the work's dedicatee, Angus Morrison, and in 1929 by no less a personage than Sir Hamilton Harty).

The form of the piece is brilliantly unconventional. The text is an impressionistic evocation of a South American carnival, but Lambert's setting absorbs the manners and style of North American jazz even more thoroughly than those of Latin American music; indeed he once said he wished to perform *The Rio Grande* with a black American choir. This jazz element is expressed not only in the effervescent rhythms of the faster sections but in the extreme soulfulness of the slower ones, where echoes of Delius's *Appalachia* – another work inspired by Black American music – suggest one possible progenitor for Lambert's piece.

The work begins with an exuberant Allegro for the full forces, although as early as the trumpet solo at 'and fright the nightingales' there is a hint of the languors to come. A big cadenza for piano and percussion leads to a slow, romantic central section, rising to a torrid climax in a sensuous habanera rhythm. A return and development of the Allegro material (heralded by a kind of cakewalk in the piano) rises to the biggest climax of all, after which a briefer piano cadenza introduces a languorous, bluesy coda, dominated by the voice of a solo mezzo-soprano and a humming chorus. Piano and percussion have the final quiet word.

© Malcolm MacDonald

György Ligeti (b. 1923)

A Jew born in Transylvania, Ligeti attended the Budapest Academy where his studies were interrupted by the war. His father and brother were killed at Auschwitz; Ligeti survived and began teaching at the Academy from 1950. His dissonant, chromatic style was banned under the Communist regime and in 1956, following the failed uprising in Budapest, he illegally crossed into Austria. Now able to explore Europe's musical experimentalism, he worked at West German Radio's electronic music studio in Cologne (1957–8). The shifting sound clusters of his orchestral work *Atmosphères* aroused attention in 1961, and seven years later Stanley Kubrick featured his *Atmosphères*, *Aventures*, *Requiem* and *Lux aeterna* in the film *2001: A Space Odyssey*. After the seminal, concise Chamber Concerto (1969–70) and the anarchic opera *Le grand macabre* (1974–7), he developed an intricate polyrhythmic style as heard in the Piano Concerto (1985–8). A heart condition slowed down his output from 1979, by which time he had held teaching posts in Stockholm, Stanford and Hamburg. In 1985 he began his still-ongoing series of Études for piano; these wonderfully innovative pieces are establishing themselves as modern classics of the genre.

∾ Requiem (1963–5)

1 Introitus
2 Kyrie –
3 De die judicii sequentia
4 Lacrimosa

Why would György Ligeti – a composer of the unusual, the surprising, the notoriously experimental – want to write a work steeped in so much tradition as a Requiem? Mozart, Berlioz, Brahms – the very backbone of the Western musical tradition – had each written one but, in the 1950s and 1960s when Ligeti first came to be noticed, setting the mass for the dead was not in vogue. Ligeti's headline-grabbing *Poème symphonique* of 1962 – scored for 100 metronomes – doesn't sound like a work from which a Requiem might follow, and yet Ligeti embarked upon his first large-scale choral piece the very next year. It remains one of the most impressive items in his output. The fact that bits of it were used (without permission) on the soundtrack for Stanley Kubrick's film *2001: A Space Odyssey* hasn't hindered its cause either.

Ligeti's *Requiem* makes the most of its composer's interest in extremes of vocal technique, instrumental colour and rhythmic experimentation. The movements of the mass that Ligeti chose to set concern the fervour of hope for eternal rest, the submission to God's mercy and the terror of the Day of Judgement. Like his predecessors in setting these verses, such as Berlioz and Verdi, Ligeti relishes the opportunity to exploit the inherent theatricality and drama of extremes within the text.

Ligeti's distinctive sound-world is apparent right from the start of the first movement. The Introit, which sets the words 'Requiem aeternam' ('Grant them, O Lord, eternal rest'), begins with bass voices and trombones right at the bottom of their registers singing and playing extremely slowly, as if from the very bowels of the earth. The voices, as so often in this piece, appear to be not quite in sync with each other and thus the whole effect is extraordinarily unsettling and stark. The two soloists (soprano and mezzo-soprano) enter imperceptibly and then are left unsupported by the choir as a solo flute provides the barest of accompaniments.

The second movement – Kyrie ('Lord have mercy upon us') – develops the atmosphere of the Introit into a particularly modernist vision of hell: one where the torments are not so much of the Devil and his minions, but rather a musical equivalent of the kind of living nightmare that Sartre portrayed in *Huis clos*, where dislocation and uncertainty reign. The subdivided choirs sing clusters of similar lines that Ligeti referred to as 'micropolyphony'. As so often, the text turns into mere syllables or sounds and it is easy to hear how the eerie, wordless blend of chorus and orchestra suggested alien life to Kubrick in *2001*.

The third movement – 'De die judicii sequentia' – follows without a break and the opening is marked 'with extreme vigour and excitement'. In contrast to the long lines with which the Kyrie ended, the atmosphere of the 'Dies irae' has the madness of a Bruegel vision about it. (Bruegel is one of Ligeti's favourite painters.) There are certainly distant echoes too of Verdi's own famous 'Dies irae' setting in the archetypal brass volleys, whispering chorus at 'mors stupebit' ('death . . . shall stand amazed') and agonised female soloists so frightened that they are forced to the extremes of their registers against the drama of the orchestra's batterings and brayings. What makes Ligeti's version of the Day of Judgement so distinctive is that the soloists' exaggerated leaps suggest horrors from which no theology can save us. (Ligeti is of Jewish origin and suffered his own share of terrestrial persecution in Hungary before, during and after the war.)

The 'Lacrimosa' last movement, marked 'very slowly', is a quiet and sustained lament. The resources are used sparingly: the chorus is silent and the soloists often sing entirely unaccompanied. Gradually, from very low and very high orchestral sounds heard together, the voices move tremulously towards the end and an uncertain plea to be granted eternal rest. The pianissimo high strings fade away into silence, leaving only a long held note from the two lowest of the woodwinds (bass clarinet and contrabass clarinet), before that too dies away – finally and without hope of resurrection.

Robert Stein © BBC

Gustav Mahler (1860–1911)

More than any composer since Beethoven, Mahler radically altered the course of symphonic form, broadening its scale and instrumentation, imbuing it with vast emotional range and incorporating autobiographical references. Born in Bohemia, he went to study in Vienna, aged fifteen, before developing a conducting career in a succession of opera theatres. In 1897 he became Kapellmeister at the Vienna Court Opera, converting from Judaism to Catholicism in order to do so. The demands of his conducting commitments left only the summers for composing, when he would retreat to the mountains and lakes. He was heavily drawn to the folk-like poetry collection *Des Knaben Wunderhorn* (*The Youth's Magic Horn*, 1808), writing over twenty *Wunderhorn* songs and incorporating its texts into his Symphonies Nos 2–4. Five of his siblings died in infancy, as did his own elder daughter – lending further poignancy to his *Kindertotenlieder* (*Songs on the Death of Children*, 1904). He worked in New York at the Metropolitan Opera and Philharmonic Orchestra, but fell victim to heart disease: he died before completing his tenth numbered symphony, soon after the bitter discovery of his wife Alma's affair with the architect Walter Gropius.

❧ *Das klagende Lied* (1878–80; rev. 1892–3, 1898–9)

1 Waldmärchen (Forest Legend)
2 Der Spielmann (The Minstrel)
3 Hochzeitsstück (Wedding Piece)

From his beginnings as a composer, Mahler felt the need to dramatise his inner life. At first it was not at all obvious that the symphony was to be his chosen medium. In his early works his chief concern was with the human voice. His first achieved piece was a cantata – *Das klagende Lied* (*The Song of Lamentation*) – and this was followed by songs with piano, the song cycle *Lieder eines fahrenden Gesellen*, and the earliest settings of the folk collection *Des Knaben Wunderhorn*. Out of the *Lieder eines fahrenden Gesellen* came the generating ideas for the First Symphony, although this was initially conceived as a symphonic poem called *Titan*, after Jean Paul's novel, with whose hero Mahler strongly identified. The first movement of the Second Symphony began life as an independent symphonic poem called 'Totenfeier' ('Funeral Rites'); its fourth movement is a setting of a *Wunderhorn* poem and the 'Resurrection' finale is virtually a cantata. The Second Symphony expands several musical and dramatic ideas first found in *Das klagende Lied*. Throughout this early period, song, symphony, symphonic poem and cantata are closely interwoven. They remain so in his later work: much of the Eighth Symphony is as much cantata or oratorio as symphony; *Kindertotenlieder* is a symphonic song cycle; *Das Lied von der Erde* a song cycle expanded into a symphony. *Das klagende Lied*, with its mixture of song, quasi-operatic chorus and symphonic episodes, is therefore not such an exception in Mahler's oeuvre as some have thought.

Mahler began *Das klagende Lied* in 1878, when he was seventeen and a student at the Vienna Conservatoire. He finished it in 1880 and entered it for the prestigious Beethoven Prize in 1881, but it failed to win. Mahler wrote his own text around a folk tale familiar to him from childhood. Two brothers seek the hand of a queen; the younger finds the red flower which will win her favour; the elder brother kills the younger, steals the flower and claims the queen for his bride. A minstrel finds one of the younger brother's bones and makes a flute from it; the flute, when played, tells the story of the murder; the minstrel plays the flute at the wedding to the horrified guests, and the castle falls to the ground, engulfing all.

Mahler's own favourite younger brother, Ernst, had died of a painful illness when Mahler was thirteen. Mahler was deeply affected by Ernst's death, and his name appears several times in the margin of the manuscript of *Das klagende Lied*. When much later he came to revise the score for publication, Mahler decided to omit the first part of the cantata, 'Waldmärchen', which deals with the younger brother's murder. A psychoanalytical interpretation of Mahler's suppression of 'Waldmärchen' is only too easy to make, and has been used to justify reinstating the original three-part version. Whether there is any truth in this interpretation or not, the fact remains that there were valid reasons for omitting 'Waldmärchen' on purely musical grounds. Much of 'Waldmärchen' is recapitulated in 'Der Spielmann', and the two parts are quite similar in concept, both beginning with a lengthy orchestral prelude and employing a good deal of leisurely narrative. Altogether, the revised, two-part version is tighter and more effective. 'Waldmärchen', however, contains much attractive music and the original version deserves the performances which it has had since the manuscript resurfaced in 1969, and it is certainly of interest to hear the work in the way Mahler first conceived it.

Mahler always remained fond of his 'fairy-tale from my youthful days', as he called *Das klagende Lied* when sending the libretto to his future wife, Alma. In 1893, when he was engaged on the revision, he wrote to his friend Natalie Bauer-Lechner:

> . . . all the 'Mahler' whom you know was revealed at one single stroke. What surprises me most is that even in the instrumentation nothing has to be altered, it is so characteristic and new . . . I cannot understand how so strange and powerful a work could have come from the pen of a young man of twenty.

Mahler's pride in his youthful achievement is absolutely justified. *Das klagende Lied* presents us with the authentic Mahlerian sound, precisely imagined, masterfully orchestrated. Several passages in the cantata were reused or developed by Mahler in later works. The passage in 'Waldmärchen', where the younger brother lies down to sleep under a willow tree just before his murder, appears again almost identically at the end of *Lieder eines fahrenden Gesellen*, where the hero falls asleep beneath a lime tree. The opening of 'Der Spielmann' is a sketch for the opening of the Second Symphony, in the same key (C minor) and with the same funereal associations. When we hear the gentle F major second theme of this introduction, which soon subsides into a pastoral evocation complete with bird-calls, we are in the world of the first movement of the First Symphony; while the climax of 'Hochzeitsstück' – the collapse of the castle – is repeated note for note in the First Symphony's finale.

The landscape evoked in *Das klagende Lied* is the landscape where Mahler was brought up – the hills and woods of Bohemia. Mahler remained all his life a passionate lover of the countryside, and natural sounds and scene-painting found a permanent place in his music, as did the sounds of Bohemian folk music, whose imprint is felt on all his melodic writing. He was already bypassing both the advanced chromaticism of the later Wagner and the sophisticated post-Schumann idiom of Brahms in favour of a simpler, broader musical language: a return, almost, to the early Romantic world of Weber, Marschner and Wagner's first operas. But the voice is already personal, and its daring was bound to shock (the shrill off-stage band at the start of 'Hochzeitsstück', for instance).

Das klagende Lied was not performed until 1901, and so missed the full brunt of the hostility that it would have incurred had it been performed twenty years earlier; nevertheless the Viennese critics attacked it, as they attacked all Mahler's premieres. Though his language was strongly rooted in the past, and was always to be so, his sensibilities were, from the start, thoroughly modern.

© David Matthews

Felix Mendelssohn (1809–47)

The grandson of a philosopher, Mendelssohn combined musical precociousness of a Mozartian order with a lifetime of learning and travelling. He gave his first performance as a pianist aged nine, and composed thirteen early string symphonies between 1821 and 1823. By the time of his first visit to London, aged twenty, he had already spent time in Paris. After returning to Berlin, where he had studied philosophy with Hegel, he undertook a major tour of Europe, which inspired the 'Scottish' and 'Italian' Symphonies as well as the *Hebrides* overture. He became conductor of the Lower Rhine Music Festival, Music Director of the Leipzig Gewandhaus Orchestra (1835), and founded the Leipzig Conservatory (1843). He showed vivid scene-painting ability in his overtures (especially *A Midsummer Night's Dream* and *Calm Sea and Prosperous Voyage*), but he produced some of his best work in the standard classical forms: an enduringly popular Violin Concerto, six string quartets and two piano concertos. Of his three oratorios, *Elijah* was especially favoured by the English choral societies of the Victorian era.

✎ *Elijah*, Op. 70 (1845–6; rev. 1847)

Mendelssohn began to plan an oratorio on the subject of Elijah as early as 1837, a few months after the great success of his first oratorio, St Paul. During the next two or three years he carried on detailed discussions with two of his literary friends, Carl Klingemann and Julius Schubring, about the work, but then put the project aside. In June 1845, however, he was commissioned by the Birmingham Festival Committee to 'provide a new oratorio, or other music' for the following year's festival. This stimulated him to return to his work on *Elijah*. With the assistance of Schubring he prepared the German libretto, completed the music in the early months of

1846, and corresponded at length with his chosen English translator, William Bartholomew. He conducted the first performance at Birmingham Town Hall on 26 August 1846. Its reception was rapturous: as *The Times* said, 'Never was there a more complete triumph – never a more thorough and speedy recognition of a great work of art.'

Mendelssohn himself was far from satisfied, and he soon set about making wholesale changes in the score, completely rewriting (for instance) the scene with the Widow, and several of the recitatives. The final version was performed four times by the Sacred Harmonic Society of London in April 1847, again under the composer's baton. The second of these performances, on 23 April, was attended by the Queen and Prince Albert. The German premiere was at Hamburg in October 1847, but by that time the composer was too weak to conduct it; he died on 4 November.

For most Victorians, 'the' *Elijah* (as they soon began to call it) immediately jumped to a position near the summit of the oratorio mountain, which to them was the highest in the whole range of music. Only 'the' *Messiah* overtopped it. Mendelssohn also regarded it as his greatest achievement. Neither of these judgements would be unquestioningly accepted today. But we may gain a fuller understanding of the work if we grasp what it meant to its composer and to its intended audience.

At first thought, it seems surprising that the gentle Felix should have been attracted to such a character as Elijah, fiercest and most vengeful of the prophets. In *St Paul* he had chosen a story that was an allegory of his own experience: his family had converted to Christianity when he was a small boy. But although there is no reason to doubt the sincerity of his Lutheran faith, at a deeper level his inherited Jewishness perhaps craved emotional expression. *Elijah* is in no way inconsistent with Christianity – indeed, the final movements explicitly look forward to the coming of Christ. Yet the story is extremely Jewish. The God whose will must prevail is entirely the fearsome Jehovah of the Old Testament. Jack

Werner has convincingly suggested a Jewish origin for what he calls the 'Mendelssohn cadence', a kind of drooping descent on the notes of the tonic-minor triad, for instance at the end of 'Lord! Bow thine ear' (which also begins with an unaccompanied chant of Hebrew flavour), and at the end of 'It is enough'. But there is more to it than a general identification with Judaism. Mendelssohn was a deeply conservative man, convinced that the world was in a state of moral decay: he had experienced the evils of court intrigue at Berlin, dashing his hopes of political reforms that would have allowed him to lead a Prussian musical resurgence. In a revealing letter to Schubring (1838) he wrote:

> I imagined Elijah as a real prophet through and through, of the kind we could really do with today; strong, zealous, and yes, even bad-tempered, angry, and brooding – in contrast to the riff-raff, whether of the court or of the people, and indeed in contrast to almost the whole world – and yet borne aloft as if on angels' wings.

It is difficult to resist the impression that he felt himself to be an Elijah, though he was far too modest to say so. More and more, he saw himself as the guardian of true values in music: that is to say, of the styles of the eighteenth-century masters. He was dismayed equally by the virtuoso schools of singing and piano playing, and by the irreverent and impatient radicalism of composers such as Berlioz and Wagner. 'Will then the Lord be no more God in Zion?'

His answer was to bring forth a work that would reassert the moral and musical power of the old values. Like Brahms later on in his *German Requiem*, he confined himself to well-tried, familiar musical idioms and procedures. However much original invention there may have been in the work, its style was thoroughly predictable in 1846, and could be immediately embraced by the public: 'O show to all this people that I have done these things according to thy word!' In destroying the Baal-worshippers, *Elijah* strikes a satisfying blow against all the corruptions of modern times.

There can be little doubt that Mendelssohn wrote *Elijah* chiefly for an English audience. It was the great success of *St Paul* at Birmingham that spurred him on to completion. Though he worked with a German text – his English was, after all, imperfect – he supervised the translation in minute detail, and spared no pains to ensure that his music would fit the English words. (A few false accents escaped his attention, eg 'ex-tir-pate' in 'Hear us, Baal!'.) He told Bartholomew he would alter the notes to preserve the English Bible version of the text. He came to England in person to conduct the premieres of both the original and the revised versions. There was a continuing love affair between him and the English public (and royalty) that must have been exhilarating, especially when compared with the contention he had faced in Germany.

Nevertheless, the unprecedented success of the work in England was partly due to causes that had little to do with Mendelssohn's own feelings about it. It appealed above all to Nonconformists and Evangelical Anglicans: Birmingham was a great stronghold of dissent, and the Sacred Harmonic Society was run by Dissenters (Exeter Hall, where the London performances were held, was also used for their great religious meetings). It was a time when anti-Catholic feeling was running high. John Henry Newman had just (1845) defected to Rome, along with many of his followers, confirming the worst suspicions of orthodox churchmen about the Oxford Movement. (Newman himself, it is interesting to note, declared in 1871 that he was 'very much disappointed, the one time that [he] heard the *Elijah*, not to meet with a beautiful melody from beginning to end!'.) Ordinary middle-of-the-road Anglicans were perhaps equally troubled by the steady erosion of faith, resulting from the growth of rationalism and the progress of science. They joyfully accepted a work that confirmed the old faith, miracles and all, with the full expressive power of anti-materialistic musical Romanticism. Henry F. Chorley spoke for the majority of English listeners when he wrote in the *Athenaeum*: 'The world owes good thanks to Dr Mendelssohn for having conformed his manner to his subject – for having treated the same religiously yet romantically.'

So when the devout Victorian witnessed the destruction of Baal and the discomfiture of Ahab and Jezebel, he could take satisfaction in the punishment of all who threatened his beliefs, whether they were Roman 'idolaters' or heathen 'scoffers'. The reassertion of stern Old Testament morality was in perfect harmony with the dissenting tradition, going back to the early Puritans. Victorian audiences, as more than one observer noted, were apt to treat an oratorio concert almost as an act of worship. Wagner maliciously reported in 1855:

> Four hours they sit in Exeter Hall, listening to one fugue after another in perfect confidence that they have done a good deed for which they will, one day, be rewarded in heaven by hearing nothing but the most beautiful Italianate operatic arias. It was this earnest fervour in the English public that Mendelssohn understood so well, and he composed and conducted oratorios for them till he has become the veritable saviour of the English musical world.

Another factor that helped to win over the Victorians was the upright character of the composer. They found it diffi-cult, when listening to the music of Bellini, Berlioz or Chopin, to banish from their minds the rumours of these composers' sexual promiscuity or bohemian style of living. In Mendelssohn they recognised a composer whose life was as blameless as that of their queen and her consort.

The success of *Elijah* was due, then, to a tangle of issues and circumstances, some of which do not strike a chord of sympathy today. But whatever the reasons, they inspired Mendelssohn to some of his greatest music. Even if we prefer the freshness and vitality of his early masterpieces – the Octet, the concert overtures – we cannot deny the consum-mate mastery of his last major work. The libretto is most skil-fully adapted from the muddled biblical account, to make a story with a natural form and with two climaxes, one each in

Parts One and Two. The last four movements abandon dramatic form to supply the Christian moral; and there are other passages, especially the choral quartet 'Cast thy burden upon the Lord', that establish this oratorio as a religious as well as a dramatic composition.

The music, too, is both religious and dramatic. While eschewing the more obvious hallmarks of contemporary operatic style, such as the cabaletta or the second-beat 'crash', Mendelssohn drew from earlier operatic convention to convey a sense of action and situation. There is as much pictorial writing as in Handel's *Israel in Egypt*, and as much characterisation as in Bach's *St Matthew Passion* – less of individuals than of 'sides'. In Part One the chief contrast is between the frantic agitation of the supporters of Baal and the assured calmness of the prophet, the latter expressed by a rich evocation of traditional harmony ('Lord God of Abraham'), even including the modal chord on the flat seventh. In Part Two, Elijah's resignation in the face of death is the continuous element that contrasts with the varied expression of the other characters and the depiction of natural and supernatural forces.

Throughout the work there are abundant examples of Mendelssohn's wonderful musical invention, in melody, in harmony and in scoring. The Victorians found 'O rest in the Lord' the most delectable number, though it was not one of the composer's favourites – at one point he planned to cut it out. My own choice for sheer loveliness is the chorus 'He, watching over Israel'. By understanding and facing the historical overtones of the work, we can more fully savour its enduring musical quality.

© Nicholas Temperley

∾ *Die erste Walpurgisnacht*, Op. 60 (1832; rev. 1843)

For all his colossal intellect and incomparable talent as a writer, Goethe had a blind spot when it came to music. While his greatest artistic contemporary, Beethoven, confessed that he 'worshipped' Goethe, the writer remained unmoved by Beethoven's music, describing his Third Symphony as 'merely strange and grandiose'. When the young Schubert sent Goethe twenty-eight settings of his poetry, respectfully asking permission to dedicate the songs to him, Goethe failed even to reply, simply returning the manuscript without comment. The one composer for whom Goethe had any time at all was a minor figure named Carl Friedrich Zelter, whose settings of Goethe's verses – pleasant and competent enough, but far inferior to Schubert's – were tolerated and even welcomed by the poet. Zelter became an influential teacher: among his pupils were Meyerbeer, Carl Loewe, Otto Nicolai, and the young Felix Mendelssohn, who began to study theory and composition with Zelter at the age of ten. Two years later Zelter introduced his talented young protégé to Goethe at Weimar: the boy spent nearly two weeks there, and greatly impressed the aged poet with his precocious intellect. A lasting friendship sprang up between the two, who met several times during Mendelssohn's teenage years.

In 1832, shortly before Goethe's death, Mendelssohn composed a cantata for chorus and orchestra based on one of Goethe's preliminary studies for *Faust*. (Goethe originally devised a libretto himself, and sent it in 1799 to Zelter, but Zelter felt inhibited by the subject-matter, and declined the invitation to set it.) The text selected over thirty years later by Mendelssohn is not the famous 'Witches' Sabbath' from Part One, but a semi-dramatic account of the origins of the folk legend of Walpurgisnacht, the eve of the first of May, which in Germany is dedicated to the Celtic St Walpurga. On this night (as on Hallowe'en in British mythology), witches and other evil spirits are meant to roam abroad, congregating for their orgies on the Harz mountains. In Goethe's version, the legend dates from the time when Christianity was beginning to prevail in Northern Europe, forcing pagan priests and their followers to celebrate their rites secretly in the remote safety of the mountains. When their ceremonies are threatened by encroaching Christians, they disguise themselves as demons to frighten their enemies away.

Mendelssohn revised the cantata in 1843, and performed it in Leipzig. Berlioz, who was visiting Leipzig at Mendelssohn's invitation, praised the score for its 'impeccable clarity, notwithstanding the complexity of the writing. Voices and instruments are completely integrated and interwoven in an apparent confusion which is the perfection of art.'

There are nine sections. After an overture depicting the transition from winter storms to spring sunshine, the Druids and their followers celebrate the new season. As they prepare their rites, an old woman warns them of the danger from discovery by the Christians. But a priest sings of the freedom to be found in the forests, and guards are posted around the encampment. In a dramatic and highly effective central chorus, the guards assemble with torches, in grotesque disguises, to frighten away the superstitious Christians. The priests continue their ceremonies undisturbed; but in a penultimate solo, a Christian expresses his fear at being surrounded by witches and werewolves, and he and his companions flee in terror. The Druids continue to praise their ancient Gods.

© Wendy Thompson

❧ *St Paul*, Op. 36 (1836)

For most British music-lovers there is only one Mendelssohn oratorio: *Elijah* – premiered triumphantly in Birmingham in 1846, and for over a century one of the central pillars of this country's professional and amateur choral repertory. Visiting London in 1855, Wagner observed caustically that 'the real delight of the English is the oratorio . . . Mendelssohn is to the English what Jehovah is to the Jews.' In fact, *Elijah* was so successful that it came to overshadow Mendelssohn's first effort in this form, *St Paul*, completed ten years earlier. But when *St Paul* had its first performance in Düsseldorf in 1836, it too was well received.

The following year it was one of the high points of Mendelssohn's much-acclaimed visit to the Birmingham Festival. Many eminent musicians of the day spoke well of it. A performance in Linz in 1847 (the year of Mendelssohn's death) made a deep impression on the twenty-three-year-old Anton Bruckner – when Bruckner combined chorale and fugue in the finale of his monumental Fifth Symphony (1876), he almost certainly had the Overture to *St Paul* at the back of his mind.

It is true that Mendelssohn had doubts about *St Paul*. But then he had set himself very high standards. After the British premiere, in Liverpool in October 1836, the bass Henry Phillips expressed his admiration of the work to its composer. 'Thank you! Thank you!' Mendelssohn replied. 'If I could once write a chorus equal to Handel's, I should be content.' As well as championing Handel's music, Mendelssohn had also famously conducted a performance of Bach's *St Matthew Passion* at the Berlin Singakademie in 1829 – probably the first performance of the work since Bach's death in 1750, and a crucial event in the history of the nineteenth-century Bach revival. In writing *St Paul*, Mendelssohn directly invoked the examples of both Bach and Handel: his use of traditional Lutheran chorales as commentaries on the story derives straight from the former, while the writing in the dramatic choruses is just as clearly influenced by the latter.

Veneration for these past masters was by no means Mendelssohn's only reason for writing *St Paul*. Mendelssohn's father had been putting pressure on the young composer to turn his back on his youthful 'elfin' manner – the spirit of his Overture to *A Midsummer Night's Dream* and the Scherzo of the precociously brilliant Octet – and proceed to something 'graver': oratorio, for instance. Mendelssohn seems to have come to regard this as his duty – increasingly so after his father's death in October 1835.

The young Felix's sense of indebtedness to his father was intense. Abraham Mendelssohn had done all he could to encourage his son's phenomenal talents. Fanny Mendelssohn

– the composer's older sister – wrote that 'such intense sympathy as theirs is very rarely found in this world'. It could be that Mendelssohn's choice of subject in *St Paul* was a tribute to his father. Like the biblical Paul, Abraham Mendelssohn was a Jew who converted to Christianity; also like Paul (originally known as Saul), Abraham had in the process changed his name, from Mendelssohn to Mendelssohn-Bartholdy – the surname Abraham's brother-in-law had adopted after his conversion.

But that leaves one problematic issue. In the Acts of the Apostles – the biblical book from which *St Paul* is mostly derived – the Jews are portrayed as the villains of the story: they have collectively rejected Christ, the Messiah sent to them by God, and now they turn against his disciples. Not surprisingly, the Acts of the Apostles has been a favourite text for Christian anti-Semites. How did Mendelssohn feel about the depiction of his ancestors in such morally uncompromising terms? Serious as he was about his Protestant Christianity, Mendelssohn was no narrow evangelical. There is no evidence that he regarded unconverted Jews as – in the words of the Book of Revelation – 'the synagogue of Satan'. His friend, the actor, director and singer Eduard Devrient, tells us that normally Mendelssohn 'avoided all reference to his Jewish descent'. But Devrient recalled one occasion when the mask slipped. It was just before that historic performance of the *St Matthew Passion* in Berlin. 'And to think', said Mendelssohn triumphantly, 'that it should be an actor and a Jew that give back to the people the greatest of Christian works.' His attitude towards the unconverted hostile Jews in the Acts of the Apostles is likely to have been complicated, to say the least.

As a whole, *St Paul* may not have the dramatic momentum of the first part of *Elijah*, but there are many fine things. The use of the chorale 'Wachet auf' ('Sleepers, awake') in the fugal Overture is more than ingenious – especially the ending, where the final phrase of the chorale emerges in triumph from the busy orchestral texture. The chorus 'Dieser Mensch hört nicht auf zu reden' ('This man ceaseth not to speak'), with its dramatic trumpet calls, is Handelian in spirit, if not in style, as too is the moment of Paul's conversion: female voices and high woodwinds proclaim the words of God, 'Saul! Was verfolgst du Mich?' ('Saul, why persecutest thou me?'), tenor and bass soloists, trombones and low strings darkly express Paul's fearful response. (Handel had used a very similar idea in setting the words of the angels in *Messiah*: 'Glory to God in the highest, And peace on earth.') The chorus that follows, 'Mache dich auf!' ('Arise! Shine!'), is Mendelssohn at his best – vigorous and muscular, with an exciting introductory crescendo for orchestra alone; the return to the high woodwind chords of the conversion scene at the end is another inspired touch.

One of the dangers of basing a narrative work on the Acts of the Apostles is that the two dramatic high points – the stoning of Stephen and the conversion of Paul – happen early on. But Mendelssohn manages to make good musical drama out of later events. When Paul and his fellow apostle Barnabas heal a lame man at Lystra, the people are convinced that they must be the Roman gods Mercury and Jupiter. The chorus of Gentiles that follows, 'Seid uns gnädig, hohe Götter!' ('O be gracious, ye gods'), is in Mendelssohn's most seductive manner – in the words of his biographer Philip Radcliffe, the music 'has so much charm that we almost suspect him of a secret sympathy for the heathen'.

A compelling recitative is followed by an aria and chorus in which Paul proclaims the true faith. Interestingly, Mendelssohn resisted pressure from his co-librettist Julius Schubring to make this a clear statement of Protestant dogma. St Paul's declaration that Christians are justified by faith, rather than by good works, was central to the teaching of the great religious reformer Martin Luther, and it remains the backbone of evangelical teaching today. But Schubring tells us that Mendelssohn 'would not accept my suggestions for the Paulinian doctrine of justification by faith, but at the appropriate place substituted merely the general assertion:

"Wir glauben all' an einen Gott" ["We all believe in one God"]' – which, Schubring adds, 'did not satisfy my theological conscience'.

Many nineteenth-century Protestants would have shared Schubring's qualms. The phrase is sung to a chorale theme in slow-moving notes, sounding clearly through the austere contrapuntal texture of the chorus 'Aber unser Gott ist im Himmel' ('But our God is in the heavens') – another very Bachian device, and one of the most impressive things in the entire work. So at this focal point of Part Two, Mendelssohn avoids pushing home a specifically Christian message, opting instead for a universalised credo. In its message, then, as well as in its many fine musical moments, *St Paul* is a more subtle and interesting work than some would have us believe.

Stephen Johnson © BBC

Claudio Monteverdi (1567–1643)

Born in Cremona, Monteverdi had already had motets and madrigals published while in his teens. In around 1582 he was employed as a string player at the court of Duke Vincenzo Gonzaga. He was passed over for promotion to *maestro di cappella* in 1596, eventually winning the honour in 1601. With his third book of madrigals (1592) he became a recognised – and criticised – exponent of a modern style known as the *seconda prattica* (as opposed to the more established *prima prattica*), in which the musical expression was servant to greater clarity and expression of the words. This style naturally lent itself to theatrical settings, and in 1607 his first opera, *Orfeo*, was performed at the Mantuan court, soon followed by *Arianna*, of which only the moving 'Lament' survives. His Vespers, published in 1610, may have drawn attention to him as a likely candidate to succeed Giovanni Gabrieli as *maestro di cappella* at St Mark's, Venice, which he did in 1613. Alongside his church music he continued to develop the dramatic form, in *Combattimento di Tancredi e Clorinda* (1624), and, following the opening of the first Venetian public opera house, *Il ritorno d'Ulisse in patria* (1640) and *L'incoronazione di Poppea* (1642/3).

℘ Vespers (1610)

1 Deus in adiutorium (chant) – Domine ad adiuvandum me festina
2 Dixit Dominus
3 Nigra sum
4 Laudate pueri
5 Pulchra es
6 Laetatus sum
7 Duo Seraphim
8 Nisi Dominus

 9   Audi coelum
10   Lauda Jerusalem
11   Sonata Sopra Santa Maria
12   Ave maris stella (Hymn)
13   Magnificat

Those who feel that their musical experience of a work is enriched by imagining the circumstances of its original performance will find Monteverdi's 1610 Vespers frustrating. There have been several theories to account for its composition, but none has met with universal approval. It is not even agreed that it is a single composition rather than an anthology of separately created movements, and there is controversy as to how the music in the 1610 edition should be ordered for a performance. In addition, there are a host of specific problems of performance practice, many of which fundamentally affect the whole character of the work.

The sole source for the music and information about it (apart from a German reprint of a couple of movements in 1615) is the edition of 1610. The title-page reads:

Sanctissimae Virgini Missa senis vocibus [ad ecclesiarum choros], ac Vespere pluribus decantandae, cum nonnullis sacris concentibus, ad Sacella sive Principlum Cubicula accomodata. Opera a Claudio Monteverde nuper effecta ac Beatissimo Paulo V. Pontifici Maximo consecrata. Venetiis, Apud Ricciardum Amadinum. MDCX.

(Of the most holy Virgin, a mass for six voices [for church choirs] and Vespers to be sung by several voices, with a few sacred songs suitable for the chapels or chambers of princes; a work by Claudio Monteverdi recently composed and dedicated to the most holy Pope Paul V. Published in Venice by Riccardo Amadino 1610.)

The phrase in brackets occurs only in the *bassus generalis* (organ continuo) part-book. That part-book alone has a separate heading after the Mass:

Vespro della Beata Vergine da concerto composto sopra canti fermi.

(Vespers of the Blessed Virgin in the concerto style composed on plainchant.)

Like virtually all music of the time, the Vespers were published in parts, not score: as in orchestral music, each performer can only see the line he is performing, though the *bassus generalis* continuo part has some of the more elaborate sections printed in score to help the organist follow the singers and direct the performance. There was no full score. The volume begins with a Mass for six voices; then comes what is normally performed as the Vespers, followed by another version of the Magnificat for six voices and organ. The full version of the title-page makes a clear distinction between the Mass (intended for church choirs), and the music for Vespers (for the private chapels or chambers of princes). Some have tried to make a further distinction, linking the Vespers to the chapels and the sacred songs to the chambers. This point was particularly an issue when it was thought that the smaller-scale pieces in the collection could not have been performed liturgically. But that is forcing the language of the title-page too far, and more recent research has shown that the liturgical objections were invalid: Monteverdi is merely suggesting that the smaller pieces can be performed as independent solos.

Three cities have been associated with the Vespers: Mantua (where Monteverdi was employed from about 1590 until 1612), Rome and Venice. Rome features little in Monteverdi's life, apart from the dedication of the Vespers to the Pope and his visit there in 1610. The dedication may have been intended to show that he would be a suitable candidate for a senior papal musical position. The Mass, in a learned and polyphonic style, was certainly appropriate for the conservative Roman ecclesiastical taste. Monteverdi might have expected the Psalms to win favour for the way that they showed how the traditional intonation formulae could be combined with the latest compositional style – though his music was like nothing else sung in Rome at the time. But he may have had other reasons for the dedication. A letter he wrote on his return shows that at least one object of the visit was to secure a scholarship at a seminary for his son Francesco; he also reports on singers there, so may have been sent as a talent scout for the Mantuan court.

Venice was the centre of the music-publishing industry, so Monteverdi perhaps felt the need to visit the city to see through the press so complicated a publication as the Vespers: but the imperfections of the edition (such as the inconsistencies between the voice and the organ parts) make this unlikely. It has been suggested that the publication was intended to impress those who appointed the *maestro di cappella* at the Ducal Basilica of St Mark's. But the then holder of the position, Giulio Cesare Martinengo, had been appointed only a few days after the death of his predecessor Giovanni Croce in 1609, leaving no time for applications from as far as Mantua, and, although Martinengo's health was poor, there was no reason to suppose that he would need replacing quite so soon. Monteverdi may have performed the Vespers at St Mark's after he was appointed in 1613, perhaps even at his audition; but he can hardly have conceived the work with that in mind.

For most of his time at Mantua, Monteverdi had not been required to write church music. But Giacomo Gastoldi, the director of music at the ducal chapel, the Basilica of Santa Barbara, retired through ill health at the end of 1608, and no composer of distinction was found to replace him. So it is possible that Monteverdi was asked to provide music for the chapel. Various occasions have been suggested for which Monteverdi might have been requested to compose a lavish service of Vespers, but none has met with any degree of musicological consensus. The adaptation of the fanfare from *Orfeo* to open the Vespers, however, suggests that it was associated with some Mantuan celebration.

The service of Vespers comprises five psalms, a hymn and the Magnificat. The hundred and fifty psalms were divided among the daily services so that the whole Psalter was recited each week. This pattern, however, was broken on major festivals, which had their own particular groups of psalms. The psalms, originally Jewish hymns, were made more appropriate for Christian worship in two ways: a doxology – a form of praise, such as 'Gloria patri . . .' ('Glory be to the Father . . .' – was added to each of them praising the Holy Trinity, and each psalm was framed by a verse (called an antiphon) relating the psalm to its place in the church year. By special papal licence or ancient tradition, a few churches (such as the ducal chapel in Mantua and St Mark's in Venice) had their own variant selection of psalms and antiphons; otherwise, the same texts were said or sung throughout the Catholic Church. The numbers given after the titles show those of the Vulgate (the standard Latin translation of the Bible) and those of Protestant Bibles.

Monteverdi published the collection as Vespers of the Blessed Virgin. There are several Feasts of the Virgin throughout the church year: her Purification (2 February), Annunciation (25 March), Visitation (2 July), Our Lady of the Snow (5 August), her Assumption (15 August), her Nativity (8 September) and her Conception (8 December) being the ones for which a celebration on the scale of the 1610 publication might be appropriate. Each Feast began with the Vespers on the preceding evening, with the Second Vespers service on the evening of the day itself. Modern performances often surround Monteverdi's music with the chant for specific feasts.

Monteverdi's publication provides music for the five Marian psalms, the hymn and the Magnificat. He also includes a series of smaller-scale pieces (the 'sacred songs' of the title page) which are interspersed between the psalms and look as if they might well function as antiphons. When editors and performers first started to present the Vespers in a liturgical context, this caused problems. The texts of these pieces, though sometimes corresponding with antiphon texts, did not belong to the cycle of antiphons for any single Marian feast. So it was postulated that the antiphons were extraneous items merely thrown in as chamber music. But there were still problems, since the modes of the psalm settings do not correspond with the modes of the chant antiphons of any Feast, and some editions have included antiphons whose modes match but which would never have been sung together at a single service. When sung entirely in chant, the tone chosen for a psalm should agree with the mode of the antiphon; but Monteverdi seemed, almost perversely, to have avoided matching his psalms with the mode of the antiphons for any of the Marian feasts.

More recent research has shown that the supposed problems came from expecting medieval or modern practices to be relevant to the seventeenth century. There were a variety of ways of relating psalm and antiphon. At services of lesser import, the antiphon before the psalm was reduced to the opening words and only sung in full after the psalm; on major feasts, it was sung in full before the psalm, but could be replaced after the psalm by an independent motet or an instrumental piece (in this context described as an antiphon substitute), liturgical propriety being satisfied as long as it was spoken (not necessarily loudly enough to interrupt the music). Some modern performances set the music into a complete Vespers service or at least include plainsong antiphons. It is, however, likely that the smaller-scale pieces were intended to function as antiphon substitutes, replacing the need for chant after the psalms and Magnificat, and chant before them may well have been said inconspicuously by the clerics.

The heading in the organ part-book 'Vespers of the Blessed Virgin in the concerto style, composed on plainchant' draws attention to a feature of the work of prime significance: in the Vespers, Monteverdi allies the most modern musical language (the *concertato* style) with the old technique of composing on the chant. Each psalm is constructed upon one of the tones to which psalms had been chanted for the preceding millennium – as far as Monteverdi knew, since the time of King David! At a time when traditional music of the Church was under attack for its barbarity, Monteverdi chose to make it the centre of his first ambitious church-music publication.

The work calls on a wide range of musical styles, almost as if Monteverdi is trying to show off his capabilities to the full. The most conservative are the double-choir settings of 'Nisi Dominus' and 'Lauda Jerusalem'. In both, the melodic base of the chant (the *cantus firmus*) is hardly varied; but the other voices have an extraordinary suppleness and vitality, and that feature is even more noticeable elsewhere. Generally, the textual declamation of church music was relatively staid; the model for this aspect of the Vespers was not so much previous church music as the more subtle word-setting of vocal chamber music.

Monteverdi was known to the musical world primarily for his madrigals: his fifth book had been published in 1605. He had learned, primarily from Marenzio, the ability to encapsulate a word or short verbal phrase into a musical phrase which characterised the words while permitting a flexible contrapuntal treatment: it is this skill which makes the larger-scale music of the Vespers so original. The final section of 'Audi coelum' is a fine example. A lesser composer could easily have set it virtually homophonically, with all the voices moving together, and on a casual listening (especially when sung chorally with some parts brought out, others virtually suppressed) it might sound thus. But it is built up from a series of short, highly individual and memorable phrases and the total effect depends on the subtle balance of all the lines: 'benedicta es', with its falling fifth, 'virgo Maria' with its rising third and leaning on the 'i', and the duet in thirds of 'in seculorum'. Even the line one seems to hear may not be the part of a single voice: the chances are that if you sing to yourself the first 'benedicta es', you will in fact sing a combination of the two soprano parts.

A distinctive feature of the Vespers is the series of Glorias which conclude each psalm and the Magnificat. In the first psalm, we hear the *cantus firmus* for the first time by itself, but abruptly and movingly transposed a tone lower. In the Magnificat, the texture is again reduced, with two tenors calling to heaven in echo with a florid declamation that seems utterly unrelated to the psalm tone which is being sung by a soprano. For most of the settings of 'sicut erat in principio' Monteverdi adopts a style of slow chords with extremely close canonic imitations between the parts.

Until recently, the Vespers was thought of as a choral work, and it is still often performed thus. As with the Bach Passions, however convincing the musicological arguments that the choruses should be sung one to a part, choirs enjoy the experience of singing them. In some movements of the Vespers (e.g. 'Nisi Dominus') it is easy to distinguish sections that are evidently for soloists from sections that can be sung chorally, but in others there are no clear dividing lines; conductors or editors make their own decisions. Such problems vanish when one forgets the modern assumption that a large-scale vocal work must have a chorus and approaches it as a work in the *concertato* style, as implied by the heading to the organ part. It is now generally assumed that the instrumental sections require only one instrument to a part; if one also approaches the rest of the music from the viewpoint that it is for soloists unless there is any good reason otherwise, one finds some sections in which the doubling of voices is acceptable but none where it is necessary.

There has been controversy over the performance pitch of two sections: 'Lauda Jerusalem' and Magnificat. Music from the sixteenth and early seventeenth centuries appears on paper to be written at two pitch levels, but in performance they were more or less the same. Failure to understand that convention has led the modern ear to expect a gratuitous excitement from the high pitch levels of those movements. But the aesthetics of the time were generally opposed to the tension generated by high notes: voices and instruments should sound in the richest part of their range, and the solemnity of low sounds was favoured. Irrespective of the relative pitch of these movements, there is some evidence that North Italian pitch may have been a little higher than that of today.

It has been customary to supplement Monteverdi's instrumental parts. We can well imagine someone like Michael Praetorius, whose publications from a decade after the Vespers tell us much about how music for voices and instruments was performed north of the Alps, buying the 1610 edition and performing some of the music with choirs scattered around the church and supported by groups of instruments. Perhaps because he gives so much fascinating information about performance at the time, his suggestions have been applied to music for which it was not necessarily suited: there is no reason to assume that music was performed the same way in Wolfenbüttel and Mantua. Some performances are given with strings, cornetts and sackbuts doubling the choir: this is optional, but can be useful in giving choral performances a greater degree of precision.

Monteverdi's reputation (in his own time as now) was as an avant-garde composer: the leading figure of the new style of composition heralded by the Florentine operas (*Dafne* and *Euridice*) and Caccini's *Le nuove musiche*. But in both *Orfeo* and the Vespers he is evidently striving to combine new and old. The former leans heavily on the *intermedio* tradition. In the Vespers, he bases music in the new style on the old *cantus firmus* procedures, and even when writing a secular-sounding strophic aria for the hymn, he retains, though rhythmically transforms, the plainsong melody. As so often in artistic matters, the revolutionary is firmly rooted in tradition.

© Clifford Bartlett

Wolfgang Amadeus Mozart (1756–91)

More than two hundred years after his death, Mozart stands as a focal figure of Western classical music, not only for his astonishing precocity and inventiveness, but for the staggering range and quality of his music. His father Leopold, a violinist, paraded his son's talents around the European capital cities when he was as young as six. By sixteen, Mozart had absorbed a variety of musical fashions, having travelled to England, Germany, France, Holland and Italy. He worked for the Prince-Archbishop in Salzburg during his teens, producing symphonies, concertos and masses as well as operas. In 1780 he went to Munich to compose *Idomeneo*, his first great opera, and the following year he moved to Vienna, where in the four years beginning in 1782 he wrote fifteen of his twenty-seven piano concertos. *The Marriage of Figaro*, the first of his three operatic collaborations with the court poet Da Ponte, appeared in 1786, followed swiftly by *Don Giovanni*. In his last three years he produced his last Da Ponte opera, *Così fan tutte*, the three final symphonies (Nos 39–41) and the gem-like Clarinet Concerto, leaving his Requiem incomplete at his death.

∾ Mass in C major, K317, 'Coronation' (1779)

1 Kyrie
2 Gloria
3 Credo
4 Sanctus
5 Benedictus
6 Agnus Dei

Mozart's sixteen completed mass settings all date from his Salzburg years, in particular from the period during the

1770s when, as Konzertmeister to the archiepiscopal court, he was required to compose liturgical music both for the cathedral and for the local churches. After his move to Vienna in 1781 to try his luck as a freelance composer and performer, he attempted only two more large-scale sacred works and finished neither – the first (the great C minor Mass) apparently through loss of interest, and the second (the Requiem) because of his death.

That might seem to imply that for Mozart sacred music was not a high priority, a supposition that gains substance from a letter he wrote in 1776 to his former teacher, Padre Martini, stating that in the absence of operatic opportunities in Salzburg, 'I am amusing myself by writing chamber music and music for the church.' But it should be remembered that few chances to compose for the Church came Mozart's way in Vienna, and also that in 1791 he was given a guarantee of succession to the position of Kapellmeister at St Stephen's Cathedral on the death of the incumbent, a clear indication of the course his career might have taken had he lived. And it would certainly be wrong to suppose that Mozart relaxed his standards in his sacred compositions. It is true that little church music dates from the time of his greatest maturity, but the best of the Salzburg masses show the familiar easy skills in counterpoint and fluid vocal melody in works of elegance and charm which, while not greatly radical, nevertheless success-fully marry their composer's particular strengths to the accepted Austrian church idiom of the day.

That idiom had its roots in Italy, and the so-called 'cantata masses' of Neapolitan composers such as Alessandro Scarlatti and his successors. In these works the text was set in small chunks, the resulting sections throwing up a sometimes uneasy mixture of styles: choruses in the strict contrapuntal manner; homophonic, declamatory choral movements with busily independent instrumental accompaniments; and unashamedly operatic solo numbers. Such masses were enor-mously influential during the eighteenth century (one has only to think of Bach's B minor Mass), and in Austria that influence was felt as strongly as anywhere. Mozart was happy to follow these examples in his earliest masses, while the unfinished Mass in C minor of 1782–3 is a particularly fine example of the genre. But certain local preoccupations – among them the rise of sonata-based forms such as the symphony – contrived to create a more homogeneous Austrian style, one in which the sections became fewer and less diverse, with contrasts tending to be established within movements rather than between them. The main portions of the mass thus became single movements which might accommodate both contrapuntal and homophonic choral writing, as well as music for solo singers.

Other factors, too, were responsible for shaping the mass in Austria. Reforms introduced by the Enlightenment-inspired Emperor Joseph II discouraged the indulgences of elaborate church music, and in Salzburg Mozart found that his like-minded Prince-Archbishop set more precise limitations still: 'Our church music is very different from that of Italy,' he told Martini; 'a Mass with the whole Kyrie, the Gloria, the Credo, the Epistle sonata, the Offertory or Motet, the Sanctus and the Agnus Dei must not last longer than three quarters of an hour.' Paradoxically, perhaps, Mozart seemed to benefit from this situation in terms of his development as a composer of masses: his efforts now became more compact, with the smaller number of component sections compelling him to find more subtle ways – among them the increasing use of sonata procedures – to maintain interest. The result was a church music that was simpler, more direct and more popular in conception, with what learned elements there were assumed naturally and without self-consciousness into the music's frankly lyrical, at times even song-like manner. Significantly, it was mainly through his church music that Mozart was known to the Salzburg general public during the 1770s (his symphonies and serenades having been destined for the smaller audiences found in courtly circles); it is possible that far from being frustrated by the restrictions imposed on him by his austere employer, the composer was quite happy to tailor his style to suit a less sophisticated audience.

The Mass in C major, K317, is one of his last Salzburg settings, dating from March 1779. Mozart obviously thought well of it, for he used it again on a number of occasions during the 1780s. It was a performance arranged by Antonio Salieri, however, which brought the work its nickname: in 1791 Salieri conducted it in Prague at the coronation of Leopold II as King of Bohemia, and the Mass soon became known locally as the *Krönungsmesse*. It was heard again the following year at the coronation of Franz I, Leopold's successor as Holy Roman Emperor, and it is possible that Salieri also directed it at Leopold's own imperial coronation in Frankfurt in 1790. The work is a fine example of a mass which combines Neapolitan and Austrian elements in a varied but concise score. On the Neapolitan side there are declamatory choruses with busy string accompaniments (for instance in the Credo, or the 'Hosanna' sections of the Sanctus and Benedictus) and strikingly operatic moments such as the Agnus Dei, a soprano solo whose relationship to the later 'Dove sono' from *The Marriage of Figaro* is unmistakable. There is counterpoint, too, though not in the form of fugues but rather in the tuneful, unobtrusive species of part-writing found here in the outer sections of the Credo – which came easily to Austrian composers in general and to Mozart in particular.

More clearly Austrian, though, is the quasi-symphonic concern to achieve some sort of unity. The reappearance of material from the Kyrie in the concluding 'Dona nobis pacem' is an obvious example, but more significant is the sonata-like organisation of the Gloria: take away the chorus, and from the forte–piano contrasts of the opening, through the 'second subject' at the words 'Domine Deus' and the modulating central ('development') section starting at 'Qui tollis' and ending with 'Qui sedes ad dexteram Patris, miserere nobis', to the clear recapitulation at 'Quoniam tu solus sanctus', this section could almost be the sonata-allegro of an amiable classical symphony or overture. The orchestrational style of the Mass, too, is up to date, save only for its omission of violas, a curious Salzburg church tradition.

If these stylistic elements are received ones, features which are to be found in the work of a number of other eminent Austrian church musicians of the time, there are also moments of inspired individuality: such a moment comes at the heart of the Credo, where the movement's boisterous progress is interrupted by a slow passage in which Mozart expresses with sinuous muted string figures and agonised harmonies both the mystery of the Incarnation and the agony of the Crucifixion.

© Lindsay Kemp

∽ Requiem in D minor, K626 (1791), completed by Franz Xaver Süssmayr (1766–1803)

No last work by a great composer has been more surrounded by myth and mystery than Mozart's Requiem. The story of its genesis is the very stuff of legend: how the work was commissioned by a mysterious messenger dressed in grey; how the ailing composer was convinced he was writing a Requiem for himself; how he died before he could finish it; how the score was completed by his pupils. Small wonder that dramatists from Pushkin (*Mozart and Salieri*) to Peter Shaffer (*Amadeus*) found themselves drawn to the scenario, though it is true that no member of Mozart's intimate circle ever went so far as to suggest that the court composer Antonio Salieri had poisoned Mozart out of envy for his patently superior genius, or – equally improbably – that he had anything to do with the completion of the Requiem.

The mystery of the grey-clad messenger, and why his employer had been so keen to preserve his anonymity, was eventually solved with the publication of a long-suppressed document written nearly half a century after the event. In it, a choirmaster called Anton Herzog told how he took part in quartet parties at the castle of a certain Count Walsegg von Stuppach. The Count used to indulge in the harmless game of making believe that the works being played were his own; and when his wife died at a tragically early age on 14 February 1791, he decided to commission a Requiem from Mozart, and to offer it as his own personal tribute. What he could not have foreseen, of course, was that Mozart himself would die before the commission could be fulfilled. At the time of his death Mozart had, in fact, fully composed and scored only a single section of the work – the opening 'Introitus'.

One of the eye-witnesses to Mozart's death on 5 December 1791 was his sister-in-law, Sophie Haibl. Years later, she described how she had heard the dying composer giving instructions to his pupil Franz Xaver Süssmayr as to how the Requiem should be completed. Yet it was only as a last resort, and after two other candidates had shown themselves unequal to the task, that Mozart's widow, Constanze, turned to Süssmayr. Her reluctance to enlist his help may be connected with the fact that he had lost no time in joining the Salieri camp, and by 1792 was taking lessons from Mozart's arch-rival himself.

Just how much of the Requiem was completed in line with Mozart's instructions we shall never know; but in 1960 a pair of hitherto unknown sketches came to light. One of them shows Süssmayr actually to have ignored Mozart's intentions. Mozart, it turned out, had planned to end the 'Lacrimosa' with a double Amen fugue in D minor. It is possible, of course, that Mozart himself rejected this idea, and briefed Süssmayr accordingly; but judging from the cheerful and perfunctory 'Osanna' fugue Süssmayr provided for the Sanctus, his contrapuntal skill would hardly have extended to elaborating Mozart's projected Amen fugue in any case. As it was, Süssmayr set the word 'Amen' to a simple plagal cadence.

Perhaps it was bad luck for Süssmayr that he was left to carry out the difficult task of composing a Sanctus in a bright D major (which would surely also have been Mozart's choice

of key). Much more successful is his Agnus Dei, whose
sweeping, impassioned violin figures have a genuinely
Mozartian feel, and whose alternations between intense
entreaty and gentle supplication are carried out with considerable imagination. It is difficult not to feel that Süssmayr
must have had help of some kind from Mozart for this section. After it, for the concluding 'Lux aeterna', he resorts to a
reprise of the music of the Introitus and Kyrie.

From those portions of the score Mozart did complete, we
can see how sombre a work he was planning. Its sonority,
with a wind section limited to two basset-horns and two bassoons, and with a trio of trombones reinforcing the chorus, is
extraordinarily austere; and in the opening 'Introitus' Mozart
adds to the solemnity by introducing a plainchant melody in
the soprano line (at the point where the solo soprano first
enters, with the words 'te decet hymnus'). Much of the material of the Introitus appears to have been borrowed from
Handel's funeral anthem *The Ways of Zion Do Mourn*; and the
following Kyrie, too, is in the style of a Handelian fugue. Its
subject is very similar to the famous chorus 'And with his
stripes' from *Messiah* (of which Mozart had made an arrangement two years earlier). As for the 'Tuba mirum', its trombone solo is unique in Mozart's output. Following the baritone soloist's first passage, the entry of the tenor in the minor,
rather than the expected major, is a wonderful stroke, and
may remind listeners of the similar gesture in Act II of *Così
fan tutte*, where Ferrando's sudden minor-mode intervention
fatally undermines Fiordiligi's resistance.

The 'Lacrimosa' apart, the first ten sections of the
Requiem (down to and including the 'Hostias') stood complete in outline in Mozart's manuscript, though in all but the
first two it was left to Süssmayr to flesh out the often skeletal
scoring. As for the 'Lacrimosa', it is surely the most tantalising of the many fragments Mozart bequeathed to posterity.
After two bars of sobbing phrases for the violins, the chorus
enters with a melody of infinite sadness and yearning. It is an
unforgettable moment, rendered more poignant by the fact

that Mozart's manuscript breaks off after only eight bars. It is tempting to think that this haunting page was the last music he ever wrote, and it may indeed be so; but it is equally likely that, having mapped this movement out in his mind, he moved on to the more demanding Offertorium.

© Misha Donat

Carl Orff (1895–1982)

Orff was precocious as a child, writing songs from the age of five, and completing his first choral work (*Also sprach Zarathustra*, 1912) and opera (*Gisei*, 1913) while still a teenager. After studying at the Akademie der Tonkunst from 1913–14 he worked as conductor and repetiteur at the Munich Kammerspiele, where he developed an interest in theatre. After the war he wrote several suites of incidental music, before meeting Dorothee Günther, with whom he co-founded the Güntherschule in Munich, an institution aimed at integrating training in music and movement and encouraging the use of the voice and simple percussion instruments. He published the first part of his influential *Schulwerk* in 1930 – a music-training system for children which emphasised the use of primitive rhythms and repeated ostinato patterns. The system was adopted in Berlin schools before the war, and became the basis of post-war educational radio broadcasts for children. Orff's *Carmina burana* (1937) became his most popular work, dwarfing the other two parts of what became his *Trionfi*: *Catulli carmina* (1943) and *Trionfo di Afrodite* (1953).

❧ ***Carmina burana****: cantiones profanae cantoribus et choris cantandae comitantibus instrumentis atque imaginibus magicis* ['profane songs to be sung by soloists and choirs with accompanying instruments and magical images'] (1937)

Fortuna imperatrix mundi
  1 O Fortuna
  2 Fortune plango vulnera
I Primo vere
  3 Veris leta facies

4   Omnia sol temperat
5   Ecce gratum
    Uf dem Anger
6   Dance
7   Floret silva
8   Chramer, gip die varwe mir
9   Round dance
    Swaz hie gat umbe
    Chume, chum geselle min
    Swaz hie gat umbe
10 Were diu werlt alle min
II In taberna
11 Estuans interius
12 Olim lacus colueram
13 Ego sum abbas
14 In taberna quando sumus
III Cour d'amours
15 Amor volat undique
16 Dies, nox et omnia
17 Stetit puella
18 Circa mea pectora
19 Si puer cum puellula
20 Veni, veni, venias
21 In trutina
22 Tempus est iocundum
23 Dulcissime
    Blanziflor et Helena
24 Ave formosissima
    Fortuna imperatrix mundi
25 O Fortuna

Until 1935, when he celebrated his fortieth birthday, Carl Orff had merely been developing his highly original ideas for the theatre. As a child he had written both words and music for puppet plays, utilising kitchen utensils as percussion instruments, at the same time as setting his own texts as songs, helped in writing them down by his mother. His tonal imagination was stimulated by his work as repetiteur and conductor at Munich's Kammerspiele from 1915 to 1917, where the focus was on theatre rather than opera.

Orff's collaboration with Dorothee Günther in creating the Güntherschule in 1924 (in which they devised a unity of music and movement that was 'not based on incidental and subjective experience, but on their elemental relationship, in that they arise from a single source'), led to new dance creations, inspired by such ballet leaders as Mary Wigman, and also to the five-year *Schulwerk* project in which the unity of music and movement was forcefully realised.

A significant success in 1931 was Orff's adaptation of the *St Luke Passion*, then still wrongly attributed to Bach, for the Munich stage, Orff treating it as a Passion Play in South German peasant style. The following year he found Johann Andreas Schmeller's edition of *Carmina burana*. The work which was to bring him international fame was first staged on 8 June 1937 at the City Theatre in Frankfurt am Main, produced by Oskar Wälterlin. After the premiere the composer told his publisher: 'Everything I have written to date, and which you have, unfortunately, printed, can be destroyed. With *Carmina burana* my collected works begin.'

The cantata's title translates as *Songs of Benediktbeuern*. Johann Andreas Schmeller was a Bavarian specialist in dialects who had made an in-depth study of a collection of some two hundred medieval poems and songs discovered in the library of the ancient Abbey of Benediktbeuern in Upper Bavaria during the 1803 secularisation. Schmeller's edition of the collection was published in 1847.

The poems and songs, dating from the thirteenth century (and mostly anonymous), would appear to have been written down from the repertories of minstrels and jesters. Poets from a wide area, including England, France, Germany and Italy, are represented. While many are essentially intellectual poems cast in medieval Latin, there are also Middle High German love songs and dances, as well as texts that combine French and Latin, or German and Latin. The poems cover every facet of life. Eating, drinking and love-making are praised in poems that celebrate the joys of the senses, inevitably found in delightful pieces on spring and young love. The importance of money and a decline in moral values are emphasised in clever satire, as keenly felt seven centuries ago as they are today.

Orff subtitled the work (in Latin) 'profane songs to be sung by soloists and choirs with accompanying instruments and magical images' and told friends that his theatrical imagination had been caught by the opening text: 'O fortuna, velut luna', invoking the Wheel of Fortune. The twenty-four songs and poems he selected are divided into three parts – 'Spring', 'In the Tavern' and 'The Court of Love' – the whole work opening and closing with the 'O Fortuna' chorus, thus emphasising the traditional belief that, for all our devotion to the joys of Nature, Love, Beauty and Wine, we humans are still nothing more than the powerless playthings of Fate.

Orff accepted the Latin language as a vital, living thing, and enhanced the verses with a directness that makes an immediate impact. His tunes are catchy and easy on the ear, yet the strong rhythms and bold orchestration combine to whet the aural appetite. Carl Orff returned to the Latin language in 1943, setting *Catulli carmina*, or *Songs of Catullus*, and again in 1950, when he spent a year creating *Trionfo di Afrodite*, a setting of poems by Sappho and Catullus. These three works became the stage triptych *Trionfi*, referring to the triumphal processions of the late Renaissance, which were accompanied by music and dancing, appropriately anticipating Orff's ideal marriage of music and theatre.

© Denby Richards

Charles Hubert Hastings Parry
(1848–1918)

Largely through his choral song 'Jerusalem' and church anthem *I Was Glad*, Parry has come to convey the musical essence of Victorian and Edwardian England. He was educated at Eton and Oxford and published some songs and church music during his late teens, but first won recognition for his Piano Concerto (1878–9). In 1883 he began teaching at the Royal College of Music – where his pupils included Vaughan Williams and, later, Herbert Howells – becoming director in 1894. Despite these duties, and, from 1900 to 1908, those as Professor of Music at Oxford University, he composed over thirty cantatas and oratorios for chorus and orchestra due to his popularity with British choral societies. Most of these are forgotten, except for his setting of Milton, *Blest Pair of Sirens* (1887), and his oratorio, *Job*, for the Three Choirs Festival of 1892. Despite his admiration for Wagner and his willingness to seek out new trends, his music remained stylistically conservative and was soon eclipsed by that of Elgar. He wrote five symphonies, an opera and numerous songs, mostly collected in his twelve sets of *English Lyrics*.

∾ *Blest Pair of Sirens* (1887)

The more we learn about the English musical renaissance that took place in the last quarter of the nineteenth century, the greater appears the achievement of Hubert Parry. With a rare determination and sense of purpose he succeeded in overcoming a desperately timid and conservative musical background by concentrating on the real strengths of English culture, particularly its great verse and fine choral tradition.

Blest Pair of Sirens was composed in 1887 for the Bach Choir, which had been founded a decade earlier by Otto Goldschmidt, husband of Jenny Lind, 'the Swedish Nightingale'. The choir's new director, Charles Villiers Stanford, wanted to perform

Parry's 1883 setting of James Shirley's 'The Glories of Our Blood and State', but since the planned concert was to form part of Queen Victoria's Silver Jubilee celebrations, objections were raised to the inappropriate text ('Death lays his icy hand on kings: / Sceptre and crown / must tumble down').

It was decided instead to commission a new work, and it was Sir George Grove (of music-dictionary fame) who suggested Milton's 'Ode at a Solemn Music' – a text that Parry had first considered for musical setting as far back as 1867. And as the composer recorded in his diary after a rehearsal, Grove was particularly delighted with the result: 'At the end old G jumped up with tears in his eyes and shook me over and over again by the hand and the whole choir took up the cue . . . and applauded vociferously.'

The performance of *Blest Pair of Sirens* at St James's Hall in London on 17 May 1887 was a notable event both for Parry and for the development of English music. Elgar, who played as an orchestral violinist in several performances of the work, paid tribute to the composer (in one of his 1905 Birmingham lectures) as 'Sir Hubert Parry, the head of our art in this country', and certainly his own achievements in the field of choral and orchestral music would hardly have been possible without the older composer's example.

Blest Pair of Sirens displays a masterly sense of vocal style, with the eight-part chorus exploited subtly and effectively in a clear and powerful response to the words. Parry's beautifully proportioned form both reflects and illuminates the three-part structure of Milton's text, where the marriage of music and verse (the 'Blest Pair of Sirens') symbolises man's desire for union with the heavenly music of the spheres.

© Andrew Huth

❧ Coronation Anthem: *I Was Glad* (1902, rev. 1911)

The coronation of King Edward VII took place in Westminster Abbey on 9 August 1902, after a last-minute delay of six weeks because the new King had had to undergo an emergency operation for appendicitis. For the service, Elgar was commissioned to write a hymn, and Parry his processional anthem *I Was Glad*, on words from Psalm 122. He laid it out on a lavish scale, for the Abbey Choir, a large special choir and the King's Scholars of Westminster School, together with a full orchestra, organ and the Kneller Hall trumpeters. He revised the work for the coronation of George V in 1911; and in this version it has been heard on several subsequent royal occasions, including the coronation of Queen Elizabeth II in 1953 – as well as becoming part of the ceremonial end of the cathedral repertoire, more modestly accompanied by organ.

Parry's revisions chiefly involved the orchestral prelude, which (as Jeremy Dibble illustrates in his biography of the composer) he rewrote to include a clearer anticipation of the rising third to which the opening words are set. The first choral section, intended to be sung by the Abbey Choir at the West Door before the monarch's arrival, is followed by a passage of sonorous antiphony between the two choirs. A processional interlude, reusing the rising third in a new context, leads to trumpet fanfares and the Westminster scholars' vocal fanfare 'Vivat Regina Elizabetha' (in the 1953 version), taken up by the full choir. A passage for semi-chorus, 'O pray for the peace of Jerusalem', provides a more lyrical interlude, before the full choir and the processional melody return in the build-up to the grandiose ending.

The majestic sweep of Parry's anthem suffered a minor bruising at its first outing on that coronation day in 1902. The King's procession was delayed; the Director of Music began the piece before receiving the right signal, and finished it before the royal party had entered the Abbey; even the organ cadenza which Parry had written for emergencies was not enough to fill the gap; so when the King did arrive, the whole of the second part of the anthem had to be repeated. Concert performance is obviously a safer option.

© Anthony Burton

❧ *Jerusalem* (1916; orch. Edward Elgar, 1922)

William Blake's preface to his long poem *Milton* (1804) includes four four-line stanzas inspired by the ancient legend that Jesus had been brought to this country as a child, and culminating in a vision of the building of a new Jerusalem 'in England's green and pleasant land'. Parry made his famous setting of these lines in March 1916, only two and half years before his death, as a unison song (with soloist in the first verse) accompanied by organ. The idea was suggested by the Poet Laureate, Robert Bridges, who wanted a simple setting 'that an audience could take up and join in' for a meeting of the patriotic wartime Fight for Right organisation.

Parry, a man of radical and decidedly unjingoistic beliefs, must have been more thrilled by the invitation to set Blake's idealistic poem than by the narrowly nationalist context of the first performance. He was happier to see his work taken up by the women's movement, and gladly assented to it being adopted as the official Women Voters' Hymn. Later, it was to become the national song of the Women's Institute movement, and also to find a place in many hymn-books. So it already had something of the status of an alternative national anthem when Malcolm Sargent first invited the audience to sing it at the Last Night of the Proms in 1953.

Parry made an orchestral version of *Jerusalem* in November 1916, and this was widely used for some years. But it has now been universally supplanted by the orchestration for larger forces made by his younger friend and colleague Elgar for the 1922 Leeds Festival. The flashing ascent through the strings which represents Blake's 'arrows of desire' has become almost as essential a component of the piece as Parry's magnificent melody itself.

© Anthony Burton

Francis Poulenc (1899–1963)

Poulenc's first published work, the vocal/ensemble piece *Rapsodie nègre* (1917) established his place in chic avant-garde Parisian circles: there he had met Satie and was drawn into the group that became known as Les Six. After three years' study (1921–4) with Charles Koechlin he scored further success with his Diaghilev ballet *Les biches* (1924). Poulenc's urbane wit triumphed in the *Concert champêtre* (1927–8; a harpsichord concerto written for Wanda Landowska), and the Concerto for Two Pianos (1932). Later in the 1930s, the death of a friend and a visit to the shrine of Notre Dame de Rocamadour inspired a return to Catholicism; the *Litanies à la vierge noire* (1936), Mass (1937) and *Quatre motets pour un temps de pénitence* (1938) followed in close succession. For the rest of Poulenc's life devoutness and ironic wit formed characteristic strands in his work, exemplified by his two full-scale operas, the surreal comedy *Les mamelles de Tirésias* (1939–44) and the religious tragedy *Dialogues des Carmélites* (1953–6). His songs were largely written for the baritone Pierre Bernac, with whom Poulenc collaborated as pianist until the end of his life.

∾ *Gloria* (1959)

1 Gloria
2 Laudamus te
3 Domine Deus
4 Domine Fili unigenite
5 Domine Deus, Agnus Dei
6 Qui sedes ad dexteram Patris

Poulenc's *Gloria* brought forth frowns of disapproval on the face of the ecclesiastical establishment, being thought by some especially devout Roman Catholics to contain music too frivolous for a religious work. Poulenc seems to have been puzzled by this reaction to his uninhibited delight in praising his Lord. Indeed, the *Gloria* is a natural musical extension of his secular style, here projected to honour the beliefs he had first embraced as a child in an ardently Catholic family, then tended to neglect, and eventually allowed to lapse, only to renew them after the tragic death of his friend and fellow composer Pierre-Octave Ferroud in a motor accident on 17 August 1936.

Poulenc heard of the accident while he was on holiday in the Auvergne, and he went to the shrine of the Black Virgin of Rocamadour, not far from Uzerche, where he was staying. It was at the shrine that he found himself recalled to the religion that had played such a major role in his early life. He began to express himself in music that evening, his first religious work being the *Litanies à la vierge noire*, scored for three-part female chorus and organ. For the next quarter of a century choral works flowed from his pen.

During the Second World War Poulenc steadfastly remained in occupied France, using his music to declare his resistance to the Nazi invaders. In 1943, the blackest year of the occupation, he composed *Figure humaine*, to a text by Paul Eluard, set for twelve voices, in which his deep study of Bach's chorales bore fruit in a complex masterpiece which superbly projects the mood of supplication.

In 1944 Poulenc declared himself to be primarily a composer of music for the Church. The fact that he had composed more secular than sacred music may have left some of his admirers sceptical, particularly when his next choral offering was the *Chansons françaises* (1945–6). However, the *Quatre petites prières de Saint François d'Assise*, for male voices (1948), and more especially the *Stabat mater* (1950), provided music of expressive quality. The *Stabat mater* was scored for soprano, mixed chorus and orchestra, the same forces that Poulenc uses in the *Gloria*, its natural musical successor, composed nearly a decade later, in 1959.

The *Gloria* was commissioned by the Koussevitzky Foundation of the Library of Congress and first performed on

10 February 1961, with the soprano soloist Adele Addison, and the Boston Symphony Orchestra and Pro Musica Chorus conducted by Charles Munch. It is dedicated to the memory of Serge and Nathalie Koussevitzky. The *Gloria* was Poulenc's penultimate choral work, and its maturity owes more than a little to his most extensive score: his opera based on Georges Bernanos's *Dialogues des Carmélites*, produced at La Scala, Milan, on 6 February 1959, with which his assertion that he was a religious composer was triumphantly proven. The liturgical text is the greater Doxology (or Gloria of the Mass), and falls into six sections, with the soprano soloist prominent in the third and fifth, as well as making contributions to the last.

Poulenc's songs, which are among his most personal expressions, are often built on short two- or four-bar phrases, and the *Gloria* employs these within its structure. The first phrase recurs in the final section, and also permeates the whole work. Those establishment eyebrows must surely have been most active during the 'Laudamus te': this is music that praises God in joyous energy, from the flourishes of the wind at the outset to the cheerful melody in the homely key of C major with off-beat basses. The ebullience is muted for the soprano's delivery of 'Gratias agimus tibi'. Poulenc certainly felt no irreverence, suggesting that he had once seen Benedictine monks enjoying a game of football, and also recalling the fifteenth-century Benozzo Gozzoli frescoes in which angels poke their tongues out in good-humoured fun.

The 'Domine Deus' takes us back to the religious intensity in which the wonder of the majesty of the Lord is expressed by the soprano, warmly supported by chorus and orchestra, a mood contrasted by the exuberance of the choral writing in the 'Domine Fili unigenite', itself further contrasted with the firm dignity of the 'Domine Deus, Agnus Dei'. This again is coloured by the solo soprano, whose interjected Amens in the final 'Qui sedes' dispel the vestiges of drama and then usher in a true serenity to enhance the final moments of Poulenc's religious ecstasy.

© Denby Richards

❧ *Litanies à la vierge noire* (1936)

'I am religious by deepest instinct and by heredity,' Poulenc once observed. 'I am a Catholic. Nevertheless the gentle indifference of the maternal side of my family had, quite naturally, led to a long fit of forgetfulness of religion. From 1920 to 1935 I was admittedly very little concerned regarding the faith.' The death of his friend Pierre-Octave Ferroud in a car accident and a visit soon after to the shrine of the Black Virgin at Rocamadour in the summer of 1936 rekindled Poulenc's faith. Yvonne Gouverné, who accompanied Poulenc to the small chapel at Rocamadour, recalled how her companion was deeply moved by the place and its black wooden statue of the Virgin Mary:

> Outwardly, nothing happened, yet from that moment everything in the spiritual life of Poulenc changed. He bought a little picture with the text of the Litanies to the Black Virgin, and as soon as we were back in Uzerche he began to write that very pure work for female choir and organ, *Litanies à la vierge noire*.

The pilgrimage to Rocamadour helped ease the composer's grief, as did the process of writing his *Litanies*, completed between 22 and 29 August. 'In this work,' he wrote, 'I tried to depict the mood of "country devotion" that so deeply struck me in that mountain locale. That is why this invocation must be sung simply, without pretension.' Before Ferroud's death, Poulenc had gained a reputation as a master of frivolity, a skilled craftsman whose work lacked spiritual depth and relied on superficial display. The *Litanies*, his first religious composition, proved Poulenc capable of heartfelt, honest expression, notably unsentimental and direct in its treatment of the Rocamadour prayers.

Following a piquant organ introduction, the spirit of Gregorian chant influences the choral writing. Each verse, clearly articulated by the choir, is interrupted by organ interludes, the chromatic cast of which contrasts with the modal harmonies adopted for the vocal ensemble.

Nadia Boulanger conducted the first performance of the *Litanies* with BBC forces in London on 17 November 1936.

© Andrew Stewart

✑ *Sept répons des ténèbres* (1960–2)

1 Una hora non potuistis vigilare mecum
2 Judas mercator pessimus
3 Jesum tradidit
4 Caligaverunt oculi mei
5 Tenebrae factae sunt
6 Sepulto Domino
7 Ecce quomodo moritur justus

One of the most powerful symbolic acts associated with the Holy Week liturgy comes with the snuffing out of fifteen candles during the Office of Tenebrae, the nocturnal service observed on Maundy Thursday, Good Friday and Holy Saturday. The Tenebrae responsories were frequently set to polyphonic music by continental European composers in the years immediately after the Counter-Reformation, notably so by Palestrina, Gesualdo and Victoria. Francis Poulenc revisited the Tenebrae texts for what proved to be his final choral work, selecting the fifth and eighth responsories for Maundy Thursday (descriptions of Judas's betrayal and the vigil on the Mount of Olives); the fifth, eighth and ninth responsories for Good Friday (powerful texts on the pain and despair of the Crucifixion); and the sixth and ninth responsories for Holy Saturday (concerned with Christ's interment).

On 7 February 1960 Poulenc wrote to his friend Pierre Bernac from New York, 'The New York Philharmonic wants to commission . . . a choral work! I have more or less decided to write an *Office du Vendredi saint* for children's choir (rather than female voices), male choir and orchestra, with perhaps a baritone solo . . . I only hope the music comes to me.'

Later that year he confessed to Bernac that the work's birth pangs were painful and protracted. 'You might say that I am *dans les ténèbres* as, for the moment, it feels as if I am entering a tunnel. It is always like this. I am not too worried. I am passionate about this work but it also terrifies me!'

The following spring Poulenc scrapped his first draft and began afresh, crafting a work for treble soloist, mixed boys' and adult choir, and orchestra. In November 1961 he wrote to Leonard Bernstein, music director of the New York Philharmonic, that the work was 'very simple (because of the children) but, I think, very moving, not at all decorative like [my] *Gloria*, and completely inward'.

The *Sept répons* were commissioned for the opening of the Lincoln Center on 23 September 1962, although the score and parts were apparently not finished in time for the New York Philharmonic's inaugural concert there. The work received its premiere shortly after Poulenc's death, performed by the New York Philharmonic under Thomas Schippers at Avery Fisher Hall on 11 April 1963.

Poulenc likened his treatment of the Tenebrae responsories to the 'mystical realism' of the paintings of Andrea Mantegna (1431–1506), one of two artists consistently chosen by the composer to represent the spirit of his religious choral music (the other being Francisco de Zurburán). Although such dramatic moments as the betrayal of Christ ('Judas mercator pessimus') are boldly stated and the opening of 'Caligaverunt oculi mei' is cast in a suitably aggressive style, the prevailing mood of the *Sept répons des ténèbres* is one of meditation. Sorrow and despair are presented in music of austere simplicity, subtly underlined, for example, by the haunting treble (or soprano) solo in 'Jesum tradidit', the unaccompanied choral passages in 'Tenebrae factae sunt' and the dignified brass fanfare at the opening of 'Sepulto Domino'. Poulenc reserves his most direct and impassioned writing for the final response, 'Ecce quomodo moritur justus', at the same time sensuous and yet profoundly spiritual in expression.

© Andrew Stewart

Sergey Prokofiev (1891–1953)

An *enfant terrible* in his earlier years, Prokofiev entered the St Petersburg Conservatory aged thirteen, creating a stir with his early taste for rhythmic energy and grating dissonance. A rich period around the time of the Revolution brought the lyrical First Violin Concerto and the 'Classical' Symphony, before a spell in the USA, where his ballet *The Love for Three Oranges* and the Third Piano Concerto were badly received. He went on to Paris, drawn to the epicentre of the avant-garde, before moving his family to the USSR in 1936. Adopting a more direct, lyrical style in line with prevailing socialist-realist ideals, he produced the ballet *Romeo and Juliet* and the children's tale *Peter and the Wolf* (both 1936), the film music for Eisenstein's *Alexander Nevsky* (1938) and *Ivan the Terrible* (1945), and the epic opera based on Tolstoy's *War and Peace* (1943). Despite his compliant efforts, Prokofiev was denounced by Communist officials in 1948 ('the unfeeling essence of his music is alien to our reality'), though he had managed to placate them by 1951, when he won the Stalin Prize.

✺ *Alexander Nevsky*, cantata, Op. 78 (1938–9)

1 Russia under the Mongolian Yoke
2 Song of Alexander Nevsky
3 The Crusaders in Pskov
4 Arise, Russian People
5 The Battle on the Ice
6 The Field of the Dead
7 Alexander's Entry into Pskov

Prince Alexander Yaroslavovich (1220–63) ruled over the principality of Novgorod at a time when the greater part of

Russia to the south and east had been overrun by the nomadic army of Tartar-Mongol horsemen led by Genghis Khan and his successors. The greatest challenge to Novgorod's independence, however, came from the west. In 1240 Alexander defeated a Swedish force on the river Neva (hence his name of 'Nevsky'), but two years later faced an even greater threat from an invasion led by the Teutonic Order of the Sword-Bearers. The invaders had the double objective of colonising the lands on the eastern shores of the Baltic and of suppressing Russian Orthodoxy – they bore plenary indulgences from the Pope and wore the insignia of crusaders. They captured the Novgorodian town of Pskov and approached to within seventeen miles of Novgorod itself before Alexander's forces defeated them in a savage battle fought on the ice of the frozen Lake Peipus.

When Prokofiev accepted Sergey Eisenstein's invitation to provide music for the film *Alexander Nevsky* in May 1938, it was vital for both men that the project should be a popular success. Prokofiev had returned to live permanently in the USSR in 1936, the period of the first great wave of Stalinist purges. Politically naive, he seems to have been quite unaware of any immediate danger to himself; but his reputation as a European modernist provoked unease in official musical circles. The gratifying success of *Peter and the Wolf* was hardly enough to compensate for the fact that the state commissions he expected were not forthcoming, and his more serious works had generally been badly received. Eisenstein's position was even more delicate since a 1937 attack in *Pravda* had branded his experimental work with the meaningless but sinister taint of 'formalism'. *Alexander Nevsky* was to be a means of rehabilitating himself with a patriotic film of mass appeal, based on one of the proudest episodes in Russian history, and one, moreover, with obvious topical relevance to the threat from Nazi Germany.

The collaboration between Eisenstein and Prokofiev turned out to be ideal for both of them. Each stimulated the other: Eisenstein's bold, epic approach drew from Prokofiev music that was both accessible and strikingly apt for the subject; often a passage of Prokofiev's music would suggest a new cinematic idea to Eisenstein, and he was quite prepared to adjust the action of the film to fit in with the pace of a musical sequence. The director's musico-visual imagination, the composer's scrupulous sense of timing, flexibility on both sides, and a fanatical attention to metronome and stopwatch all contributed to a marriage of image and sound which was to set entirely new standards for film music.

Given the circumstances of time and place, the scenario of the film could hardly allow for much subtlety of characterisation. The Russian goodies are fearless, upright, home-loving, occasionally humorous and invariably noble; the Teutonic baddies are very, very nasty, never more happily employed than when throwing a baby onto a bonfire. Prokofiev's music faithfully reflects this black-and-white approach. He had been attracted to the idea of using authentic thirteenth-century music in his score, but soon discovered that 'this music has in the past seven centuries become far too remote and emotionally alien to us to be able to stimulate the imagination of the present-day film-goer'. He settled instead on a raucous, dissonant, brassy sound world to portray the invaders, and for the Russians a broadly melodic style deriving from the nineteenth-century nationalist composers, but fortified by his own more pungent use of rhythm and harmony.

The cantata *Alexander Nevsky*, which Prokofiev conducted for the first time on 17 May 1939, closely follows the narrative sequence of the film. The first, second, fourth and sixth sections are taken almost directly from the film score. The third, fifth and seventh had to be substantially recast to provide a more satisfactory independent musical form, and the orchestration of the whole work was revised to take into account the differences between recording studio and concert hall.

© Andrew Huth

∾ *Cantata for the Twentieth Anniversary of the October Revolution*, Op. 74 (1936–7)

1 Introduction
2 Philosophers
3 Interlude
4 Marching in Close Ranks
5 Interlude
6 Revolution
7 Victory
8 The Pledge
9 Symphony
10 The Constitution

Prokofiev and his wife Lina spent the New Year of 1936 in Moscow, celebrating with friends and making final preparations to move back to the Soviet Union with their children. In an interview published in the *Moscow Evening News* on 28 January, Prokofiev announced: 'I've thought up for the twentieth anniversary of the October Revolution a big cantata on texts from the works of Lenin. As far as I know, this will be the first time that Lenin's words have been used as the basis for a large-scale musical work.'

Prokofiev made several public announcements at this period about his new piece, even though almost nothing had yet been written. Perhaps this was a gamble to ensure that his return to his native land would be a resounding success. If so, it was a gamble that failed. According to Rita McAllister, the composer began sketching the *Cantata* while he was in Paris. As he often did, he included several ideas which had been written years before. The text, which he himself appears to have compiled by degrees, seems at this stage to have involved only words from Lenin, although it eventually came to include quotations from Marx, Engels and even Stalin.

Back once again in Moscow in March (his wife was still looking after the children in Paris), Prokofiev moved into the Metropol Hotel, where, within a few weeks, he wrote *Peter and the Wolf* for the Moscow Children's Musical Theatre. This enchanting piece became a huge success within days of its first performance on 2 May. On 15 May his wife and children arrived, and by the end of June the whole family had moved into a new flat on the east side of the centre of town.

By the beginning of July the hot weather had begun and Prokofiev and his wife and children left the dusty city to spend the summer in the countryside. In fact he did little work on the *Cantata* at this point as he was preoccupied with three Pushkin projects: a film score for *The Queen of Spades* and incidental music for theatrical productions of *Boris Godunov* and *Eugene Onegin* (1937 was to be not only the twentieth anniversary of the October Revolution, but the centenary of Pushkin's death).

Towards the end of the summer, the family came back to Moscow, arriving home at the same time as the news of the start of the great show trials of Zinoviev and Kamenev, marking the opening of the floodgates of the Stalinist Terror. How this ghastly historical episode touched Prokofiev we do not know, but even he cannot have remained indifferent to the general atmosphere of mounting fear, and to the increasing number of arbitrary arrests.

In November, Prokofiev set off on a tour of Europe and the USA. That he was able to go at all, at a time when most Soviet citizens had no chance of travelling abroad, is a remarkable indicator of the deal that he thought he had struck with the authorities when he decided to return home. For the time being, those authorities were sticking to what they had promised. His well-publicised departure also coincided with the Eighth Extraordinary Congress of Soviets, at which Stalin forced through the ratification of his new Constitution. Extracts from Stalin's speech at this Congress would eventually form the text of the final section of Prokofiev's *Cantata*.

In the early months of 1937 Prokofiev returned to Moscow (with a smart new blue Ford purchased in America) and it was possibly at this time that he began to get down to serious work on the music.

By the time summer came he had again removed his family from the city, this year to a pretty little village beyond the suburbs to the south-west, Nikolina Gora. Here, in the place where he was eventually to spend most of his time in his later years, Prokofiev completed the composition and orchestration of the *Cantata for the Twentieth Anniversary of the October Revolution*, finishing the enormous full score on 16 August 1937.

Soon afterwards, he gave a performance of the piece (playing the score on the piano and singing the vocal parts himself) to a closed session of the Committee for Artistic Affairs, chaired by its president, the ideologist and propagandist Platon Mikhailovich Kerzhentsev. In a transcript of this occasion which appeared only in 1967, Moisei Grinberg, who was present, recalled: 'I remember how Platon Mikhailovich said: "What on earth do you mean, Sergei Sergeyevich, by taking such texts, which have become the people's, and setting them to such music?"' Grinberg added: 'It must be pointed out that Prokofiev sang very nastily, although he played the piano brilliantly . . .'

Against this story must be set a diary entry by the composer Nikolai Myaskovsky (one of Prokofiev's closest friends), who heard the piece at the same time: 'Prokofiev showed us his cantata for the twentieth anniversary of October – tremendous.'

Nonetheless, and despite Myaskovsky's opinion, the result of this secret session was that the new cantata was declared unworthy of performance. For a while Prokofiev seems to have clung to the idea that the decision was not final. He wrote to a friend: 'I sat for two months at Nikolina Gora . . . scribbling a cantata for the twentieth anniversary, and it has already provoked more indignation than rapture. What will happen when it is performed?'

Even months later on 31 December 1937, he defiantly told a journalist from *Pravda* that:

My main work this year has been a large cantata dedicated to the twentieth anniversary of October. The main

themes of this composition are the Great October
Socialist Revolution, its victory, the industrialisation of
the country and the Constitution.

The cantata is written for two choruses (professional
and amateur) and four orchestras (symphony, brass band,
sound effects and accordionists). It needs no fewer than
five hundred people to perform it.

I wrote this cantata with great enthusiasm. The complex events which it treats demanded an equal complexity
of musical language. But I hope that the impetuosity and
sincerity of the music will carry it to our listeners.

These last words are particularly interesting as they give
the first hint that Prokofiev is trying to defend himself publicly against the attacks of Kerzhentsev and his cronies. In
fact, the *Cantata for the Twentieth Anniversary of the October
Revolution* was never performed in the composer's lifetime.
Only on 5 April 1966, more than twelve years after his death,
did it receive its premiere in Moscow under the conductor
Kirill Kondrashin. Even then the eighth and tenth movements were cut because of their texts by Stalin, the ninth
movement ('Symphony') was given only in fragments, and
the performance ended with a peculiar reprise of the second
movement, presumably in order to find some way of finishing
the piece in C major. Only in very recent years has it had its
first complete performances.

The *Cantata*, for all its immense size, the massive forces it
demands, its cumbersome title and its repulsive texts, represents one of Prokofiev's most magnificent musical utterances
on the large scale, a choral and orchestral feast to rank with
his world-famous film scores for Eisenstein's *Alexander
Nevsky* and *Ivan the Terrible*.

The work is cast in ten movements, which follow one
another without a break. It begins with a stormy prelude,
over the first page of which Prokofiev has written a quotation
from *The Communist Manifesto*: 'A spectre is haunting
Europe, the spectre of Communism.' The second movement

introduces the chorus with another famous quotation from Marx: 'Philosophers simply explained the world in different ways. The point is to change it.' A brief and dramatic interlude leads to the fourth movement, a setting of extracts from Lenin's writings from before the Revolution, urging his followers towards the great task ahead.

Another stormy interlude leads to the heart of the work, 'Revolution'. This, the longest section, is a gigantic choral and dramatic scena. Its texts, taken from Lenin's writings and sayings from the very first few weeks of the October Revolution, were arranged by the composer to suggest a vivid picture of an event unfolding before our eyes. It begins with the first violins alone playing a nervous message in Morse code and builds eventually to a tremendous climax, when the composer introduces the whole arsenal of special effects: shots from heavy and light artillery, machine guns, an alarm bell and a siren. As the revolutionaries gain the upper hand, the splendidly unexpected sound of an orchestra of accordions comes in, presumably to suggest the joy of the people as their cause is won. A speaker, representing Lenin himself, shouts out: 'The success of the revolution hangs on two or three days! Fight to the death, but do not let the enemy through!'

The seventh movement, 'Victory', is a haunting slow movement into which Prokofiev introduces another of his sound effects, the noise of distant tramping feet. This is followed by 'The Pledge', setting parts of Stalin's speech on the eve of Lenin's funeral in 1924. The next movement, the purely orchestral 'Symphony', was presumably what Prokofiev had in mind when he told the *Pravda* journalist that one of the themes of the piece was the industrialisation of the country. Industrial construction of some sort would seem to be suggested by the energetic first theme of this movement, while the pastoral-sounding second theme seems closer to the soundtracks of the many newsreel films of the period depicting the bliss of life in the Soviet countryside on the new collective farms.

The *Cantata* ends with a rapturous setting of fragments from Stalin's speech to the Eighth Extraordinary Congress of Soviets in November 1936. The composer's sweet and lyrical music to these extremely unlikely words brings the work to a glowing end in the home key of C major. But, as always with Prokofiev, his C major is not plain and simple, but full of surprises, harmonic twists and turns. Perhaps it was these that brought down Kerzhentsev's immediate ire on that unhappy day in August 1937, when the composer had finished singing and playing his new work, and turned to hear what the committee had to say.

© Gerard McBurney

Henry Purcell (1659–95)

Henry Purcell was England's most celebrated composer before Elgar, writing in almost all the musical genres of the time. He was a pupil of John Blow, whom he succeeded as organist of Westminster Abbey in 1679. His energies were mainly directed towards the royal court (in addition to his Westminster post he was appointed to the Chapel Royal in 1682), for which he wrote around seventy anthems, including *My Heart is Inditing* for James II's coronation of 1685. He also composed twenty-four odes and welcome songs for royal occasions, of which *Come, Ye Sons of Art* (1694, for Queen Mary's birthday) and the St Cecilia's Day ode, *Hail! Bright Cecilia*, are among the finest. He absorbed the French style in his ceremonial overtures, the Italian in his 'Sonatas of Three Parts' and the English in his string fantasias. In the last six years of his life he wrote incidental music for over thirty-five plays as well as a number of music dramas, of which the pinnacle was *Dido and Aeneas* (1689), whose expressive lament 'When I am laid in earth' remains one of the most powerful English opera arias.

∾ *Hail! Bright Cecilia*, An Ode on St Cecilia's Day (1692)

Why is St Cecilia commonly regarded as the patron saint of music and musicians? The answer may well be: by mistake. The *Acta* which describe her life and martyrdom are themselves of dubious authenticity, but they contain the sentence which has given rise to the cult. In describing her marriage to the patrician Valerian, the story shows her dedication to God and her knowledge that she could never consummate the marriage by the fact that at the wedding feast, while instruments played, she sang to the Lord in her heart. In Chaucer's *Canterbury Tales* the same idea is made the basis of the story of the second nun; the words from Cecilia's *Acta* are translated directly:

> While the organs made melodic
> To God alloon in herte thus sang sche;
> 'O Lord, my soule, and eck my body gye
> Unwemmed, lest that I confounded be.'

The implication here is clear: Cecilia turns away from the secular pleasures of musical instruments, and communes with God in silence. But in the Office of the Roman Church for her feast day, 22 November, a similar phrase is used, with a difference: 'Cantantibus organis, Cecilia Domino decantabat dicens, at cor meum immaculatum ut non confundar.'

Here there is no mention of her singing 'in her heart'; indeed we could understand the sentence to mean, 'With instruments playing, Cecilia sang in these words . . .' So Cecilia has been transformed; she no longer rejects the music-making but rather uses it in God's praise.

When this change took place is uncertain, but it is clear that for several centuries St Cecilia was the centre of much devotion without her musical skills being noted; and it is only in the fifteenth century that the long series of portraits which show her at the organ is inaugurated (of which the most famous is Raphael's, in the Church of San Giovanni in Monte, near Bologna). And it is not until 1570 that there is any record of special musical celebrations in her honour, the first being recorded at the town of Evreux in Normandy (where, from that date until 1600, there were regular yearly competitions for the best music to be written in her honour, and extended liturgical celebrations on her feast day).

It was 1683 before there was any mention of similar celebrations taking place in London. They were organised by a specially constituted body called 'The Musical Society', who appointed from among themselves two musicians and four 'persons of quality or gentlemen of note' to arrange the proceedings. Even in 1683 the feast is described as 'commemorated yearly by all musicians', and Sir John Hawkins's *History of Music* says that the meetings took place at the Stationers Hall 'from the time of rebuilding that edifice after the fire of London'; but there is no evidence of such events earlier.

The first recorded Ode on St Cecilia's Day was written by the young composer who had only a year previously been appointed an organist at the Chapel Royal: Henry Purcell. His 1683 Ode, *Welcome to All the Pleasures*, was published the following year with the note that St Cecilia's 'Memory is Annually honoured by a public Feast made on that day [22 November] by the Masters and Lovers of Music, as well in England as in Foreign parts' (which may imply, incidentally, that the celebrations were copied from abroad). And so it was for some twenty years. Many fine and even more insignificant pieces were written and composed. Without doubt the greatest (it was revived several times in the 1690s, as well as being famous in the nineteenth century) is the ode for the 1692 celebrations, *Hail! Bright Cecilia*.

What made Purcell write a work on the largest possible scale must remain uncertain. The orchestration – with oboes, recorders, trumpets and timpani – is lavish, and the writing is elaborate. Perhaps he was inspired by the text by Nicholas Brady (whose famous metrical version of the Psalms was written with another Purcell librettist, Nahum Tate), with its praise of many instruments. Such descriptions were, however, a conventional feature of such odes (as in Dryden's famous text, set first by Giovanni Draghi and then reset in the eighteenth century by Handel). Indeed, they became a butt of humour for mid-eighteenth-century cynics; in 1749 one Bonnell Thornton wrote a burlesque Ode for St Cecilia's Day which was subsequently set to music by no less an authority than Dr Charles Burney. It makes a splendid comparison with Brady, from the opening command, 'Be dumb, be dumb, ye inharmonious sounds', to its rejection of common instruments:

> The viler melody we scorn
> Which meaner instruments afford
> Shrill flute, sharp fiddle, bellowing horn,

Rumbling bassoon, or tinkling harpsichord

in favour of such delightful alternatives as the Jew's harp, played in the mouth:

> Strike, strike the soft Judaic harp,
> By teeth coercive in firm durance kept,
> And lightly by the volant finger swept.
> And, by way of contrast, the hurdy-gurdy:
> With dead, dull, doleful heavy hums,
> With dismal moans
> And mournful groans
> The sober hurdy-gurdy thrums.

Nevertheless, inadequate texts were a perennial feature of such celebration odes, and it was the particular skill of composers such as Purcell to rise above their near-banalities. The words of the satirist Thomas Brown are the most appropriate tribute to Purcell's achievement in a superb work such as this Ode:

> For where the Author's scanty words have fail'd,
> Your happier Graces, Purcell, have prevail'd.

And in this case they did prevail, in every sense; the *Gentlemen's Journal* reported that the work was given with 'universal applause, particularly the second Stanza which was sung with incredible Graces by Mr Purcell himself'. This refers to the solo 'Tis nature's voice', and has commonly been taken to indicate that Purcell (who we know from the Chapel Royal lists was a bass) was also a falsettist. But did he sing? His name is not on the score which lists the singers. Perhaps the sentence means only that Mr Purcell provided the elaborate ornamentation himself: that they were not the singer's own. It may well be the case that, like the story of St Cecilia and music, the story of Purcell as a male alto is based on a misreading of the texts.

© Nicholas Kenyon

Sergey Rakhmaninov (1873–1943)

For most of his life, Rakhmaninov led a dual career as pianist and composer. He graduated from the Moscow Conservatory with his first opera, *Aleko*, and also took to conducting after the disastrous premiere of his First Symphony in 1897 directed by Glazunov. The resulting three-year compositional silence was overcome by hypnosis, and Rakhmaninov soon wrote his highly successful Second Piano Concerto (1901). He made a lucrative tour of America in 1909 (for which he wrote his Third Piano Concerto), and after the Revolution in 1917 he lived in self-imposed exile, largely in the USA. His richly chromatic, broadly lyrical and unashamedly nostalgic style has found many critics, but has ensured his music's popularity among audiences. In addition to his three symphonies and two piano sonatas, he wrote two sets of *Études-tableaux* and *Préludes* for piano, a mighty Cello Sonata, three evocative symphonic poems and a rich setting of the Vespers (*All-Night Vigil*, 1915).

✍ *All-Night Vigil* (Vespers), Op. 37 (1915)

From the time of its first performance in 1915, Rakhmaninov's *Vigil* has been acknowledged as a supreme achievement in the music of the Russian Orthodox Church. By any standards, it is one of the most remarkable works ever composed for the notoriously difficult medium of unaccompanied chorus, and together with his choral symphony *The Bells*, it was Rakhmaninov's own favourite among all his compositions.

Although generally referred to as 'Rakhmaninov's Vespers', these fifteen movements for unaccompanied chorus make up the Ordinary of the All-Night Vigil service, which consists not only of Vespers, but also includes the liturgical offices of Matins, Lauds and Prime.

As the Russian Orthodox Church considers the day to begin and end at sunset, the celebration of Sundays and major feast-days would begin in the evening with the office of Vespers, and continue through the night until the morning, when the main office of the day would be celebrated. The prayers and psalms which Rakhmaninov set comprise the Ordinary of the full Vigil service: that is, those sections of the service which would be common to the celebration of all Sundays, Feasts and Saints' days. Performed in their liturgical context, these would be interspersed with the Proper of the Feast: those parts of the liturgy which change with the seasons or are applicable only to the Feast in question. In the larger monasteries and cathedrals, two choirs would be employed for the Vigil, one to sing the Ordinary, the other to sing the Proper.

Rakhmaninov was never a devout, practising Christian, but the poetry and traditions of the Church formed an essential part of his musical nature. Choral music, too, was always important to Rakhmaninov. One of his earliest surviving compositions is a six-part unaccompanied motet to a Latin text (*Deus meus*, 1890), and in 1910 he made a serious attempt to come to terms with the music of the Orthodox Church by setting the Liturgy of St John Chrysostom, which had also been set by Tchaikovsky in 1878. Rakhmaninov himself was not particularly satisfied with this setting, and perhaps it was this dissatisfaction which made him wish to make another and more ambitious attempt at church music, this time with the far more extensive Vigil service.

Rakhmaninov composed his setting of the Vigil in January and February 1915. It was his first major composition since 1913, when he had completed *The Bells* and the Second Piano Sonata. The first performance of the *Vigil* was given on 23 March 1915 at a concert to raise funds for the Russian war effort and took place not in any of the Moscow churches, but in the Great Hall of the Nobility. The work made such a deep impression that the concert had to be repeated five times.

Although Rakhmaninov was at pains to observe the general principles of Orthodox church music, his *Vigil* seems never to have been performed liturgically. This may partly be due to its practical difficulties, for his choral writing makes huge demands on even the most skilled choirs.

The choir is divided into the normal four ranges of soprano, alto, tenor and bass; but straightforward four-part writing is rare. Each voice is frequently subdivided into two, and sometimes three parts, and in the course of the fifteen movements Rakhmaninov shows astonishing resourcefulness in exploiting every possibility offered by changes of texture, timbre, register and weight.

The ranges of the voices reflect particular Russian traditions. The sopranos go no higher than A; but the basses are frequently taken down to low D, there are a number of low Cs and on three occasions (most notably at the end of the fifth hymn, 'Lord, lettest Thou Thy servant depart in peace') low B flats.

In contrast to Rakhmaninov's usually expansive melodic style, the melodic lines tend to move by steps or in small intervals (rarely larger than a third), and are closely moulded to the sound and meaning of the text. The language of the Vigil, incidentally, is not modern Russian, but Old Church Slavonic, which had been the literary language of Russia until the seventeenth century, and remains to this day the biblical and liturgical language of the Russian Orthodox Church.

Nine of the fifteen movements are based on pre-existing chants. The melodic style of the remaining six numbers is modelled so closely on original models that no one not deeply versed in Russian liturgical music would be able to tell the difference.

1 *Priidite, poklonimsya (O come, let us worship)*
The work opens with a fourfold invocation to worship (the Latin 'Venite adoremus'). The piece is freely composed, the phrasing is very irregular, and the music is written without bar lines.

2 *Blagoslove, dushe moya', Gospoda (Praise the Lord, O my soul)*
The text is taken from Psalm 104. The leading melody is given to a solo contralto against a sustained background for tenors and basses, alternating with hushed passages from the higher voices.

3 *Blazhen muzh (Blessed is the man)*
The text is taken from Psalms 1, 2 and 3. The psalm verses alternate with a threefold 'Alleluia' for a full choir which rises in pitch and intensity at each appearance until the climax of the piece, and then falls back for a pianissimo conclusion.

4 *Svete tikhii (Hail, gladdening light)*
The melody of this hymn, given at first to the tenors, is a chant confined to only four notes. It is embedded in a rich choral texture, quiet and sustained throughout.

5 *Nyne otpushachaeshi (Nunc dimittis)*
This is the Slavonic version of the 'Nunc dimittis', the Song of Simeon (Luke 2, vv. 29–32): 'And it was revealed unto him by the Holy Ghost, that he should not see death, before he had seen the Lord's Christ.' The piece opens with the chant given to a solo tenor against a gently swaying accompaniment in the higher voices; it ends with the basses' descent to a cavernous low B flat. This is the piece that Rakhmaninov wished to be performed at his own funeral.

6 *Bogoroditse Devo (Rejoice, O virgin mother of God)*
A Slavonic version of the 'Ave Maria', or Hail Mary. A relatively simple setting, freely composed, but following the intervals and melodic contours of ancient Russian chants inherited from Byzantium.

MATINS

7 *Shestopslamie (Hexapsalmos)*
This piece is in two sections: the first, a brief setting of the opening of the 'Gloria', features an imitation of bell sounds (a lifelong preoccupation of Rakhmaninov), climaxing in a sonorous piled-up chord cluster. The second section is restrained and reflective.

8 *Khvalite imya Gospodne* (*O praise the name of the Lord*)
The chant is set in relief by being given mainly to the altos and basses singing in octaves. The text comes from two Psalms of praise, Nos. 135 and 136.

9 *Blagosloven esi, Gospodi* (*Blessed art thou, O Lord*)
This hymn in praise of the Resurrection is one of the biggest and most dramatic movements of the Vigil service. Towards the end of his life Rakhmaninov quoted the section beginning 'Slava Otsu i Sinu' ('Glory be to the Father and to the Son') in the last movement of his *Symphonic Dances*.

10 *Voskresenie Khristovo videvshe* (*Having beheld the resurrection*)
A further hymn in praise of the Resurrection, with wide contrasts of dynamics and between different vocal registers. It is freely composed around a chant of Rakhmaninov's own.

11 *Velichit dusha moya Gospoda* (*Magnificat*)
A setting of the Magnificat (Luke 1, vv. 46–55). The verses of Mary's hymn of praise alternate with the antiphon ('Greater in honour than the Cherubim'): this refrain comes five times, with a magical change from minor to major at its final appearance.

LAUDS

12 *Slavoslovie velikoe* (*The Great Doxology*)
This movement is in effect the musical climax of Rakhmaninov's Vigil setting. The first section is a quickly chanted setting of the entire Gloria to the chant first heard in No. 7. There follows a succession of contrasted passages, some of which contain the most rhythmically complex passages in the Vespers.

PRIME

13 and 14 *Tropar': Dnes' spasenie* (*Today is salvation come*); *Tropar': Voskres iz groba* (*Thou didst rise from the tomb*)
These are both Resurrection hymns, and are in fact alternatives which would not both be performed in a liturgical

context. The musical material of each is very similar, although the second is longer and harmonically richer.

15 *Vzbrannoi voevode* (*To thee, our leader in battle*)
The Ordinary of the *Vigil* ends with a last hymn to the Virgin, brightly scored and rhythmically vigorous.

© Andrew Huth

∾ *The Bells*, Op. 35 (1913)

1   The Silver Sleigh Bells: Allegro, ma non tanto
2   The Mellow Wedding Bells: Lento – Adagio
3   The Loud Alarum Bells: Presto
4   The Mournful Iron Bells: Lento lugubre

Edgar Allan Poe's *The Bells* was his last major poem, appearing first in the form of a mere eighteen lines in 1849 and in its full version a year later, after the author's death. Rakhmaninov, as far as we know, had not read this poem in 1913, though he may well have done so during his later years in America; he came to it in the shape of a Russian version by Konstantin Balmont, sent to him by a female admirer. He worked on his score in Rome in a flat once occupied by Tchaikovsky's brother, and he conducted the first performance himself in St Petersburg at the end of 1913.

Rakhmaninov had always been attracted by the sound and symbolism of bells. Poe's four-part structure not only chimed in with this attraction but also suggested some kind of symphonic mould. The Beethovenian journey from tension to triumph is here replaced by one through life, from the sparkle of youth, through the profounder pleasures of marriage, to some form of mid-life crisis and death. The appeal of such a structure to conventional Russian pessimism is obvious and any misgivings Rakhmaninov might have had about ending with a slow movement may well have been allayed by the precedent in Tchaikovsky's Sixth; working in a room often visited by the great man could only have reinforced his confidence in this respect.

On the surface it may seem surprising that actual orchestral bells play such a small role, but on reflection it is easy to see how quickly an orgy of clanging and clashing would become trite and wearisome. Apart from that, Balmont had toned down some of the more startling onomatopoeic effects in Poe's original (for example, the sevenfold repetition of the word 'bells' at the end of each of the four stanzas) to produce something more logical and conventional. Rakhmaninov was therefore being true to the poem he knew in conveying not so much the brute sonority of bells as the characteristics of their movement and musical patterns and their affective influence on the human race.

In the first section, the solo tenor takes up various 'chime' motifs, against which Rakhmaninov's typical descending, chromatic lines stand out in sharp relief as a presentiment of less happy things. Other such campanological features as oscillation and long pedal-notes were already part of his vocabulary.

In the second movement, the soprano's celebration of golden wedding bells is framed by the chorus, as if to emphasise the ideally stable, enduring nature of marriage. Here the music is in the composer's most voluptuous vein, best described by a line in Poe's original: 'What a gush of euphony voluminously wells!'

With the third movement, disintegration sets in. Rakhmaninov provides no soloist to serve as a focus. Cross-rhythms and antiphonal choral effects give a terrifying portrait of breakdown (Rakhmaninov, we should remember, had suffered his own some fifteen years earlier, following the disastrous premiere of his First Symphony), and the downward chromatics are now sinister instead of yearning.

No immediate comfort comes with the iron bells of the last movement, which, being Slavic, 'seem to sing with a deeper note of lament than do those elsewhere'. The final calm of the tomb was an addition by Balmont – a fortunate one from our point of view, since this cross between the final pages of Wagner's *Götterdämmerung* and Richard Strauss's

Ein Heldenleben is a fitting end to what is possibly the finest movement of Rakhmaninov's own favourite among all his works.

© Roger Nichols

Gioachino Rossini (1792–1868)

During the early decades of the nineteenth century Rossini came to dominate the Italian operatic scene, excelling in both comic and serious genres. Unusually precocious, at the age of twelve he wrote six sonatas for strings that are still heard today. After studying at the Liceo Musicale di Bologna, in 1810 he received his first operatic commission for a one-act *farsa* (*La cambiale di matrimonio*) for Venice, where three years later he scored a double triumph with the heroic *Tancredi* and the comic *L'italiana in Algeri*, which spread his fame throughout Europe. As musical director of the San Carlo Theatre, Naples from 1815 to 1822 he produced a number of experimental works, ending his Italian career with *Semiramide* (Venice, 1823). Moving to Paris in 1824 he adapted to the French style two of his Neapolitan stage works before composing the newly minted *Le Comte Ory* (1828) and *Guillaume Tell* (1829), the latter among the grandest of Parisian grand operas. But he wrote no more for the stage: only a couple of liturgical compositions, the *Stabat mater* and *Petite messe solonnelle*, and a miscellany of piano and vocal pieces.

Although by his own account classical by temperament, Rossini laid down the formal ground-rules of Italian romantic opera, to be followed by Bellini, Donizetti and the young Verdi. His reputation may have fluctuated over the years, but his comedy *Il barbiere di Siviglia* (Rome, 1816), described even by the severe Schumann as 'life-enhancing', has never left the repertoire.

∾ *Stabat mater* (1832; rev. 1841)

In 1829, at the age of thirty-seven, Rossini wrote his last opera, *Guillaume Tell*. As the years passed and nothing further in the way of theatrical music came from his pen, people began to talk about the 'Great Silence', and the 'Great

Renunciation' (referring to a Pope who figures in Dante's *Inferno*). As if, where Rossini was concerned, operatic music was the only kind that counted! For he had by no means ceased to compose – witness the *Soirées musicales*, the *Stabat mater*, the *Petite messe solennelle* and the vast number of piano and vocal pieces which he termed collectively *Péchés de vieillesse* (sins of old age).

Nonetheless it remains true that in the early 1830s Rossini did suffer a crisis of self-confidence. Some say it was due to ill health, others ascribe it to the death of his parents, and others, more plausibly, to the new wind of Romanticism that was beginning to blow through Europe, creating a musical climate in which he felt ill at ease. So it was that when, during a visit to Madrid in 1831, a wealthy Spanish prelate called Varela wanted to commission from him a *Stabat mater*, Rossini at first stoutly refused. To him the perfect setting of that poem had been made by Pergolesi, and he had no wish to compete with it. Eventually he gave in to Varela's request, stipulating, however, that the work should never be published, and for it he received the gift of a gold snuffbox studded with diamonds.

In 1837 Varela died, and his heirs, finding the *Stabat mater* among his effects, sold it to a French publisher for five thousand francs. Apprised of this, Rossini wrote to the firm threatening legal action if his wish that the work remain unpublished were not respected. He had good reason for so doing, for of the ten pieces that made up the *Stabat mater* only six were written by him (debilitated by a severe attack of lumbago, he had had the rest set by his friend Tadolini). During the wrangles which followed Rossini completed the setting and offered it to his own publisher, Troupenas, who immediately brought an action against the other firm for 'forgery and theft'. The court ruled that the original agreement with Varela did not amount to a contract of sale, and therefore the music was Rossini's to do with as he thought fit, but it acquitted the defendants of the graver charge.

The first public performance of the *Stabat mater* was given in the Salle Ventadour in Paris on 7 January 1842, with a cast of soloists that included Giulia Grisi, Mario and Tamburini. Among the audience was Heine, who pronounced the work more truly Christian in spirit than Mendelssohn's *St Paul*. Adolphe Adam, the composer of *Giselle*, had already published a detailed analysis of the score based on a partial hearing a few weeks previously. In general the press and the public were enthusiastic, the only discordant note being struck by a young musical hack in the employ of the publisher Schlesinger, by the name of Richard Wagner, who sent to the *Neue Zeitschrift für Musik* a laboured, would-be satirical report on this 'momentous event': a *Stabat mater* jotted down by Rossini in a moment of repentance for all the money of which he had cheated a gullible public; of the music, not a word. The first Italian performance took place at the Conservatory in Bologna, of which Rossini was in practice, if not in name, the director. The soloists on this occasion included the British soprano Clara Novello and the Russian tenor Nicolai Ivanov. The conductor was Donizetti.

The case of Rossini's *Stabat mater* forms a parallel with that of Verdi's Requiem. Both works are by composers associated with the theatre rather than the Church. Both were lauded to the skies by those to whom the composers were national heroes; and both were attacked on principle by distinguished German musicians who never bothered to listen to them (in Verdi's case the detractor was the conductor and pianist Bülow who, however, later ate his words). Finally, the religious character of both compositions is still sometimes called into question. This is especially true of the *Stabat mater*, which not only retains links with Rossini's operatic style (the Cavatina 'Fac ut portem' is identical in mood and even key with Arsace's entrance aria in *Semiramide*), but frequently strikes a note of hedonism at variance with this most desolate of texts. How, for instance, does one reconcile the image of the Virgin Mary contemplating the crucified Jesus with the cheerful march tune for tenor to which Rossini sets the words 'Culus animam gementem', or the sensuous interweaving of soprano and mezzo-soprano voices in 'Quis est homo'?

The truth is that, as he was to tell a mature and more respectful Wagner nearly twenty years later, Rossini did not believe in adhering too closely to the sense of the literary text; for to do so, he considered, would ruin the musical form – a point of view which was shared by Schopenhauer. Nor was he convinced of the power of music to express exact shades of meaning. So, for instance, in his French opera *Moïse et Pharaon*, Sinaïde's cabaletta of joy is precisely the same as that which had accompanied Elcia's outburst of grief in the earlier *Mosè in Egitto*. Music, Rossini told his friend and biographer Zanolini, should define the 'moral atmosphere' of a text. Indeed, it is only when certain numbers from the *Stabat mater* are taken in isolation that they sound inappropriate to a religious poem. Heard in context, the martial swing of the 'Cujus animam', the jaunty syncopation of the 'Sancta mater', the 'Pro peccatis' with its startling epigram of modulation, all combine with the austere writing of the opening number, the 'Eja, mater', and the final fugue, to form a perfectly balanced and consistent musical canvas. Even at his most naive, Rossini's taste and sense of proportion never deserted him.

© Julian Budden

Arnold Schoenberg (1874–1951)

Schoenberg was largely self-taught until he took lessons during his teens from Zemlinsky (whose sister he later married). Schoenberg held rigidly to his compositional beliefs throughout his career, subjecting himself to regular criticism. In 1899 he wrote his hyper-Romantic *Verklärte Nacht* ('Transfigured Night') for string sextet, soon followed by the symphonic poem *Pelleas and Melisande*. He rejected the constraints of established harmony and tonality with his First Chamber Symphony (1906), producing his first properly atonal works after 1908: the two sets of piano pieces, Opp. 11 (1909) and 19 (1911), and the Five Orchestral Pieces, Op. 16, performed at the Proms in 1912. *Pierrot lunaire* (1912), a setting for *Sprechstimme* ('speech-voice') and five instrumentalists (playing eight instruments) of twenty-one poems by Albert Giraud, was an important success which had a major impact on later composers. In the early 1920s he developed the technique of serialism, his 'method of composition with twelve notes related only to one another', and used it in works such as the Suite for Piano and Wind Quintet. His methods greatly influenced his pupils Berg and Webern, who along with Schoenberg formed the basis of the so-called Second Viennese School. From 1925 Schoenberg taught at the Berlin Academy of Arts but was forced into exile in 1933, eventually settling in Hollywood, where he wrote his last works.

❧ *Gurrelieder* (1900–11)

Schoenberg's *Gurrelieder* is one of the largest choral-orchestral works in the repertoire, and also one of those very rare achievements that sum up an entire era and aesthetic. Not merely because of its length and huge performing apparatus but because of its unique mix of genres: part song cycle, part cantata (or indeed 'nature-oratorio'), part melodrama, with an overall quasi-symphonic thrust. The very nature of the work metamorphoses from nineteenth-century giganticism to twentieth-century filigree (and back). The whole adds up to a kind of unstageable opera of the mind.

Its origins go back to January 1900, when the Vienna Tonkünstlerverein announced a competition for a new song cycle. The young Schoenberg resolved to enter, and in March began setting some poems for voice and piano from the *Gurresänge*, an extended verse sequence written in 1869 by the Danish novelist, poet and botanist Jens Peter Jacobsen (1847–85), in a recently published German translation by the Viennese critic and philologist Robert Franz Arnold. (Schoenberg may have been led to Jacobsen by his future brother-in-law, the composer Alexander Zemlinsky, who was an enthusiast for Jacobsen's works – and was to be a judge for the competition.) Soon, however, a much larger conception erupted from Schoenberg's imagination: scorning the competition's May deadline, he went on to set Jacobsen's entire sequence, on a vast scale, for a larger performing body than any previous composer had dared to ask for. His *Gurrelieder* demands an ensemble of five solo singers, speaker, three large men's choruses (and he meant large: several of his performances entailed upwards of five hundred male singers), eight-part mixed choir in proportion, plus an orchestra that includes eight flutes, five oboes, seven clarinets, ten horns, a quartet of Wagner tubas, seven trumpets, seven trombones, much percussion and four harps. In its ambition and expressive orientation the work owed an immense amount to Wagner, and Schoenberg employed his own leitmotivic technique, accumulating motif after evocative motif, each one an additional thread woven into the lustrous tapestry of a score that teems with a plethora of detail.

The twenty-five-year-old Schoenberg was already a prolific writer of songs and had composed his first chamber music masterpiece, the sextet *Verklärte Nacht* ('Transfigured Night'). He had copious experience scoring the works of other composers, but had completed nothing of his own for large (or even standard) orchestra. So in its very size – and the sovereign confidence and imagination with which he handles his forces – *Gurrelieder* was an astonishing feat.

The gigantic ensemble is deployed to tell the legend of the medieval King Waldemar of Denmark and his love for the beautiful maiden Tovelille, whom he established in his favourite castle of Gurre, on a lakeside near Elsinore. The name Gurre, incidentally, is supposed to represent the sounds made by the doves that throng the castle, and there are doveish associations in the story, both in Tove's name and in the vatic Wood-Dove who narrates her death. For Waldemar's jealous queen, Helwig, discovers the affair and has Tove murdered. In his grief, Waldemar curses God – for which, after his own death, he and his followers are condemned to rise from their graves and ride abroad every night.

Parts One and Two of this immense project were composed in short score by mid-1900, but Schoenberg had then to abandon work for almost a year while he earned enough to live on. The rest was drafted in mid-1901, then laid aside again because he had more pressing matters: Mathilde Zemlinsky announced that she was pregnant in May, and Schoenberg married her in October. In the meantime, he ordered music paper of unheard-of size (forty-eight staves) on which to score *Gurrelieder*. This orchestration, itself a gigantic undertaking, had to be abandoned in 1903, in the middle of Part Three, so that Schoenberg could devote his time to new works which now interested him more, and to supporting himself and his new family by teaching.

It was only in 1910 that he took it up again, after a private performance of Part One, with a piano accompaniment jointly arranged by his pupils Alban Berg and Anton Webern, had convinced him that the work could not remain unfinished. In the intervening years his musical language had evolved unimaginably far from the style of *Gurrelieder*. He had become a controversial figure, widely considered a dangerous revolutionary and iconoclast. The work's world premiere, given in Vienna on 23 February 1913 under the baton of

Franz Schreker, was in fact the most overwhelming public success of Schoenberg's career. The audience was taken aback by the beauty and power of this now 'old-fashioned' work and responded with wild enthusiasm – but the composer correctly saw that this was only a temporary check to the usual hostility with which his works were greeted.

Schoenberg himself conducted the second performance, in Leipzig in 1914, and once the Great War was over *Gurrelieder* began to make its way in the world. The first UK performance was given in January 1928 as one of the BBC National Concerts, with Schoenberg himself conducting the BBC Orchestra.

The young Schoenberg was an incorrigible Romantic (in fact, he always remained one, even though his musical language evolved into something entirely different). *Gurrelieder* is his supreme contribution to musical late Romanticism, written to equal and maybe outdo Wagner, Strauss and Mahler at a time when the latter's 'Symphony of a Thousand' wasn't even a gleam in its composer's eye.

Schoenberg's choice of Jacobsen's text was inspired, for it has all the paraphernalia beloved of the Romantic era – a doomed love affair, defiance of heaven, ghostly warriors, a wild hunt, the imagery of starlight, forests, graveyards, lonely strands and lakeside castles. But the score testifies to something we don't always associate with Schoenberg: a passionate love of nature, caught and reflected again and again in orchestral metaphor of marvellous precision and warmth. We know that the concluding 'Hymn to the Sun' was inspired by an actual sunrise which Schoenberg saw from the Anninger Mountain near Vienna, with friends from the choral society he conducted. *Gurrelieder* would not be the masterpiece it is if it was merely huge: it is continuously evocative, gorgeous-hued, sumptuously melodic, deeply felt and profoundly humane.

In the very first bars of Part One's 'sunset' prelude, swaying, fluttering arpeggios on woodwind, harp and strings outline a triad of E flat with an added sixth. Then harmony becomes melody in a way characteristic of Schoenberg at all stages of his development: a calm, broad trumpet phrase turns the chord into a descending motif. (When, at the other end of the work, the chorus greets the rising sun, the sun will come up in C major on massed trumpets, with the original descending motif inverted into a rising one.)

The love of Waldemar (tenor) and Tove (soprano) is presented lyrically as their voices alternate in a series of nine songs. The rich profusion of melody has its own symphonic logic – thus the urgent, agitated figure introducing the third song (Waldemar's hurried ride to Gurre) becomes the main waltz theme of the fourth (Tove's triumphant welcome). The fifth song, Waldemar's ecstatic 'So tanzen die Engel', with its fine simple tune, has always been a favourite extract from the work; Tove's reply introduces what is to be the main love theme. A darker and just as persistent element, however, appears with Waldemar's next song – a premonition of the tragedy to come. The sinister chromatic cello motif heard here becomes associated, as the work proceeds, with death and the opening of graves.

Tove's reply leads to the last and greatest of the love songs, Waldemar's calm, fulfilled 'Du wunderliche Tove'. Throughout, the emotional temperature has steadily increased and motivic connections have been drawn ever tighter. A major orchestral interlude now provides symphonic development of all the principal motifs: by itself, this glorious music would be enough to place Schoenberg among the greatest of the Romantic composers. But its end is sudden and brutal; lyric is abruptly forsaken for narrative in the famous 'Song of the Wood-Dove'. Plangent orchestral bird-cries introduce a mezzo-soprano solo, telling of Tove's murder and the numbing grief that overcomes Waldemar. Part One of *Gurrelieder* ends in tragic gloom, with the suggestion of tolling bells.

Almost the same music opens Part Two – which consists of a single, comparatively short song in which Waldemar curses God for Tove's death and prays to become his fool so he may mock his injustice. With the 'Song of the Wood-Dove' Part

One had essentially ended with a self-contained episode (so self-contained that Schoenberg later arranged it for voice and chamber orchestra to enable it to be performed on its own); Part Two, returning us to Waldemar's predicament, is really the coda to the work's first half.

Part Three, 'The Wild Hunt', then begins. Baleful fanfares sound; the graves open; Waldemar calls his vassals to join him in the grisly chase. The sound of the hunt approaches: in scoring of uncanny precision Schoenberg evokes the chink of mail, the scrape of rusty weapons and the rattle of bones. Watched by a terrified peasant (bass), the skeletal horde thunders by in an almost entirely contrapuntal, often canonic chorus of barbaric force, supported by the full power of the gigantic orchestra.

Though Waldemar's longing for Tove remains unassuaged, there now arises a fool to mock his tyranny. The 'Song of Klaus the Fool', the jester and common man who has been denied the peace of an honest grave by Waldemar's obsession, is one of the work's high points, a bitter light relief that begins to put extreme Romantic attitudes into clearer perspective. Waldemar is heard once more, still threatening to storm Heaven itself; but it is mere railing. In despair and weariness, the vassals sink back to their graves with the coming of morning, in a remarkable chromatic chorus. Shimmering colours under long-held notes on four piccolos presage another 'Wild Hunt' – that of the summer wind.

This portion was scored only in 1911. In the meantime Schoenberg's musical style had moved closer to Expressionism: he now insisted on sparer, clearer textures, a web of shifting, iridescent colours, the subtlest instrumental reinforcement of polyphony. The text here is set as a melodrama: the speaker's part resembles the *Sprechgesang* ('speech-song') of Schoenberg's contemporary *Pierrot lunaire*. When he first conceived it in 1900, he was probably inspired by the model of Humperdinck's melodrama *Die Königskinder*, premiered in Vienna in 1897. Originally he thought his speaker should be male, but for the 1914 Leipzig performance the role was taken by Albertine

Zehme, also the first interpreter of *Pierrot*, convincing Schoenberg that a female speaker was equally acceptable. He came to favour either 'a singer who no longer has the necessary beauty of voice to sing great parts', or a professional actor with some musical knowledge.

Contrapuntally this melodrama is the most complex section of the work, but its complexity communicates as the mysterious swirling brightness of an elemental force. The speaker describes the richness and variety of nature, set in motion by the summer wind, and calls upon all creatures to rejoice in life and sunlight. With its filigree, chamber-music orchestration, its concentration on the natural world rather than human passions and dreams, and its substitution of the clarity of speech for the hubristic rhetoric of late Romantic song, it is as if at this point the music stands back from itself and puts its whole post-Wagnerian action and conception into context. And its context is the past: ancient history, long-forgotten tragedy, the seductive stuff of dreams and nightmares. While the ghosts fade, the world goes on, life renews itself for the living. A new day beckons. To quote an apposite line of Tennyson, 'And the new sun rose, bringing the new year': from the end of the melodrama, Schoenberg brings his gigantic conception to a close by homing in on the key of C. The full chorus enters in a triumphant 'Hymn to the Sun'. With the addition of women's voices this is, incredibly, the only place in *Gurrelieder* where the entire forces are used together. Musically the 'Hymn' transforms the materials of the work's opening Prelude, turning its descending main figures into optimistic rising ones, concluding this astounding lyric music drama in the most grandiose, unshakeably affirmative C major.

© Malcolm MacDonald

Franz Schubert (1797–1828)

Schubert is one of the greatest song composers; his gift for lyrical melody and poetic expression gave rise to the bedrock of the Lieder repertory. Along with dances, marches and other piano miniatures, these songs would be performed in social gatherings, or 'Schubertiades'. Born in Vienna, Schubert was taught by Salieri while a chorister at the imperial court chapel. He worked initially as a classroom teacher to appease his father, but left after two years. Following the success of two Rossinian overtures, he spent one summer as a music teacher at the country estate of Count Johann Karl Esterházy. His aspiration to break into opera remained unfulfilled after a handful of unsuccessful efforts but he wrote symphonies and piano sonatas which are increasingly part of the repertory. He contracted syphilis in 1822. The last years of his life brought the 'Great' C major Symphony (1825), the song cycle *Winterreise* (1827), and the three great late piano sonatas (1828).

∿ Mass in A flat, D678 (1819–22; rev. 1826)

1 Kyrie
2 Gloria
3 Credo
4 Sanctus
5 Benedictus
6 Agnus Dei

Schubert's Mass in A flat was composed over a period of three years. The first drafts date from November 1819, and the work was completed only in September 1822. This gives the lie to the image of Schubert as a composer who never sketched and never revised his works. The Mass in A flat was not composed for a particular occasion, but a clue to its importance to Schubert is found in a letter which he wrote to his friend Spaun in December 1822: 'My Mass is finished and is shortly to be performed; I still have my old idea of dedicating it to the Emperor or Empress, as I consider it a success.'

That the Mass was indeed performed is indicated by the letter Schubert wrote in support of his application for the vacant post of Deputy Court Kapellmeister in April 1826, in which he claims to have five masses ready, 'which have already been performed in various Viennese churches'. Despite his confidence in his latest Mass, which had been further revised at the beginning of 1826, Schubert's application was unsuccessful, and he was informed that his Mass was 'good, but not composed in the style which the Emperor prefers'.

The Mass in A flat is certainly a very personal statement of faith, with a strongly lyrical character. It is the music of a young man, full of confidence in his own ability. Schubert makes uncompromising demands on his large orchestra and choir. It is very busy music, whether in the sheer exhilaration of the Gloria or the harmonic adventurousness of the Sanctus.

The Kyrie flows lyrically. The choir pleads persuasively 'Lord, have mercy' and the soloists enter with 'Christ, have mercy', with the two groups subsequently combined. The choir ends the movement with lingering repetitions of 'eleison', the final petition sung to a very soft orchestral accompaniment.

The contrast between this quiet ending in A flat and the burst of E major fortissimo, which opens the Gloria, could not be greater or more deliberate; it is a musical *coup de théâtre*. Widely striding bass quavers and running semiquavers in doubled violins produce a sense of joyous hyperactivity. The orchestra is augmented by a flute, two trumpets and three trombones. The soloists introduce a calmer note at 'Gratias agimus' and alternate with the choir in a pattern of petition and response. An extraordinary intensification (more than a crescendo) begins at 'Quoniam tu solus sanctus', the sopranos rising two octaves from low B to high B. After a hushed statement of 'Tu solus Dominus', the set-piece fugue 'Cum Sancto Spiritu' concludes the movement. This extended fugue demonstrates Schubert's debt to Handel and despite the rather instrumental handling of the choir (at one point the basses hold a 'pedal' note for thirteen bars!) provides an exciting close to this extended Gloria.

Schubert, in his mass settings, consistently and deliberately omitted from the Creed the words 'et in unam sanctam catholicam et apostolicam ecclesiam' ('and in one holy Catholic and apostolic church'). His faith was not tied to one denomination. An additional feature of the present Mass is the frequent repetition of the word 'Credo' ('I believe'), making this a highly individual and sincere confession of faith. After two contrasted statements of the C major chord, the choir enters unaccompanied, making the great shout of 'Credo' on the third entry the more forceful – Schubert's sense of dramatic structure again in evidence. When, at the end of the first section, the choir states 'Credo' in successively quieter repetitions, the last with men only, one has the impression of a public declaration of faith giving way to a personal and intimate one. At the word 'Crucifixus', Schubert's graphic phrase evokes the pain, almost the very raising of the cross. 'Et resurrexit' returns to the music of the initial 'Credo'.

The choir's three chords on 'Holy' at the opening of the Sanctus emerge dramatically from shifting orchestral harmonies, but having thus passed through the mystic portal, we enter a blissful world; indeed, the pastoral atmosphere of the 'Pleni sunt coeli' and 'Osanna' suggests Elysian Fields in a rather literal way. After the fluent Benedictus, where pizzicato quavers in the cello and the omission of the bass soloist give a light spring to the music, Schubert repeats the 'Osanna', thus unifying these two sections.

Choir and soloists combine again in the Agnus Dei, the choir responding 'Miserere' to the soloists' addresses to the godhead. Alternation continues in the final 'Dona nobis pacem', with the choir bringing this great affirmation of faith to a quiet conclusion, accompanied by ornamental figures from the woodwind, which reinforce the lyrical aspect of the work.

© Paul Reid

∾ Mass in E flat, D950 (1828)

1 Kyrie
2 Gloria
3 Credo
4 Sanctus
5 Benedictus
6 Agnus Dei

Church music was, so to speak, in Schubert's blood. He learnt his notes as a choirboy, first in the parish church of Liechtental, where his family regularly worshipped, and then as a choral scholar in the Imperial Chapel, as a pupil of Ruzicka, the court organist, and Salieri, the Kapellmeister. It was his first Mass in F which brought him to public notice in 1814. His six masses and some forty liturgical and sacred works are distributed over the whole of his creative life. Moreover, there are clear signs that in his mature years he turned more and more to the possibility of an ecclesiastical appointment. In 1826 he made a formal but unsuccessful bid for the vacant post of Deputy Court Kapellmeister. In the last months of his life he wrote a whole series of liturgical works, and took the surprising decision to go to Simon Sechter, the court organist and an acknowledged authority on fugue and counterpoint, for lessons. Such a course could only mean that he was looking to the patronage of the Church to give him the status and financial security he needed.

Yet his own religious beliefs seem to have been decidedly unorthodox. It is well known that the words 'Et in unam sanctam catholicam et apostolicam ecclesiam' ('and in one holy Catholic and apostolic church') are always omitted in his settings of the Creed, and there are many other changes from the accepted text. There are four significant omissions, for instance, in the Credo of the E flat Mass. Schubert's friend Ferdinand Walcher once sent him a note, quoting the first sentence of the Credo ('I believe in one God') and adding, perhaps jocularly, 'You don't, as I well know.' The truth seems to be that he rejected the rigid orthodoxy of his father in favour of the rational deism of the Enlightenment, then still very much alive in Vienna. Many of his friends and patrons – men like Josef Spendou, the founder of the Vienna Orphanage, and Ladislaus Pyrker, the Patriarch of Venice – were liberal Christians whose beliefs were frowned on by the Church. It is true nonetheless that Schubert was a deeply religious man, with a profound sense of the transcendental meaning of life.

It should not surprise us, then, that he could not approach the text of the Mass with the simple piety of a Haydn or the philosophical depth of a Beethoven. The human aspects of the Christian story, on the other hand – reverence for the Mother of God, wonder and praise for the mystery of the Incarnation, the humble prayer for forgiveness and reconciliation – never failed to move him. The Benedictus and the Agnus Dei almost always inspired his lyrical gifts. He was not best qualified, however, to deal with those sections of the Mass normally reserved for fugal treatment, partly because he had never had any formal instruction in the art of fugue, perhaps also because he was more at home with simple ternary structures than with more complex ones. Even in the Mass in E flat, his last and greatest setting, one can hardly be unaware of the contrast in the Credo between the lyrical fluency of the 'Incarnatus' and the 'Crucifixus', and the comparative stiffness of the concluding fugue.

In his earlier Mass in A flat (D678) Schubert had imposed his own solution on the problem, restricting himself to just one fugue ('Cum Sancto Spiritu') and using a bold and original key scheme based on the 'circle of thirds' – A flat, E major, C major, F major and A flat again. Schubert revised this Mass over a long period of years; but when in 1826 he took the autograph to Josef Eybler, the Kapellmeister, he was told that it did not conform to the Emperor's ideas. In the E flat Mass, therefore, he reverted to a much more conventional form. There are fully worked fugues in the Gloria ('Cum Sancto Spiritu'), the Credo ('Et vitam venturi'), the Sanctus ('Osanna in excelsis'), and much contrapuntal writing elsewhere. The main key scheme confines itself to the tonic and its nearest neighbours – B flat major and A flat major – though within each movement Schubert exploits his flair for unexpected modulations to the full. Schubert's two mature Masses offer a contrast very similar to that of his two mature symphonies; the earlier works – both finished in 1822 – are concise, innovative, unconventional and idiosyncratic; the later ones – dating from the composer's last years – traditional in form, discursive, spacious, aimed at universality and sublimity.

To achieve this effect Schubert was prepared to take liberties with the text. Apart from the omissions already referred to, there are several unusual repeats. Most of them – for instance, the repeat of the 'Incarnatus' and the 'Crucifixus' – may be welcome to the listener, because they contain some of the finest music in the whole work, though they are difficult to reconcile with liturgical use. The repeat of the Agnus Dei and 'Dona nobis pacem' at a slightly brisker tempo may be defended on somewhat similar grounds. All of which suggests that Schubert's intention was to write a ceremonial mass suitable for public performance rather than for liturgical use. In that he succeeded admirably. The work is conceived antiphonally, and its effect is achieved by the interplay of tonal groups – brass, woodwind, strings, solo voices and chorus – with all Schubert's command of orchestral colour. Nowhere is this better demonstrated than in the 'Domine Deus', where the hushed pleading of the chorus ('Miserere, miserere nobis') answers the inexorable chant of the brass and the male voices; and in the Agnus Dei, a marvellous movement built upon a four-note motif identical with the bass line of Schubert's great setting of Heine's 'Der Doppelgänger'. The soloists are used sparingly, but with calculated effect, in the 'Incarnatus' and the Benedictus.

The Mass in E flat was written for the Church of the Holy Trinity in the Alsergrund, where Schubert's friend Michael Leitermayer was organist. Beethoven's funeral service had been held there, and it was at Schubert's request, so it is said, that the first performance of the Mass was given there on 4 October 1829, eleven months after his own death. As so often towards the end of Schubert's life, his work seems to have been motivated and inspired by Beethoven's example.

© John Reed

Robert Schumann (1810–56)

After studying Law in Leipzig, Schumann intended to embark upon a career as a pianist, but an injury to his right hand compelled him to focus his energies on composition. During the 1830s he concentrated on works for the piano: largely character pieces, often literary-inspired, such as the *Papillons* (1831), *Carnaval* (1835) and *Kinderszenen* (1838). He founded the influential *Neue Zeitschrift für Musik* in 1834 and by the end of 1835 was in love with Clara Wieck, daughter of his piano teacher, Friedrich Wieck. The year of his marriage to Clara, 1840, saw a blossoming of song composition, including the cycles *Dichterliebe* and *Frauenliebe und -leben*, and the two sets of *Liederkreise*. Encouraged by Clara to explore larger forms, he wrote the *Scenes from Goethe's 'Faust'* (1844–53), four symphonies, the concertos for piano (1845) and cello (1850) and the opera *Genoveva* (1852). In the 1840s his mental health declined; after an unsuccessful suicide attempt, he was admitted in 1854 to an asylum near Bonn, where he remained until his death.

❧ *Scenes from Goethe's 'Faust'* (1844–53)

Goethe's *Faust* has both fascinated and inhibited composers since Part One of the poetic drama appeared in 1808. Its shorter lyrics have been set to music any number of times, and the characters of Faust, Mephistopheles and Gretchen are familiar in a variety of musical incarnations. On the other hand, Part Two, which appeared only after Goethe's death in 1832, is so wide-ranging in scope, so rich in ideas and situations, that only the boldest composers have attempted any sort of musical setting. Schumann was one of these bold spirits, and his approach to composing music for *Faust* was typical both of his strange, unsettled character and of the insight he brought to the literary texts he set.

All his life Schumann was subject to extreme swings of mood, with periods of intense creativity alternating with paralysing depressions. Despite this, however, there is something remarkably systematic about his output. First came a decade of piano music, then a year dedicated to song composition. After that he turned his attention to orchestral music, then chamber music, then choral music. It was only when he had reached the age of thirty-four that he felt ready to consider music for *Faust*, a project that must have been in his mind for many years. Apart from its supreme literary qualities, Schumann would have been fascinated by its forays into the occult and the world of spirits, by its investigations of the heights and the depths of human character, and by its overall progress towards illumination and redemption – concepts to be found in almost all of his later large-scale works.

Even so, the music he eventually composed over a period of nine years was not a unified work and was never intended to be. Even if he at first thought of an operatic treatment, he soon abandoned any such idea as quite unrealistic. The title – *Scenes from Goethe's 'Faust'* – means just what it says. This is not a musical summary of the whole, nor an oratorio, but a selection of scenes taken from various parts of Goethe's drama. Each of its three parts is different in style and approach. Part One and the end of Part Two are indeed highly dramatic, but the philosophical abstractions of Part Three are completely unsuited to stage representation.

The first part to be composed was the third, which Schumann began in 1844. It cost him great effort, for he was in a very low state, both physically and mentally. He resumed work on Part Three in 1848, and on 29 August 1849, a day after the centenary of Goethe's birth, it was performed simultaneously in Dresden, Leipzig and Weimar (where the conductor was Franz Liszt). Part One was sketched in 1849 and Part Two in 1849–50. The entire score was revised and put in order in 1853. The overture was added that August, just six months before Schumann's final descent into madness and silence.

The *Scenes from Goethe's 'Faust'* were first performed as an entirety in 1862, six years after Schumann's death, and since then performances of even single scenes, let alone of the entire work, have been rare events. This is partly due to the cloud of prejudice that obscures much of Schumann's later music and has led to the neglect of such other magnificent works as the opera *Genoveva* and the oratorio *The Paradise and the Peri*. We often hear that Schumann's powers began to decline around 1842, possibly as a result of his mental illnesses; that he was essentially a miniaturist who never quite came to terms with the larger musical forms; that freshness and spontaneity gave way to density and heaviness. It is true enough that Schumann became a different sort of composer in his thirties. But by no means a worse one, as a complete performance of the *Scenes from Goethe's 'Faust'* should demonstrate beyond any doubt.

OVERTURE

This was the last music to be composed and, according to Schumann, the hardest because 'the elements that have to be mastered are too many and too gigantic'. He originally thought of writing a fugue, the most learned of musical forms, and this tense D minor movement with its obsessive dotted rhythms should probably be heard as a portrayal of Faust himself, the scholar and seeker after truth who enters into a demonic pact with Mephistopheles.

PART ONE

Part One is dominated by Gretchen, the pure girl whom Faust will seduce and ruin. Having already discovered the barrenness of scholarship, he will learn the dangers of love without responsibility and the destructive effects of unlimited power.

1 *Garden Scene*

The music describing the rejuvenated Faust's courtship of Gretchen is that of Schumann the song composer: with a few well-chosen strokes he depicts the seductive power of Faust and the girl's fresh simplicity. Mephistopheles and Gretchen's neighbour Marthe make only the briefest of appearances, enough to remind us that the whole episode is being ably stage-managed by Mephistopheles.

2 *Gretchen before the image of the Mater Dolorosa*

The girl is abandoned and ruined. With the same light scoring as in the 'Garden Scene', Gretchen offers flowers – symbolising the innocence that she has lost – to an image of the Virgin Mary. Gretchen, too, at the end of Goethe's drama, will become an archetypal Mother of Sorrows.

3 *Scene in the Cathedral*

From the air and light of the 'Garden Scene' there is a constant descent into darkness. Gretchen is now gasping for air and light. The victim of Faust's irresponsibility, she is pregnant and has unwittingly killed her own mother with an overdose of the sleeping-draught she used to keep the old woman quiet during her love-making with Faust. Soon she will be condemned to death for the murder of her new-born child. The Evil Spirit is the voice of her own tormented conscience, while the congregation add their condemnation with phrases from the Requiem Mass evoking the Day of Judgement.

PART TWO

Faust himself is the centre of attention in Schumann's setting of the beginning and end of the dramatic sections of Goethe's Part Two. His quest moves from the search for power and knowledge onto a higher moral plane where he investigates the mysteries of existence, the evolution of humanity, the development of culture and the betterment of mankind.

4 *Ariel. Sunrise*

Schumann's music for Ariel and the attendant spirits is the most delicately conceived in the whole score, as they soothe away Faust's guilt and inspire him to more worthy endeavours. Faust's huge solo as his creative will is awakened has a rare breadth and nobility of purpose.

5 *Midnight*

Of the four spectral Grey Women – Want, Debt, Care and Need – only Care has power over Faust. After all his experiences, he has come to the realisation that his highest goal is the fulfilment of his own human nature and dedication to his fellow men. Although blinded by Worry, he is spurred on to a final effort for the benefit of humanity.

6 *Faust's death*

Total darkness, night and blindness, as Faust believes the clank of spades to be workmen carrying out his grandiose plans on behalf of the community, rather than the digging of his own grave by an army of lemures ('Ghosts of the wicked dead who wander about at night . . . Their minds act as imperfectly as their bodies'). His inner vision shines all the more strongly, though, and he foresees the moment when he will at last be able to find satisfaction – the end of his quest and therefore of his life, according to his pact with Mephistopheles.

PART THREE

7 *Faust's transfiguration*

After Faust's death, the human drama is completed. With the struggle for Faust's soul, Goethe's verse moves into a realm of symbolism and metaphysics. Faust is saved through his striving, and through the intercession of the transfigured Gretchen.

Schumann sets Goethe's final scene without any alterations, and his main concern was that the music should enhance the meaning of the words. After the 1849 performances of Part Three, he commented: 'What pleased me most was to hear from many people that the music made the poem intelligible to them for the first time.'

© Andrew Huth

Jean Sibelius (1865–1957)

Sibelius established himself early in his career as Finland's national composer, helped by his ability to convey the austere beauty of his country, his passionate adoption of themes from the Finnish folk epic the _Kalevala_, and his patriotic music such as _Finlandia_ (1900). Born north of·Helsinki, he initially intended to become a violinist, but studied composition in Vienna and Berlin between 1889 and 1891. His choral _Kullervo_ Symphony and the tone poem _En Saga_ (1892, both inspired by the _Kalevala_) preceded seven purely orchestral symphonies, ranging from the Tchaikovsky-influenced First (1900) to the enigmatically brief Seventh (1924). Supported by a government pension from the age of 32, he effectively retired for the last thirty years of his life, writing no major works (though he at least started an Eighth Symphony, which he destroyed). His Violin Concerto, by turns introverted and highly virtuosic, remains among the most popular in the repertory.

❧ _Kullervo_, Op. 7 (1891–2)

1   Introduction (Allegro moderato)
2   Kullervo's Youth (Grave)
3   Kullervo and His Sister (Allegro vivace)
4   Kullervo Goes to War (Alla marcia)
5   Kullervo's Death (Andante)

The Finnish language had different adversaries when the _Kalevala_, Finland's epic collection of myths and legends, took shape in 1835 and when the young Jean Sibelius set out on a new path determined to yoke some of its more striking passages to music over half a century later. A new wave of independent feeling in the 1890s saw Russia as the enemy; but Russia had been happy enough to encourage the native scholar and district health officer Elias Lönnrot as he forged

the wealth of Finnish mythology into one idiosyncratic volume: such projects, the Russian authorities believed, could
only loosen the claims of the Swedish tongue in their then-
new Grand Duchy. (Swedish, incidentally, was the language
spoken by most members of Sibelius's family; he was fortunate enough to have a Finnish-orientated education, which
embraced study of the *Kalevala*, but he would frequently slip
into Swedish in more excitable moments.)

Music was almost as important as language in the origins of
the *Kalevala*. Lönnrot travelled the length and breadth of
Karelia consulting the runic singers, living heirs of Finland's
oral tradition. Their stories differed, of course, compelling
some artificial links in this first cohesive attempt at Finnish
epic, and the relatively recent high profile of female singers
changed some of the perspectives (women are not to be sold
as chattels; mothers scorn the wasteful act of battle). What
they had in common was that everything was sung, usually to
tunes made up of the scale's first five notes – the compass of
the five-stringed *kantele* (Finnish zither) which sometimes
served as accompaniment. In November 1891 Sibelius went
to hear one of the finest living exponents of a fast-dying art,
Larin Paraske. What she sang, and what Sibelius wrote
down, has left its palpable mark on *Kullervo*. Yet Sibelius also
wanted to avoid the charge of a narrow nationalism, and the
vast structure of *Kullervo* allowed him to try out several
approaches consecutively.

The first theme, which so proudly and strikingly launches
the work on horns and clarinets, came to Sibelius while he
was still studying in Vienna in the spring of 1891. An utterly
characteristic idea, its contours relate to the more robust type
of Finnish folk music – as distinct from runic song – and yet
both its varied orchestral treatment against an ever-changing
background and its reflective handling in the development of
what is, as he proudly pointed out to his fiancée Aïno
Järnefelt, 'strict sonata form', clearly reflect his excitement at
having recently heard Bruckner's Third Symphony. Another
theme in this vigorously projected portrait of rugged

Kullervo – we need know nothing about him at this point except what the music tells us – comes closer to the world of runic song in its narrow-intervalled, almost obsessive scope.

The art of the old pre-*Kalevala* singing is more insistently recreated in the second movement, where the story proper begins with an unforgettable string melody that becomes more intense on each of its two reappearances. The three statements reflect the favourite pattern of the runic singers' semi-improvisatory style, and indeed in the telling of Kullervo's unhappy childhood spent at his usurping uncle's house, he has three seemingly impossible tasks to fulfil, and three ways of getting his own back (least admirably, the spiteful murder of a child put in his care). The rustic woodwind episodes that provide some kind of contrast to Sibelius's grim lullaby, however, suggest that he was thinking more of Kullervo's subsequent time as herdsman to Ilmarinen the smith. The clenched-fist anguish the brass make of the opening rhythm at the climax surely illustrates his rage at breaking his knife on the stone which Ilmarinen's wife has maliciously put inside his lunchtime roll; but the horrible aftermath – he drowns the cows and drives home a 'herd' of wolves and bears to tear the wife apart – is no concern of Sibelius. He does, however, choose to narrate the climactic event of Kullervo's unhappy life in some detail.

Again the parameters change, as voices enter the action for the first time at the start of the third movement, 'Kullervo and His Sister'. The men's chorus is again runic in spirit, and as such partly responsible for the unusual 5/4 metre – before its much-quoted appearance in the second movement of Tchaikovsky's Sixth Symphony (premiered in 1893). But Sibelius kicks off with a brilliant orchestral theme in the same metre; his biographer Erik Tawaststjerna suggests a trepak-like Karelian dance as the model. Thrice-uncouth Kullervo asks a maiden into his sledge; only on the third attempt, enticed by his coffer of silver and costly clothes, does she eventually agree. The purely orchestral love scene is far removed from Wagnerian sensuousness, its powerful theme forced onwards against a highly charged rhythmic background in a way that looks forward to Janáček's most searing inspirations. Revelations unfold with Janáčekian swiftness, too, and subtle reminiscences of the childhood music from the previous movement; the girl's discovery that she is Kullervo's long-lost sister reveals a very operatic appreciation of setting Finnish text to music; and there is no attempt to provide a fluent transition to Kullervo's lament over the deed and her suicide, where the baritone's declamation resounds against curt chords from the full orchestra and abrupt silences. The twenty-minute drama leaves us in no doubt that this is the finest of the work's five movements. Indeed, it was the only one that Sibelius allowed to reappear in public – in 1935, the *Kalevala*'s centenary – having withdrawn the score shortly after its first bout of successful performances in 1892 and 1893.

The fourth movement, 'Kullervo Goes to War', is furthest in spirit from the original story, which deals more with Kullervo's desperation, his mother's pleas to forget senseless battle and her subsequent death than with the triumph over his one-time oppressors, despatched in a couple of lines. The singularity of this inappropriately spirited but once again thematically memorable sequence of war cries lies in Sibelius's avoidance of the heavier brass in all but the central episode and the coda.

The final movement, 'Kullervo's Death', brings the return of the chorus and of ideas from earlier movements, memorably developed in what is more or less a single runic line of almost unbearable intensity, followed by a disciplined funeral cortège and the most economical apotheosis of the work's opening theme. The *Kalevala* never made great claims for Kullervo as a magnificent hero, and Sibelius keeps his extra dimension of nobility within characteristically terse boundaries.

© David Nice

Igor Stravinsky (1882–1971)

Stravinsky's unrivalled impact on the course of twentieth-century music was originally brought about by the complexity and originality of his first ballets, on Russian themes, for Diaghilev's Ballets Russes: *The Firebird* (1910), *Petrushka* (1911) and *The Rite of Spring* (1913), though we now know how much they owe to the Russian folk-music tradition. With his move to Paris and another ballet, *Pulcinella* (1920), came a shift to the sharp-edged clarity of the neo-classical style, which also characterises the Octet (1923), the Piano Concerto (1924) and *Oedipus rex* (1926–7). In the eight months to June 1939, Stravinsky suffered the loss of his daughter, wife and mother in turn and, with war impending, moved to the USA, where he undertook numerous conducting tours, and composed his Mass and *The Rake's Progress* (1951). In the 1950s, ever in tune with the times, Stravinsky made another compositional change, in which he embraced serialism (the ballet *Agon*, 1957; the cantata *Threni*, 1958). He made many recordings of his own music, as both conductor and pianist.

❧ Mass (1947–8)

1 Kyrie
2 Gloria
3 Credo
4 Sanctus
5 Agnus Dei

Stravinsky the worldly, Stravinsky the master of theatre, Stravinsky the brilliant interpreter of Baroque and folk manners, Stravinsky the evoker of circus, the reinventor of symphony and oratorio and opera, and, constantly, of himself. To many it might seem strange that this same Stravinsky also wrote a setting of the Mass. Yet why should it? For one thing, he was a composer deeply interested in and influenced by the music of the past, a past that for him included the Renaissance, the era when the Ordinary of the Mass provided a framework for the largest, most sophisticated of musical forms. For another, many of his secular works suggest an obsession with ritual of one kind or another, be it the pagan religiosity of *The Rite of Spring*, the fairy-tale element of *The Firebird*, or even the anti-progress, relentless and predictable, of Tom Rakewell in his great neo-classical opera *The Rake's Progress*.

Yet this leaning towards ritual is not the entire explanation. Stravinsky was in any case a man with religious instincts. Although Russian Orthodox by upbringing, he saw merit in the Catholic Church's aspirations of universality. He set one or two liturgical texts in the Slavonic language of the Orthodox Church – an *Otche nash* (Lord's Prayer), *Simol veri* (Creed) and *Bogoroditse devo* (Ave Maria) – in 1926, 1932 and 1934. Then, in 1948, came this Latin Mass, which was first performed in Milan on 27 October of that year under the direction of Ernest Ansermet.

The Mass is scored for four-part chorus – Stravinsky specified boy trebles – and a wind ensemble of two oboes, cor anglais, two bassoons, two trumpets and three trombones. It was intended primarily for liturgical use rather than concert performance, and even includes the traditional chant incipit at the beginning of the Credo. One can see in its instrumentation, perhaps, a kind of substitute, more flexible, for the organ. The spur for composing the work, or so Stravinsky claimed, was his discovery of some Mozart masses in a second-hand music store in Los Angeles in the early 1940s. Unusually, it was not the result of a commission. 'As I played through these rococo-operatic sweets-of-sin,' he wrote, 'I knew I had to write a Mass of my own, but a real one.' The implications of that remark were clear. Mozart's music, for Stravinsky, failed to achieve sufficient gravitas befitting the words it set. It flouted one ritual – the high solemnity of the Mass – by resorting to another, the decorativeness of coloratura writing.

Stravinsky's style of word-setting is therefore distinctly syllabic. Indeed, it has been argued that a contributory reason for his writing the Mass in the first place was that he liked the expressive sound of the Latin syllables themselves. He certainly loved the ancient language. And syllabic though the Mass may be, it would be wrong to label the work as severe, or as simply and purely functional. In fact, the solo voices are allowed one or two melismas, though the choir responds with austere block sounds. What it does have – with exceptions in such passages as the 'Osanna' section of the Sanctus and Benedictus – is a quality of restraint, reverence, stillness. Still the most perceptive description of its language is that by Roman Vlad, written in 1958. Vlad writes that

> the levelling-down of expressiveness [is achieved] through an almost complete diatonic stillness. The musical fabric is woven with modal threads which hardly ever combine in polytonal or polyphonic knots; sometimes they fall into patterns on the lines of early polyphonic forms – descant and faburden – and combine in free contrapuntal clusters innocent of any model. The resulting clashes of dissonance . . . no longer generate dynamic effects; they are used to absorb the harmonies, whittling away their traditional function, performing a kind of blood-letting which relieves their tonal tension.

Stephen Pettitt © BBC

❧ Les noces (1914–17, 1921–3)

It was the ritual element that fired Stravinsky's imagination in his presentation (not description, as he insisted) of a peasant wedding in a Russian village, the subject of his 'Russian choreographic scenes with song and music'. So all-pervasive, indeed, is the symbolism, both Orthodox Church and pagan, that the composer felt that a full appreciation of the work's overtones would not be grasped other than by Russians. Such ceremonies as the plaiting of the bride's hair and tying it with

coloured ribbons, and her traditional weeping, are purely rit-
ualistic; the swan and goose in the final scene are folk characters, but also symbolic of the bridal pair; the saints Cosmas
and Damian, frequently invoked in scene 2, were also associated with fertility cults.

Les noces ('The Wedding') is no naturalistic representation
of the event: everything is stylised and depersonalised, even
to the extent of the same role being voiced by different solo
singers – the bridegroom's words, for example, are given now
to a tenor, now to two basses, now to one. The desultory,
overlapping and conflicting, often barely comprehensible
collage of chatter and wedding adages was likened by
Stravinsky to the incoherently diffused conversations in
Joyce's *Ulysses*. Yet musically the work is organised with
uncommon terseness, almost all the melodic material deriving from the initial cell announced by the solo soprano, and
with deliberately restricted contrasts of tempo and of colour.

Stravinsky's original idea, in setting the text he had himself
compiled from Kireyevsky's *Popular Poems* (a copy of which he
had picked up in Kiev in 1914), was to employ an outsize
orchestra of 150 players; but he abandoned this after writing
only a few pages of the score. Wartime conditions in
Switzerland, where he was living, would in any case have
made this quite impracticable. So, going to the other extreme
and wishing to underline the primitive force of the work (on
which he had already spent some three years, though interrupted by the composition of *Renard*) by rejecting a wide
colour palette in favour of a stark pungency, he then toyed for
a short time with the thought of scoring the instrumental
parts (which are subservient throughout to the solo voices and
chorus) for electric pianola, harmonium, two cimbaloms and
percussion. The final instrumentation – for four pianos with
pitched and unpitched percussion – was not completed until
three months before the work was produced, by Diaghilev's
Ballets Russes in Paris on 13 June 1923. The critics at first
were outraged, but Diaghilev, to whom the composer had
played parts of the score as early as 1915, 'loved the work

more than any other of mine', as Stravinsky later recorded.

Though its music is completely continuous, this cantata falls into two parts. The first, comprising the first three scenes, is predominantly solemn, even tearful, in mood: the bride, being prepared by her friends for the wedding, laments having to leave her home; the bridegroom, whose hair is being anointed by the other men, seeks his parents' blessing; the bride, too, asks a blessing of her parents and takes her leave of them, while the two mothers mourn the loss of their children. The fourth and longest scene, which makes up Part Two of the work, is given over to the bibulous and noisy merrymaking at the wedding feast; the marriage bed is warmed, and to the good wishes of the company the bridal couple retire. The bridegroom's voice is heard, talking of their future happiness, and then for the first time the singing (which has hitherto been non-stop) ceases; a purely instrumental, short postlude sums up the ritual of the occasion with clanging bell sounds.

© Lionel Salter

⤳ *Oedipus rex*, opera-oratorio in two acts (1926–7)

The idea for 'an opera in Latin on the subject of a tragedy of the ancient world, with which everyone would be familiar' was essentially Stravinsky's own, as is proved by a letter to Cocteau of October 1925, setting out the terms of their collaboration in typically businesslike fashion. But where did he get such a curious notion? There was certainly nothing new in the idea of updating Greek tragedy: Cocteau himself had presented an abridged modern translation of Sophocles's *Antigone* in 1922 (with music by Honegger and designs by Picasso and Chanel), and had recently completed a drawing-room tragi-comedy on the subject of Orpheus – Stravinsky had probably attended a reading of this *Orphée* in September 1925. But these plays were in French. For Stravinsky, the idea of a Latin text was fundamental. Why?

Hitherto all his sung theatre works except *Pulcinella* – where the Italian text was part of the received material – had been in Russian (including the ballet *Les noces* and his last theatre work, the mini-operetta *Mavra*), which may seem natural enough until we remember that Stravinsky always knew perfectly well, and in the case of *Mavra* specifically intended, that the audience for these works would be French. A certain ethnographic mystique pervades Stravinsky's music of the period. But in the mid-1920s a new factor emerged; he suddenly, after some thirty years, became a devout communicant of the Russian Orthodox Church. The reason for this abrupt reconversion is not yet fully understood; Robert Craft, Stravinsky's friend and collaborator, believes it to have been connected with the composer's complex and distressing family life (his wife was slowly dying of tuberculosis in Nice while the composer maintained an open liaison with his future second wife, Vera Sudeykina, in Paris), but it may equally well have been a product of his exile, by now obviously permanent. In any case, Stravinsky himself records a religious source for *Oedipus rex*, in the shape of Joergensen's life of St Francis of Assisi, a copy of which he picked up and read while passing through Genoa on his way home from Venice in September 1925. He was, he tells us, struck by the Italophone St Francis's habit of using his mother's native Provençal as 'the language of his most solemn times' (for instance, he always begged for alms in Provençal). 'To this reading,' Stravinsky says, 'I owe the formulation of an idea that had occurred to me often, though vaguely, since I had become *déraciné*. This idea was that a text for music might be endowed with a certain monumental character by translation backwards, so to speak, from a secular to a sacred language.' One might add to this that, for a Russian, the natural 'sacred' language is Old Slavonic, and in fact Stravinsky did begin setting his next Latin-text work, the *Symphony of Psalms*, in Slavonic. But to update a Greek tragedy into Slavonic for a French audience would plainly have been to pile obscurity on to the esoteric.

The eventual form of *Oedipus rex* suggests that Stravinsky initially took Baroque oratorio, with its alternation of recitative, aria and chorus, as model, though there is much less Handelian style in the music than is often supposed – and, after all, Italian opera (which certainly is suggested) also uses this kind of formula. The male chorus he imagined seated in a row, cowled and reading from scrolls, while the soloists would be masked and immobile, not entering or exiting, but revealed and concealed by curtains or spotlights. At this point, however, the conception begins to take on some of the boulevardier elements of Cocteau's *Orphée*. For instance, the seer Tiresias was meant to slide on and off stage through a grotto (symbolising his role of 'fountain of truth'), very much like Death in *Orphée* who enters and exits through a mirror. Stravinsky probably resisted Cocteau's more capricious ideas for staging – though the drawing for the *mise-en-scène* in the published score (allegedly by Stravinsky's son Theodore) is remarkably like Cocteau's sketch for the setting of *Orphée*. But the most boulevardier idea of all, the dinner-jacketed speaker, Stravinsky did not resist, though he later vehemently disowned it as 'that disturbing series of interruptions . . . intolerable snobbery . . . But alas, the music was composed with the speeches, and is paced by them.'

Stravinsky's whole attitude to the classical material and its modern treatment has to be understood in the light of his own later music. Since *Mavra* (1922) he had composed only instrumental music, and entirely for piano or wind instruments. Every work was accompanied by some kind of manifesto (not always penned by Stravinsky himself but probably reflecting his ideas) urging the virtues of form as an expressive category, denouncing such conventional Romantic concepts as interpretation and a phrased espressivo. On the contrary, cold, rational forms were seen as a virtue of classical thought. *Oedipus rex*, with its statue-like, masked dramatis personae, and nearly two-dimensional setting, was simply this kind of neo-classicism put onto the stage. Musically, all the same, it represents something of a relaxation from the very severe posture of the early 1920s. A full symphony orchestra returns, and though the violins are reduced in importance, they do still often assume their traditional expressive and diapason function. Stravinsky's musical models are much more eclectic than before: shades of Verdi (in the opening chorus) and Bellini (in Jocasta's aria), and perhaps Berlioz (in the bucolic music of the Shepherd and the Messenger), and even Puccini (in the final scene). Stravinsky himself called the work a *Merzbild* – the Dada term for a picture made out of junk – and was defensive about some of its stylistic excesses. But in fact *Oedipus rex* (as the composer also pointed out) makes its own coherence, and this is achieved by solid compositional means, by careful pacing and balance, and by a brilliant control of dramatic climax. Constructivist method is involved: for instance, every scene is coordinated by a meticulous use of proportional metre (though conductors don't always observe it). Notice also the powerful effect of dramatic irony set up by the speaker in describing the outcome of each scene, which then automatically rubs shoulders with the start of the same scene set to music: the violent contrasts are of course no accident, and cast doubt, in the end, on Stravinsky's fundamental rejection of the whole device, as opposed to his perhaps natural desire to play down Cocteau's contribution to a masterpiece he regarded as essentially his own.

One of the composer's supposed objections to Cocteau's text is its obscurity and implied snobbishness, which seem to assume a knowledge of Sophocles's play, *Oedipus Tyrannus*, while apparently quite deliberately confusing anyone whose knowledge is, perhaps, a little timeworn. Here, anyway, is a vade mecum:

The Oracle warned King Laius of Thebes that, as a punishment for stealing Pelops's son Chrysippus, he would be killed by his own son; so, when Oedipus was born, Laius and Jocasta exposed him on a mountainside, piercing his feet with leather thongs. There he was found and brought up by a shepherd of the Corinthian King Polybus. Polybus, being childless, adopted (and named) Oedipus; later, Oedipus was taunted about his parentage, and, when he consulted the Oracle, was told that he would kill his father and marry his mother. To avoid these crimes, and naturally, supposing them to refer to Polybus and his wife, he left Corinth for Thebes, and on the way killed an old man he met at a crossroads, not recognising him, of course, as King Laius. At Thebes he solved the riddle of the Sphinx which was laying waste the city, winning thereby the hand of the now-widowed Queen Jocasta. It is crucial that, even when he begins to suspect that he is the murderer of King Laius and thus the cause of the plague in Thebes, Oedipus still does not realise he is Laius's son. He simply believes his crime to be usurping the marital bed of a man he has killed. One other obscurity is his accusation of Tiresias's complicity with Creon, which is explained by the fact that in Sophocles it is Creon who first suggests consulting Tiresias. Finally, the listener needs to know that when, after the scene with Jocasta, the speaker announces that 'the witness to the murder emerges from the shadow', he is referring not to the Messenger but to the Shepherd, who (again in Sophocles) had been the one member of Laius's retinue who escaped at the time of the murder. On returning to Thebes and finding Oedipus already installed as king, he had discreetly requested transfer to remote mountain pastures, but has now returned at Oedipus's own summons as part of the inquest into Laius's murder.

The speaker introduces each scene, describing the events we are about to witness. He 'is in a black suit . . . [and] expresses himself like a lecturer, presenting the story with a detached voice.'

Act I

'Caedit nos pestis': the Thebans implore their king Oedipus, who vanquished the Sphinx, to rescue them now from the plague. 'Liberi, vos liberabo': Oedipus boastfully promises to do so. He reports that Creon, his brother-in-law, has been sent to consult the Delphic Oracle. 'Respondit Deus': Creon arrives and announces that the murderer of King Laius is hiding in Thebes and must be hunted out before the plague will go. 'Non reperias vetus scelas': Oedipus undertakes to find the murderer. 'Delie, exspectamus': the people implore the blind seer, Tiresias, to tell what he knows. 'Dicere non possum': Tiresias refuses, but when Oedipus accuses him directly of the murder, he retorts that Laius's murderer is a king, now hiding in Thebes. Oedipus angrily accuses both Tiresias and Creon of plotting to seize the throne. 'Gloria': at this moment the people hail the arrival of Oedipus's wife, Queen Jocasta.

Act II
'Non erubescite, reges': Jocasta rebukes the princes for quarrelling. The Oracle, she says, is a liar. It prophesied that Laius would be killed by her son, but in fact he was killed at a crossroads by thieves. 'Pavesco subito': suddenly afraid, Oedipus tells Jocasta that once he killed an old man at a crossroads. He determines to find out the truth. 'Adest omniscius pastor': the chorus greets the arrival of the Shepherd and of the Messenger from Corinth. The Messenger announces the death of King Polybus of Corinth. Oedipus, he reports, was not Polybus's son but a foundling, discovered on a mountainside and brought up by a shepherd. Jocasta understands and tries to draw Oedipus away. 'Nonne monstrum rescituri': Oedipus accuses her of shame at the discovery that he is not the son of a king, but the Shepherd and Messenger spell out the truth: that Oedipus was the son of Laius and Jocasta, abandoned to die. 'Natus sum quo nefastum est': Oedipus acknowledges the truth: that he has killed his father and married his mother. 'Divum Jocastae caput mortuum': the Messenger, helped by the chorus, relates the death of Jocasta and Oedipus's self-blinding with her golden brooch. Oedipus appears, a figure of revulsion. He is firmly but gently expelled from Thebes by the people.

Stravinsky composed the score between January 1926 and May 1927 and it was first performed at the Théâtre Sarah-

Bernhardt in Paris, as part of Diaghilev's Ballets Russes season, on 30 May 1927. Stravinsky and Cocteau had always intended the work as a present to Diaghilev for his twentieth-anniversary season, and it was only for lack of money, and in the end time, that the performance took place in oratorio form. The idea that this so-called opera-oratorio was not intended to be staged is quite unfounded – which is not to say, of course, that it is any less than extremely powerful when played in concert. The first staging was in Vienna on 23 February 1928, followed two nights later by the famous Kroll production in Berlin, conducted by Otto Klemperer.

© Stephen Walsh

✏ *Symphony of Psalms* (1930)

1 Exaudi orationem meam, Domine –
2 Expectans, expectavi, Domine –
3 Laudate Dominum

This is the work which bears the famous dedication, originally in French, 'This Symphony composed to the glory of GOD is dedicated to the Boston Symphony Orchestra on the occasion of its fiftieth anniversary'. The anniversary, which fell in the 1930–1 season, was celebrated by commissions to a number of leading composers: an indication of the importance attached to new music by the orchestra's conductor, Serge Koussevitzky. What Koussevitzky no doubt hoped for – and what Stravinsky's publisher Gabriel Paichadze certainly wanted him to write – was a concert work for full orchestra, something conspicuously absent from his catalogue since his early Symphony in E flat. However, Stravinsky chose instead to carry out a project which he had had in mind for some time, a setting for chorus and orchestra of texts from the Book of Psalms.

This decision reflects Stravinsky's own Christian beliefs. Although his parents were not churchgoers and had no strong religious feelings, he had been baptised into the

Russian Orthodox Church; but he had left it during his teens. It was only in 1926, after instruction from a Father Nicolas whom he had met after moving to Nice, that he had re-entered the Russian Church. In the same year, as he later described, he underwent a profound religious experience at the basilica of St Antony in Padua. At about this time, too, he met the philosopher and Roman Catholic convert Jacques Maritain, and they became personal friends in 1929, the year in which Stravinsky received the commission for the *Symphony of Psalms*.

Stravinsky seems, in fact, to have wavered between the Russian Church and the Roman. By his own account, the strongest factor in his decision to re-enter the Russian Church was linguistic: an affection for the Slavonic language of the Russian liturgy, in which he had prayed in childhood. This was the language of his first religious work, the *Otche nash* (Lord's Prayer) which he composed in 1926 – and to which in the 1930s he added *Simol verï* (Creed) and *Bogoroditse devo* (Ave Maria). But these were short, simple pieces for unaccompanied choir, intended for use in Orthodox services, in which instruments are prohibited. For a more ambitious concert work, the same constraints did not apply; and after beginning to compose the *Symphony of Psalms* in Slavonic, Stravinsky switched to Latin. This was not only the language of the Roman Catholic Church, but also the language in which he had in 1926–7 set his opera-oratorio *Oedipus rex*. Describing that work in his autobiography in 1935, Stravinsky wrote that he had 'always considered that a special language, and not that of current converse, was required for subjects touching on the sublime'; and he describes Latin as 'a language of convention, almost of ritual, the very nature which imposes a lofty dignity'.

What also contributes to the 'lofty dignity' of the *Symphony of Psalms* is its scoring. Stravinsky imagined it first as a work for an all-male choir and wind orchestra. The idea of a male chorus survives in an instruction on the title-page that the soprano and alto parts should be, if possible (it rarely is), taken by children's voices. The original conception of a 'wind orchestra' was refined into the final scoring for a unique ensemble of fourteen woodwind and thirteen brass instruments, with timpani and bass drum, harp, two pianos, cellos and basses. Significantly, not only the violins and violas of a conventional orchestra are missing, but also the Romantically expressive clarinets.

This orchestra, with its predominance of woodwind and brass, seems at first a puzzling choice for a serious, religiously inspired work. For most of Stravinsky's contemporaries, including Les Six, wind instruments were associated primarily with lightness and frivolity, and with the colouring of jazz. This is indeed reflected in Stravinsky's own one-act opera *Mavra* of 1921–2, in which the orchestra contains twenty-three wind instruments and nine strings, and even more in his Wind Octet of 1922–3. But in larger groupings, wind instruments could also take on more solemn associations: as they must have done in Stravinsky's lost *Chant funèbre* in memory of Rimsky-Korsakov; and as they certainly did in his 1920 *Symphonies of Wind Instruments*, dedicated to the memory of Debussy, and in the slow sections of his Concerto for Piano and Wind Instruments of 1923–4.

In any case, most of the distinctive sonorities of the *Symphony of Psalms* are made possible not simply by the choice of a wind band, but more crucially by the enlargement of some of the sections and the addition of the keyboard and string instruments. In the first movement, for example, there are the brittle punctuating chords of E minor, including the pianos and harp; the chattering of eight double-reed instruments, in a subtle mixture of staccato and slurs, which accompanies the altos' first entry; the patterns of arpeggios moving at two different speeds in the woodwind and pianos. In the central movement, one can point to the spider's web of oboes and flutes in the opening fugal exposition; the warmth of the cellos in the instrumental accompaniment to the choral fugue; the starkness of the culminating near-*tutti*. In the finale, the slow introduction is lit up by the radiance of Cs and Gs spread through many octaves on pianos, harp, cellos and basses and five flutes; the quick sections are propelled forwards by pizzicato cellos and basses, and galvanised by sudden explosions of dazzling brilliance on upper woodwind, brass, pianos and cellos; the coda moves in a great surge of legato counterpoint, with cellos divided into three, before the final grey, gleaming chord of C major.

If the forces used in the work are unconventional, so too are the proportions and formal outlines of the three movements. These have virtually nothing to do with traditional ideas of the symphony (although there is a genuinely 'symphonic' treatment of minor and major thirds both in motives and figuration and in large-scale tonal relationships). The first movement is short and preludial, static in its use of ostinato figures, though building towards its final cadence. The second, considerably longer, begins with two fugal expositions, the first for instruments and the second for voices (accompanied by fragments from the first), and later combines elements of both. The finale, considerably longer again, consists two extended quick sections, the second a varied repetition of the first, each preceded by a slow introduction, and the whole crowned by a slow coda.

But this formal shape, so odd in abstract terms, makes sense in relation to the texts of the Psalms chosen by Stravinsky, and to the order in which he set them. His first idea was to set Psalm 150, a psalm of universal praise; and so he began with what were to be ultimately the fast sections of the finale. These were inspired, he said, 'by a vision of Elijah's chariot climbing the heavens'; this is represented in the whirling triplets which twice break into the music – as literal a musical image as Stravinsky ever composed.

Next Stravinsky turned back to the first two movements. The first is a setting of verses from Psalm 39, a psalm of prayer, which he composed in 'a state of religious and musical ebullience'. The second sets the opening verses of Psalm 40, in which Stravinsky found a musical symbol for expectation and fulfilment in what he called 'an upside-down pyramid of fugues': the first limited to solo instruments in the treble register; the second introducing human voices in a wider compass; the final section uniting the two.

Finally, and crucially, came Stravinsky's realisation that the 'new song' referred to in this psalm should form the introduction to the finale; and that this music should also end the symphony. Linked with this was his perception, slowly arrived at, that 'God must not be praised in fast, forte music, no matter how often the text specifies "loud"'. Thus it is that the exultant word 'Alleluia', in its three appearances in the movement, is set so memorably to a slow, quiet rising phrase; and so it is, too, that the final verses of the psalm are treated not as the paean of praise that they undoubtedly are, but as a measured, restrained processional, over a bass line which rotates slowly, like the swinging of a giant censer.

© Anthony Burton

Thomas Tallis (*c.*1505–85)

Hailed as the 'father of English cathedral music', Tallis began his church-music career as organist at the Benedictine priory in Dover from 1532, moving to London, then Waltham Abbey, before taking up a post as a lay clerk at Canterbury Cathedral. In 1543 he became a Gentleman of the Chapel Royal in Windsor, where he remained until his death. At Windsor he met and taught Byrd and together they published a volume of *Cantiones sacrae* ('Sacred Songs', 1575). He wrote both elaborate music for the old Latin liturgy, and much more concise, spare music for the new English liturgy. Though not as forward-looking as Byrd, his contrapuntal skill can be heard in his forty-part motet *Spem in alium* and his first setting of the *Lamentations*. He also wrote a small amount of instrumental and keyboard music. Tallis's reputation was enhanced in the twentieth century by Vaughan Williams's use of a melody from the Archbishop Parker's psalter of 1567 in his *Fantasia on a Theme by Thomas Tallis*.

℘ *Spem in alium* (*c.*1573?)

According to the eighteenth-century musical antiquarian Dr Charles Burney, Tallis's *Spem in alium* survived as a 'wonderful effort of harmonical abilities', its contrapuntal design quite unlike that of other known works for multiple choirs. Each voice part, he explained, shares 'in the short subjects of fugue and imitation, which are introduced upon every change of words . . . and thus this stupendous, though perhaps Gothic, specimen of human labour and intellect, is carried on in alternate flight, pursuit, attack, and choral union to the end.' Burney was writing about a work from the distant past, one that deserved coverage as a curiosity, even a freak of musical nature. His suggestion that Tallis's 'Song of 40 Parts' should be performed alongside Handel's choral works at

Westminster Abbey's annual congress of musicians was not put into practice, and its revival was delayed until the publication in 1888 of an inaccurate transcription.

One theory runs that *Spem in alium* was written in honour of Queen Elizabeth I's fortieth birthday in 1573, although recent research favours the rival theory that Thomas Howard, the music-loving fourth Duke of Norfolk, commissioned the work to serve as an English answer to another forty-part showpiece, Alessandro Striggio's motet *Ecce beatam lucem*. Tallis upheld national pride by creating a monumental composition in which eight choirs of five voices each weave a complex web of polyphony around a simple underlying progression of chords.

Andrew Stewart © BBC

Michael Tippett (1905–98)

Tippett studied at the Royal College of Music, but he was unhappy with his early works and withdrew them, seeking a period of further study – of counterpoint with R. O. Morris – which prepared the ground for his first mature works, the String Quartet No. 1 (1935; rev. 1944) and the Piano Sonata No. 1 (1936–7). His moral and political convictions pervaded his life and music: he conducted in Oxted, Surrey, in the 1930s, then organised the South London Orchestra of Unemployed Musicians, and was imprisoned for three months in 1943 for refusing to comply with military exemption requirements. After the war he was a leader of the revival of early music at Morley College. His first major success was the oratorio *A Child of Our Time* (1939–41), a public statement against persecution, which included settings of Negro spirituals. He wrote five operas, also to his own texts, as well as four symphonies, four piano sonatas, five string quartets, and two major choral works concerned with Man's relationship to Time, *The Vision of St Augustine* (1965) and the vast, eclectic *The Mask of Time* (1980–2).

✣ *A Child of Our Time* (1939–41)

In his five operas and three oratorios, Michael Tippett gave artistic expression to some of the crucial questions and dilemmas of our time. He was a composer who felt a passionate obligation to speak on behalf of his public, whether as prophet or exponent of communal myth. In his operas and oratorios, therefore, he tried to objectify his personal emotions and to distil them into generalised statements. Beethoven had done this for his own time; but Beethoven was a child of the French Revolution and of the glorious dawn of early Romanticism ('Bliss was it in that dawn to be alive'), and the twentieth century could no longer sustain such blazing optimism as was proclaimed in *Fidelio* or the Ninth Symphony. This was not so much because of the horror of recent history, as of our increased consciousness of it. Yet Tippett, who was as committed and aware an artist as any, was nonetheless able to produce music full of joy and visionary ecstasy, as well as of compassion and consolation. He achieved his ability 'to praise in spite of all' (Rilke's phrase), with Beethoven as his inspiration, during a ninety-three-year quest for self-knowledge.

Compassion, self-knowledge – these are the central themes of Tippett's art, which found their first mature expression in *A Child of Our Time*. The theme of self-knowledge is encapsulated in a line sung by the solo tenor near the end of the oratorio: 'I would know my shadow and my light, so shall I at last be whole.' The imagery here is Jungian (Tippett had been a student of Jung's work since the early 1930s, and at the time of writing *A Child of Our Time* was conducting his own self-analysis), though the strongest influence on the language of *A Child of Our Time* is that of T. S. Eliot, who had originally agreed to write the libretto but then advised Tippett to write it himself. Tippett had long been contemplating some kind of large-scale work on the theme of compassion, arising out of the political situation of the 1930s and his own active participation in it as a socialist, and later as a pacifist.

In November 1938 a particular act of political violence brought the as yet darkly glimpsed work into focus. A German diplomat in Paris, Ernst vom Rath, was shot by a young Polish Jew, Herschel Grynspan; the Nazis retaliated by launching an especially brutal pogrom (*Kristallnacht*). By September 1939, the outbreak of the war, Tippett had written his libretto and begun the composition of the music, which it took him a further year and a half to complete.

Tippett intended *A Child of Our Time* as a kind of modern equivalent of the Bach Passions: a work involving the audience in the drama leading up to a central tragic event – in the Passions, the death of Christ; in *A Child of Our Time*, the fate of the Jewish people – set against the universal background of human suffering. In trying to create a work that would communicate directly, Tippett deliberately kept his musical language as straightforward as possible. Much of the melodic material derives ultimately from folk song. He employed all the characteristic musical forms found in the Bach Passions: recitative, aria, chorus and congregational hymn. The last posed problems, for he wanted to find a contemporary equivalent for the Lutheran chorales, which draw the people more closely into the drama of the Passions. One day he heard a black singer on the radio sing the spiritual 'Steal Away', and he realised that the spiritual, a genuinely popular form with a breadth of appeal that transcends any particular doctrine or faith, was exactly what he was looking for. So he used five spirituals at critical moments in the oratorio, when the accumulated tension needs to spill over into communal involvement.

As important as the Bach Passions, as a background work to *A Child of Our Time*, was Handel's *Messiah*. The musical shapes of the recitatives, arias and choruses – which are mostly fairly brief – and the overall contemplative content of the words are closer to *Messiah* than to the Passions (and Tippett too even has his own little 'Pastoral Symphony', at the beginning of the finale). Tippett also derived his formal scheme from *Messiah*: the first part establishing a general background, the second part narrating a particular story, and the third part drawing a moral. In *A Child of Our Time*, Part One speaks in general terms of the oppression and violence of the age. Part Two tells the story of the boy's shooting of the official and its terrible consequences: the boy is not named, but is presented as a symbol of the scapegoat, 'the child of our time'. Part Three attempts a reconciliation, culminating in the tenor's great plea for self-knowledge, already quoted. At the very end of the work, before the closing spiritual, the predominantly wintry imagery softens as the mezzo-soprano sings of the coming of spring: 'Spring with an ache in it', as Tippett described it.

© David Matthews

ॐ *The Mask of Time* (1980–2)

Part 1
1 Presence –
2 Creation of the World by Music
3 Jungle
4 The Ice-Cap Moves South–North
5 Dream of the Paradise Garden
Part 2
6 The Triumph of Life
7 Mirror of Whitening Light –
8 Hiroshima, mon amour
9 Three Songs:
    I The Severed Head
    II The Beleaguered Friends
    III The Young Actor Steps Out –
10 The Singing Will Never Be Done

Modern man – so Michael Tippett used to say – suffers from a profoundly divided consciousness. For himself, Tippett knew well what that meant. Though not a believer in any kind of god, he had an innate tendency to view human thoughts, feelings and events in the context of the universal, the eternal – to ask, as Mahler did before writing his 'Resurrection' Symphony, 'What is Life? What is Death? Have these things a meaning?'

It was Tippett's yearning for some kind of transcendence that drove him to explore the experience of timeless serenity recounted by one of the greatest Christian writers in his *Vision of St Augustine* (1963–5). But the image of the all-powerful, all-loving Christian God, presiding over a world that contained the possibility of Auschwitz and Hiroshima, also provoked one of his angriest outbursts – in his Third Symphony (1970–2) the soprano soloist sings:

> But if the cherub stands before God,
> Let him demote himself to man,

> Then spit his curses across the celestial face,
> Though he be answered (Answered?!)
> With annihilation from the whirlwind.

For a while, Tippett thought he had found the answers he needed in the writings of Jung. Jung believed that gods and goddesses were legitimate symbolic expressions of the mysteries of the human mind, and that a religious understanding of the universe and of the individual's place in it was possible even to the modern agnostic. But Tippett felt he had to go on questioning – even Jungian dogma was still dogma, and therefore limiting. He was enormously affected by watching Jacob Bronowski's epic thirteen-part BBC television series *The Ascent of Man* (1973), which traced the rise of humankind and its ability to understand and master its environment through science. And yet, when it came to summing up his own understanding of human nature and the meaning of life, Tippett felt that it was only through art – especially through music and poetry – that this was possible. Categorical statements were out of the question. Metaphor, symbol, paradox, and the mysterious language of music itself, were the only terms in which he could express his intuitions. And the work in which he explored these most thoroughly, extensively and energetically was *The Mask of Time*.

Given Tippett's awareness of the split in modern consciousness (religious yearning versus the revelations of science), the failure of established religious creeds, the reckless cruelty of nature and the appalling suffering inflicted by man on man, *The Mask of Time* could easily have been a pessimistic work; but Tippett was also driven to portray the striving of human beings, not merely to survive, but also to sustain and celebrate their humanity – in other words, to give the modern listener reason to rejoice.

Tracing the 'argument' of *The Mask of Time* is difficult. The text skips from snippets of poetry to scientific observations, from real events to ancient myths, with the bewildering logic of a dream. But, like a dream, it can reveal profound truths –

or at least surprising new perspectives – if the listener/reader doesn't cramp it with logical, 'common sense' expectations. And there is a grand scheme drawing it all together – not so very far removed from the scheme of Haydn's great religious work *The Creation*. Haydn begins with the sudden emergence of light amid chaos and darkness. For Tippett, thinking poetically, the first event is 'Sound / Where no airs blow'. (This is, of course, scientifically impossible; but mystical writing thrives on paradox – think of the opening verse of St John's Gospel: 'In the beginning was the Word, and the Word was with God, and the Word was God.') 'Presence', *The Mask*'s first movement, thus begins with an echoing single chord on the word 'Sound', after which the chorus ponders the elemental story of the universe, 'Exploding / Into time / Into space . . . / Turning / Returning'. At the same time, the tenor soloist (quoting W. B. Yeats) observes the miraculous birth of light, 'Night splits and the dawn breaks loose', while reminding us (in a poem addressed to a circus stilt-walker!) that everything is 'metaphor'.

The rest of Part One is Tippett's own *Ascent of Man*. In 'Creation of the World by Music' (No. 2), we hear how music brings order out of chaos, particularly as represented in the myths of the Ancient Greek poet Orpheus and the Hindu god Shiva; then a depiction of Halley's comet (which returns roughly every seventy-five years – last in 1985) reminds us that the history of the universe is also one of 'Eternal Reversal'. No. 3, 'Jungle', depicts the horrors of nature (familiar through David Attenborough's television series *Life on Earth*) – with some wonderful onomatopoeic rhythmic chanting for the chorus. Then, in 'The Ice-Cap Moves South–North' (No. 4), we trace the emergence of human civilisation – agricultural, organised and religious. Finally, in 'Dream of the Paradise Garden' (No. 5), Tippett creates his own religious myth: mankind loses its 'innocent', direct relationship with nature and with God, and with it the possibility of creating heaven on earth. In the end, all that is left is the nostalgic dream of Eden, and 'the bitter-sweet songs of, ah, music'.

In Part Two, the questioning individual enters the story. 'The Triumph of Life' (No. 6) is the title of Shelley's final, unfinished poem. Shelley sees life as a chariot, conveying a 'captive multitude' of human beings, all of whom are eventually thrown off. Tippett's setting builds to a huge climax above a dragging repeated bass. Then comes a depiction of Shelley's own death by drowning.

The title of the seventh movement, 'Mirror of Whitening Light', comes from alchemy – an alluring but ultimately vain scientific attempt to make order from chaos. The use of the plainchant *Veni creator spiritus* ('Come, creator spirit') in the movement's three increasingly fantastical instrumental Preludes is ironic – hinting at the medieval Church's own bizarre attempts to make rational sense of the universe. The final powerful image – 'unbind the structured atom / to a whiteness that shall blind the sun' – leads inevitably (via a fusillade of percussion and threatening brass chords) to the eighth movement, 'Hiroshima, mon amour', where atomic devastation stands for modern man's greatly enhanced capacity to destroy life. Above a hummed male-voice accompaniment (so simple, but so telling), a soprano sings some especially moving words from the Russian poet Anna Akhmatova's *Requiem* and *Poem without a Hero*.

The themes of return and reversal are heard again in the first of the 'Three Songs' (No. 9). Orpheus, who brought order through music in Part One, is now torn to pieces by the Thracian women. But in the second song, the ancient Chinese oracle, the I Ching, reveals that return may also bring good fortune. How does the individual understand his place in these great, but seemingly impersonal cosmic schemes? In the third song, a young actor in Ancient Olympia puts this question – or something like it – to the oracle of Zeus. The answer is enigmatic, but challenging, and it brings us to the apotheosis of *The Mask of Time*, and to the kernel of Tippett's message: 'O man, make peace with your mortality, / for this too is God.'

Having delivered these words, soloists, chorus and orchestra rise in a great wave of wordless singing (No. 10). The end is extraordinary: brief but ecstatic eruptions of song, alternating with harsh brass chords. Transcendent human warmth and cold emptiness face each other across space. Humanity has the last word.

© Stephen Johnson

Ralph Vaughan Williams (1872–1958)

Unlike Elgar before him, Vaughan Williams received a traditional musical education, at the Royal College of Music in London, but he also studied abroad – in Berlin with Bruch and in Paris with Ravel. Soon after his return came the *Fantasia on a Theme by Thomas Tallis* and *A Sea Symphony* (1910); he became active as a collector of folk music and edited *The English Hymnal* (1906). After completing his second symphony, *A London Symphony* (1913), he joined the army. As well as choral works such as *Sancta civitas* (1925) and *Serenade to Music* (1938), he wrote a mass and made many choral arrangements of English folk songs. Apart from *The Lark Ascending* for violin and orchestra, his concerto-type works – for viola (*Flos campi*), piano, oboe and tuba – remain rarely performed. After the death of his first wife, he remarried aged eighty, and produced two more symphonies before his death.

∾ *A Sea Symphony* (Symphony No. 1) (1903–9, rev. 1918)

1 A Song for All Seas, All Ships (Andante maestoso)
2 On the Beach at Night Alone (Largo sostenuto)
3 Scherzo – The Waves (Allegro brillante)
4 The Explorers (Grave e molto adagio)

When completed, *A Sea Symphony* was incomparably Vaughan Williams's most ambitious and extensive work to date. It had cost him considerable labour over six years, with many false starts and changes of plan. Originally the work was entitled 'Songs of the Sea', later 'Ocean Symphony'; many passages – including a complete movement entitled 'The Steersman' – were composed and then rejected; the slow movement was written three times before the composer was satisfied. Vaughan Williams himself conducted the world premiere, on 12 October 1910 in Leeds Town Hall as part of the Leeds Festival, with Cicely Gleeson-White and Campbell McInnes as the soloists and the composer Edward Bairstow at the organ; the work was first heard in London at the Queen's Hall in 1913, conducted by Hugh Allen.

In its epic scale and ardent idealism, probably no work did more to solidify Vaughan Williams's growing reputation as the chief spokesman for a new generation of British composers. The mingled subject of the sea, sailors and exploration was almost a national obsession in the Imperial island of Britain, and doubtless Vaughan Williams had in mind Stanford's popular *Songs of the Sea* and his choral ballad *The Revenge*. Yet he chose not an English poet but the speculative, metaphysical rhapsodies of the American, Walt Whitman, for whom the ocean evoked limitless spiritual possibility, the 'cohesion of all'. Like many British creative artists (such as his great friend Gustav Holst, and also Frederick Delius), Vaughan Williams was much impressed and involved with Whitman's poetry at this time. Three years before *A Sea Symphony* was performed, he had already made his mark at the Leeds Festival with a choral setting of Whitman, *Toward the Unknown Region*, one of his first characteristic utterances of mystical idealism; and, in addition to the *Sea Symphony*, he also worked on a set of three choral Nocturnes to Whitman texts, which he never brought to final form.

In its huge scale and large forces, however, *A Sea Symphony* was clearly his principal Whitman-inspired work. Outranking in size and scope even Delius's *Sea Drift*, it more resembles some of the idealistic series of 'ethical oratorios' that Vaughan Williams's teacher Parry was currently composing to non-denominational, or even agnostic, texts. Parry tended to call such pieces 'sinfoniae sacrae' and they do reveal a quasi-symphonic organisation. But, although it contains no extended passages for orchestra alone, *A Sea Symphony* is more obviously symphonic, with a first movement that respects the broad outlines of sonata form, a ternary-form slow movement, a scherzo with trio, and an epic if episodic finale that draws the musical threads together and provides a 'cyclic' return to opening ideas. And, although Parry established new standards in the idiomatic setting of English verse, Vaughan Williams succeeded in the even more difficult task of shaping Whitman's voluble and irregular free-verse lines to clear and characterful melodic ideas, freely selecting passages (from five different poems from the poet's principal collection *Leaves of Grass*) and omitting others, to conform to his musical scheme.

The symphony is unified by two motto-themes that are heard in all four movements. The first is the oscillation of minor and major triads (B flat minor to D major) heard in the trumpet fanfare and choral outcry of the very opening bars, to the words 'Behold the sea itself'; and the second is the broad surging melody, characterised by an almost Brahmsian combination of duplet and triplet rhythm, that follows immediately to the phrase 'and on its limitless heaving breast, the ships'. These elements introduce a sonata-style exposition with a lively Allegro subject beginning at 'Today a rude brief recitative' (led off by the baritone soloist) and a more lyrical, hymn-like one for the 'chant for the sailors of all nations' (introduced by the soprano). The soprano also begins the development-like central section with the injunction to 'flaunt out the separate flags of nations'. In the recapitulation a sonorous climax is reached at the invocation of a 'pennant universal', subsuming those separate flags, before a quiet close.

The slow movement opens in meditation for baritone and a semi-chorus of altos, in a mood of deep, tranced thought, 'on the beach at night alone'. The central section develops into a march involving the full chorus, still meditative on the subject of 'this vast similitude' and rising to a climactic profession of faith for unison chorus and brass. The opening music returns to create a peaceful, nocturnal epilogue.

A suggestion of the first-movement fanfare opens the Scherzo, a brilliant piece of blustery writing for voices and chorus, with plenty of suggested wind and wave effects and a grand C major tune for the Trio that contemplates 'the great vessel sailing'. Vaughan Williams wove two nautical folk tunes about ships, 'The *Golden Vanity*' and 'The Bold *Princess Royal*', into this movement.

The text Vaughan Williams fashioned for his finale charts an ambitious course from the creation of the world, through Adam and Eve 'from the gardens of Asia descending', to the emergence of the poet, who symbolises the creator and whose songs set the soul on its exploration, in deep waters, for the goal of the infinite. The movement begins with a mysterious quiet prologue and is fashioned in a series of large, increasingly climactic spans. The descent from the 'gardens of Asia' is achieved in an extended slow-march passage, and the arrival of the poet 'singing his songs' prompts a majestic climax. The soprano and baritone soloists now enter, and for much of the remainder of the movement they are in quasi-operatic duet or in dialogue with the chorus. The mood grows increasingly ardent and Romantic, until at 'Away O soul!' a very nautical Allegro sets the music once more upon the waves, rising to a grand and visionary climax at 'Steer for the deep waters only!'. In an extended quiet epilogue for the full forces (Holst surely remembered it when writing 'Neptune' in *The Planets*), the mind's eye seems to be drawn to an ever more distant horizon, beyond which everything sinks, perhaps over the edge of the world.

Malcolm MacDonald © BBC

❧ *Serenade to Music* (1938)

Serenade to Music is a prime example of a score composed for a specific occasion (in this case, moreover, for a specific collection of voices) that has wholly transcended its origins to become a repertoire piece. Indeed, for many people it must be one of the works that best define the essence of Vaughan Williams as the great musical exponent of English pastoral and poetry.

He designed the *Serenade* – written as a present for Henry Wood in celebration of his fifty years as a conductor – to be sung by an ensemble of sixteen leading British singers with whom Wood had worked over the years. Wood conducted the premiere at his own Golden Jubilee Concert in the Royal Albert Hall on 5 October 1938. The orchestra was drawn from the four with which he had been most closely associated (the Queen's Hall Orchestra, the BBC Symphony, the LPO and the LSO) and the voices were that specific 'sixteen' of the 1930s: the sopranos Isobel Baillie, Lilian Stiles-Allen, Elsie Suddaby and Eva Turner; the contraltos Margaret Balfour, Muriel Brunskill, Astra Desmond and Mary Jarred; the tenors Parry Jones, Heddle Nash, Frank Titterton and Walter Widdop; and the basses Norman Allin, Robert Easton, Roy Henderson and Harold Williams.

A recording – in every sense historic – was subsequently made by the same artists. In this original version, the *Serenade* most closely resembles a very large-scale modern madrigal in its interweaving and harmony of so many different parts; and the parts themselves were individually characterised, each tailored to the singing style and musical personality of the vocalist who first sang it.

This sixteen-voice form is still performed on special occasions, although it is now more common to hear the *Serenade* with only four soloists and a chorus, or with a chorus singing the sixteen parts but with several voices to a part. Vaughan Williams even made a version for orchestra alone (Henry Wood gave the first performance of this, too, in February 1940), which demonstrates that the music of the *Serenade* retains its magic without the aid of words.

Yet the words – some of the greatest poetry in English – are of course tremendously important. Vaughan Williams deftly sifted the dialogues of Lorenzo and Jessica, Portia and Nerissa from the final scene of *The Merchant of Venice* to create a seamless nocturnal meditation on the power not just of music but of hearing, and the meaning which we, hearing music, assign to it. So total is the fusion that the music seems to arise directly out of the words and to give them perfect expression: some feat, when the author is Shakespeare. Vaughan Williams's master, Hubert Parry, had performed a similar feat with Milton in his *Blest Pair of Sirens*, but the *Serenade*, more intimate and metaphysical, takes us nearer the heart of its composer.

A great deal of Vaughan Williams is recalled or suggested within the languorous compass of this ecstatic nocturne. The tranced lyricism of the instrumental prologue, with its solo violin, evokes the world of *The Lark Ascending* (here the violin is perhaps a nightingale, though that bird, according to Portia in an unset line of Shakespeare's, would be 'no better a musician than the wren' if heard by day).

Yet there is also a suggestion that the whole piece is a kind of symphonic slow movement. Throughout the voices' choric first entry and the ensuing succession of solos, the material – all highest-quality Vaughan Williams – continually presages major works yet to be written: the Fifth and Sixth Symphonies, *The Pilgrim's Progress*, *Sinfonia Antartica*, *Hodie*. By the time the epilogue brings us back to the songful violin, we have not merely celebrated harmony but glimpsed the potential, at least, of 'true perfection'.

Malcolm MacDonald © BBC

∾ *Toward the Unknown Region* (1905–6)

British music of the early twentieth century is often criticised by its detractors as either epitomising the brash, patriotic pomp and circumstance of the Edwardian era, or else degenerating into anaemic maunderings after 'lands of lost content' or 'blue remembered hills' – as if England's boundaries could be defined by the Forest of Dean, the Malverns and the Vale of Evesham. The preoccupations of what has been unkindly termed the 'cowpat' school represented one form of reaction against the bonfire of the certainties caused by *fin-de-siècle* political upheavals, but it soon became clear to thinking musicians that mellifluous nostalgia (where would English music be without the triplet?) was leading them up a blind alley. Between these two extremes, however, a third strand appeared, nourished by a preoccupation with abstract spiritual values. These visionary voyages into uncharted territory, crossing boundaries and widening horizons, are one of the most appealing features of late Victorian and Edwardian philosophical thought, both sacred and humanist. Elgar's *The Dream of Gerontius* belongs to this tradition, as do many works by Gustav Holst, Frederick Delius and Vaughan Williams himself.

These last three composers found inspiration in the works of the American poet Walt Whitman (1819–92), whose central theme was the eternal power of rejuvenation within the Great Scheme of Things. Unlike the self-pity of a Housman, Whitman could lament the loss of love and life without losing sight of a greater order, a 'life-force' which survives all catastrophe. Vaughan Williams was a young, relatively unknown composer with only a handful of pieces to his credit when he had the idea of setting Whitman's *Toward the Unknown Region*, a metaphysical poem which begins:

> Darest thou now, O Soul
> Walk out with me toward the unknown region,
> Where neither ground is for the feet nor any path
> to follow? . . .

Years later, Vaughan Williams told Imogen Holst how the work had come into being: 'Gustav and I were both struck – so I suggested we should both set the words in competition – suggesting "Darest thou". The prize was awarded by us to me.'

Toward the Unknown Region was first performed at the Leeds Triennial Festival on 10 October 1907, with the composer conducting. The audience received the piece with enthusiasm. The critic of *The Times* wrote that the piece showed a 'nobility and earnestness of invention which mark the composer as the foremost of the younger generation'. Vaughan Williams received his success with typical modesty:

'They sang and played magnificently – but the twenty minutes I stood there conducting were like a thousand years of purgatory,' he wrote to a friend. 'But after all it's only a step and I've got to do something really big some time. I think I am improving. It "comes off" better than my earlier things used to.' The 'something big' turned out to be *A Sea Symphony*, another setting of Whitman, which was first performed three years later.

© Wendy Thompson

Giuseppe Verdi (1813–1901)

Along with his contemporary Wagner, and with Mozart, Verdi ranks among the greatest of all operatic composers. He was born in a village near Busseto, and became the town's *maestro di cappella*. In 1839 he moved to Milan, where his first opera, *Oberto*, was staged with great success. Following the failure of his second opera, *Un giorno di regno* (1840), and the loss of his wife and two infants, he considered terminating his operatic career, but was inspired by a libretto for an opera on the story of Nebuchadnezzar (*Nabucco*, 1842). Over the next decade he wrote sixteen operas, culminating in his three middle-period hits, *Rigoletto* (1851), *Il trovatore* and *La traviata* (both 1853), all of which regularly feature in opera houses across the world. He later accepted commissions from St Petersburg (*La forza del destino*, 1862), Paris (*Les Vêpres Siciliennes*, 1855, and *Don Carlos*, 1867) and Cairo (*Aida*, 1871, set in ancient Egypt and connected with the opening of the Suez Canal). In semi-retirement from operatic composition, he wrote his String Quartet (1873) and *Requiem* (1874), following them with his last great Shakespeare operas, *Otello* (1887) and *Falstaff* (1893).

∾ *Four Sacred Pieces* (1888–9, 1895–7)

1   Ave Maria
2   Stabat mater
3   Laudi alla Vergine Maria
4   Te Deum

Verdi was not the only composer to crown an operatic career with religious composition. Rossini's last work of importance was the *Petite messe solennelle* of 1863, Verdi's a set of sacred pieces that the poet-composer Arrigo Boito, his collaborator on *Otello* and *Falstaff*, likened to 'Correggio domes'. (He was referring to the frescoes in Parma Cathedral and the Church of S. Giovanni Evangelista, now revealed in all their splendour with the aid of electric lighting.) The *Ave Maria* owes its origin to a letter published by a professor of music, one Adolfo Crescentini, in the *Gazzetta musicale di Milano* in 1888, together with an 'enigmatic scale' of his own invention (the usual octave split up into bizarre intervals), which he invited composers to harmonise. Evidently both Verdi and Boito had puzzled over it – it represented the kind of conundrum that Boito loved – for early the next year we find Verdi writing to the poet with a request for that 'ramshackle scale' which he had thrown into the fire by mistake:

> You'll say that it isn't worth my while to be bothered with this nonsense, and you'll be right. But what of it? They say that when you're old you go back to being a boy . . . Besides, I think one could base a piece with words on this scale – say an Ave Maria. Another one! It would be my fourth. So perhaps I may look forward to being beatified after my death!

It need hardly be said that Verdi's solution, which takes the form of a full-scale polyphonic motet, towered over the other contributions, just as Beethoven's *Variations on a Theme of Diabelli* far surpassed those of his fellow composers.

A similar interest in sixteenth-century polyphony inspired the *Laudi alla Vergine Maria*, a setting of lines from Dante's *Paradiso*, probably conceived a few months before the *Ave Maria* and clearly intended as an 'hommage à Palestrina'. But in composing the *Te Deum* and *Stabat mater* during the years 1895–7, Verdi had no thought of archaising. Both were to be set for instrumental forces even greater than those that had served him in the Requiem some twenty years earlier. His search for a model for the *Te Deum* took him to the archives of the basilica of S. Antonio in Padua. He wrote to the director of music, Giovanni Tebaldini:

> I know several of the old Te Deums and I've heard some

modern ones, and I've never been convinced by the way this canticle has been interpreted – quite apart from the musical value. It is usually sung during grand, solemn and noisy ceremonies for a victory or a coronation etc. The opening lends itself to that since Heaven and Earth are rejoicing . . . 'Sanctus, sanctus, Deus Sabaoth' . . . But towards the middle the colour and the expression change . . . 'Tu ad liberandum' . . . Here Christ, born of the Virgin Mary, opens to humanity the 'regna coelorum'. Humanity believes in the 'Judex venturus', invokes him in 'Salvum fac', and ends with a prayer, 'Dignare, Domine, die isto' . . . moving, sad to the point of terror. All this has nothing to do with victories and coronations.

In the event, no suitable precedent was forthcoming, and Verdi, not for the first time in such cases, decided to go his own way, thus producing one of the most powerful and original of all settings of the canticle.

Less is known about the genesis of the *Stabat mater*; yet here, too, it is possible to discern a tribute, albeit indirect, to Palestrina, whose own setting of the poem attributed to Jacopo da Todi (known to nineteenth-century audiences mostly in an edition by – of all people – Richard Wagner) shares with Verdi's the unusual distinction of presenting the text simply and without repetition.

Somewhat reluctantly, Verdi agreed to the publication of all four pieces as a set. But, to begin with, he allowed only the last three to be performed together: the *Ave Maria* he regarded as a mere technical exercise – a *sciarada* (charade), as he liked to call it. The premiere of the *Laudi* and its two companions took place in Paris at the Conservatoire on 7 April 1898; the Italian premiere followed a month later in Turin under the baton of Toscanini. In both, as also in the first British performance at the Three Choirs Festival that same year, the *Laudi* were sung by solo voices. The practice of using a small choir, and also of adding the *sciarada*, evidently began with the Viennese *prima* given the following November. It was not, in fact, a first hearing for the *Ave Maria*, which had been tried out as early as 1895 by the students of Parma Conservatory.

Though written over a number of years and never designed as a unity, the *Four Sacred Pieces* form a complete and satisfying musical experience – from the austere experiment of the *Ave Maria* to the rapt introspection of the *Stabat mater*, from the limpid sweetness of the *Laudi* to the grandeur and sublimity of the *Te Deum*, the most thematically organised of the four. Parisian audiences awarded the palm to the *Stabat mater*; and one or two critics, including our own Charles Villiers Stanford, suggested that it might be the most appropriate piece to end with. Certainly the more obvious uplift of the penultimate bars before the opening image returns suggests a stronger affirmation of faith than does the close of the *Te Deum*.

But faith never came easily, if at all, to Verdi; and it is surely more fitting that, like the Requiem, his last musical testament should end on a note of awe and uncertainty in the face of the Unknown.

© Julian Budden

∾ Requiem (1874)

1   Introit and Kyrie
2   Dies irae
3   Offertory
4   Sanctus
5   Agnus Dei
6   Lux aeterna
7   Libera me

In November 1868 Rossini died in Paris at the age of seventy-six. Plans were immediately set afoot to commemorate the anniversary of his death both in Pesaro (where he was born) and Bologna (where he had grown up). For the Bologna commemoration, it was Verdi who suggested to the publisher Tito Ricordi the idea of a composite Requiem Mass to which the leading Italian composers of the day would all contribute. He himself volunteered a 'Libera me', one of the prayers which he remembered with most pleasure from the church-going days of his youth. Ricordi responded with alacrity; a committee was formed and a list of composers drawn up to which Verdi gave his blessing. But the plan foundered on the unwillingness of the Bologna impresario to put his chorus and orchestra at the disposal of the organisers. Ricordi then considered mounting the Requiem in Milan, but to Verdi that would have destroyed the point of the enterprise; the Mass should be given in Bologna or nowhere. 'The best course', he wrote, 'is to restore the pieces to their respective authors and to say no more about it.'

He did not remain adamant for long. More than once during the next two years he allowed the committee to take another look at the Mass and see whether it would stand up to public performance. Evidently the members were doubtful, for nothing was done about it. One of them, however, Alberto Mazzucato, a professor at the Milan Conservatory and a rival of Verdi in his younger days, wrote to him after having examined the 'Libera me': 'You, my dear Maestro, have written the finest, grandest and most vastly poetic page of music that can be imagined. Nothing more perfect has been written, nor ever will be.' Much gratified, Verdi wrote back that Mazzucato's praise almost persuaded him to complete the Requiem on his own, 'especially since with a little more working out I would find that I had already written the Requiem [aeternam] and the "Dies irae" of which there is a reprise [*riepilogo*] in the "Libera me".' And indeed he had. The main section of the 'Requiem aeternam' is there in its entirety, sung by soprano and chorus; so too the principal theme of the 'Dies irae', not as cataclysmic as in its final real-isation, but unmistakably the same idea. In this first version of the 'Libera me' the soprano line, having been written for Antonietta Fricci, is without the trumpet-like high notes and sudden changes of register which Verdi included for the more dramatic Teresa Stolz. But in all essentials the 'Libera me' of the 'Rossini' Requiem is the same as that which forms the last movement of Verdi's later Mass, only without those little improvements which he never failed to bring to a revision. If the reminiscences of the earlier prayers had not been reminiscences at all (since the other composers had set them quite differently), Verdi would not have been particularly concerned, for he set no great store by the musical unity of the work as a whole. It was to have been a historical gesture, no more.

For the moment Verdi assured Mazzucato that the temptation to finish the Requiem would soon pass. There were enough requiems in the world; one more would be pointless – 'and I detest pointless things'. He protested too much. In April 1873 Ricordi returned the autograph of the 'Libera me' to the composer, presumably at his request. A month later the poet Alessandro Manzoni died at the age of eighty-eight after a fall on the steps of a church. In June Verdi wrote to Ricordi proposing to write a requiem to be performed a year hence ('it will have somewhat vast proportions, and besides a large orchestra and large chorus it will need four or five soloists – I can't as yet specify the exact number'). It would seem, then, that Verdi had already decided to complete the Requiem even before Manzoni's death provided its ostensible *raison d'être*.

Although usually described as a poet, Manzoni's claim to immortality rests on his historical novel, *I promessi sposi* ('The Betrothed'), one of the masterpieces of European literature, whose characters are as familiar to every Italian as those of Dickens are to the English. To Verdi it was 'not just a book – it's a consolation to all mankind'. The paradox is that while Manzoni's novel is permeated by its author's liberal Catholicism, Verdi was not only anti-clerical in his views but disclaimed any religious feeling whatever. Giuseppina Strepponi-Verdi, the composer's second wife, put it very well: 'There are some who are really virtuous by nature and need to believe in God. There are others, no less perfect, who are quite happy not to believe in anything at all, while observing to the letter every precept of the strictest morality. Verdi and

Manzoni – these two are for me a subject of endless meditation.' The same paradox extends to the music of the
Requiem, which scales vast spiritual heights while avoiding
all trace of conventional piety.

The first performance took place under Verdi's own direction at the church of S. Marco in Milan, the four soloists
being Teresa Stolz, Maria Waldmann, Giuseppe Capponi and
Ormondo Maini. It was a predictable success. Only the great
German conductor Hans von Bülow, then resident in Italy,
had, after a 'stealthy glance' at the score, refused to attend
'this latest arrival from the world of *Il trovatore* and *La traviata*'.
But he lived to eat his words and humbly beg the composer's
pardon.

Performances in Paris, London and Vienna soon followed
– the last attended by Richard and Cosima Wagner. One
would give much to have Wagner's own judgement on it, but
we must be content to infer it from Cosima's withering
description – 'a work of which it would certainly be best to
say nothing'. Brahms thought differently. 'Bülow', he
remarked, 'has made a fool of himself for all time. Only a
genius could write something like this.'

In the meantime Verdi had made an important modifica-
tion to the score. He replaced the choral fugue to which he
had originally set the 'Liber scriptus' with a solo for Maria
Waldmann – a fine example of a declaimed melody in Verdi's
maturest manner. This was first heard at the London premiere, given on 12 May 1875 in London's Royal Albert Hall.
Yet England was one of the countries where the Requiem had
the greatest difficulty in making its way. The problem was
one of musical language. Great liturgical works were scarcer
in the nineteenth than in earlier centuries, since the
Romantic age was less attuned to the idea of collective devotion. Religion was felt to be a private matter, and many of the
greatest composers did not scruple to draw for its expression
upon the idiom in which they were most at home (Berlioz,
Brahms and Fauré are all notable examples). Verdi, like
Rossini in his *Stabat mater*, makes use of a theatrical idiom,

since, as Giuseppina put it, 'Verdi must write like Verdi.' Just as Rossini's 'Fac ut portem' speaks the language of Arsace's cavatina from *Semiramide*, so a number of passages in Verdi's Requiem evoke memories of similar moments in his operas. The harmonic side-slip in that miracle of thematic economy, the Offertory, recalls the death of Gilda in *Rigoletto*; the heavily charged harmonies of the 'Requiem aeternam' take us back to the chorus of exiles in *Macbeth* (second version). The 'Lacrimosa' has a more directly operatic origin in a duet for tenor and bass with chorus from *Don Carlos* which Verdi discarded before the opera's Paris premiere in 1867 (though it has now been reconstructed and is occasionally heard in performances). But many in England believed that whereas the language of the concert hall might legitimately find a place in a religious work, that of the opera house might not. Operas were profane, if not slightly impious; and had not Hubert Parry described opera-goers as the least musical among all those who claim to love music?

Fortunately, this prejudice has diminished over the years. In any case, Verdi's theatrical manner does not make the Requiem a religious work in operatic garb. The four soloists no more represent individuals than do those of Handel's *Messiah*. Indeed, it is the absence of a story-line that enables the musical thought to develop with a freedom unknown in the operas, where the special *données* of a stage action enforce certain compromises. This is not to say that the Requiem is necessarily the greatest of Verdi's works, but it is certainly the one which shows his genius at its most concentrated.

The musical forms that Verdi here employs are difficult to classify. Variation of the simplest kind is the basis of the 'Agnus Dei'. There is a sonata-like key-scheme with two differentiated ideas in the 'Ingemisco'; a suggestion of bar-form-with-refrain in the 'Quid sum miser', the refrain itself taking its full shape only at the second statement. The 'Rex tremendae' presents that typically Verdian design of a static theme alternating with one which develops. The 'Sanctus' is a double fugue evolved in four-bar units, which give it a certain dance-like character; but, as Donald Tovey beautifully puts it, the dance is that of the 'Sons of the Morning'. Verdi's counterpoint has nothing of the schoolroom about it.

Particularly impressive is the word-painting. The 'Dies irae' is conceived as a wild storm bursting forth after the tranquil ending of the 'Kyrie' with a violent tonal non sequitur. The 'Tuba mirum', with its four trumpets in the distance and four in the orchestra, has all the vividness of Berlioz's quadrophonic setting together with a more concentrated feeling of menace. In 'Mors stupebit et natura' the bass soloist seems to be staring into a bottomless abyss. In the oboe melody beneath shimmering violins that precedes the tenor's words 'Inter oves locum praesta' ('Place me among the sheep') we hear a shepherd piping high on the mountainside. At the end of the 'Lux aeterna' tremolando violins and violas portray the 'light perpetual' to which the soul prays to ascend, while an unusually voiced chording of woodwind and brass depicts the mortal remains for which the tenor and bass implore eternal rest. No wonder that, when Bülow eventually heard the Requiem, he was contrite.

© Julian Budden

Antonio Vivaldi (1678–1741)

Vivaldi was born in Venice, where his father gave him violin lessons. At fifteen he began training for the priesthood, and in 1703, the year of his ordination, he began his long association with the Ospedale della Pietà, one of the city's four boarding schools for orphan girls for which he wrote much church music as well as instrumental works. His first works, the Op. 1 Trio Sonatas and Op. 2 Violin Sonatas, were published in 1705 and 1709, but he won wider repute with his set of twelve concertos *L'estro armonico*, Op. 3, published in Amsterdam. His *Ottone in villa* (1713), premiered in Vicenza, was the first of a large number of operas (many now lost), and his sacred oratorio *Juditha triumphans* (1716) is a testament to the musical talents of the girls at the Ospedale. From 1718 to 1720 Vivaldi was in the service of Prince Philip of Hesse-Darmstadt, governor of Mantua; during the 1720s he played for the Pope and was granted several audiences with Emperor Charles VI. However, his career declined in the 1730s, and in 1740 Vivaldi moved to Vienna, where he died in poverty.

❧ *Gloria* in D major, RV 589 (*c*. 1715)

Although Vivaldi is recognised today primarily for his many fine concertos, he was also the composer of some forty operas and of a significant quantity of church music. In this last category may be found solo motets, settings of the canticles and psalms, and what has become his best-known church composition, the *Gloria* in D major, RV 589.

Vivaldi, although a frequent traveller abroad as well as to other Italian cities, spent much of his working life as director of music at the Ospedale della Pietà, one of four state-supported Venetian orphanages. Vivaldi joined its staff in 1703, at which time the *maestro del coro* there was Francesco Gasparini, a celebrated teacher and composer. Traditionally,

the story goes that owing to some severe illness – never specified – Gasparini was gradually forced to give up his position
at the Pietà, which incidentally gave him responsibility for
instrumentalists as well as singers. It seems more probable,
however, that illness was just an excuse for the increasing
amount of time which Gasparini was spending in Rome staging his operas. Be that as it may, in 1713 Vivaldi took over
Gasparini's responsibility as official composer for the Pietà,
though not in fact the prime position of *maestro del coro*,
which was awarded to a comparative non-entity.

From now on Vivaldi was expected to provide a set quantity of church music for the chapel of the Pietà, as the following duty sheet illustrates:

> He must, every year, at least for Easter and for the Feast
> of the Visitation of the Blessed Virgin Mary . . . write two
> new Masses and Vespers, at least two motets each month,
> and any other composition which might be ordered from
> him by those appointed to direct the church in Holy
> Week, in cases of Funeral ceremonies or in any other
> case . . .

And in 1715 there is a record of Vivaldi having received a
merit award of fifty ducats for 'excellent musical compositions contributed after the absence of Maestro Gasparini'.
Among the finest of Vivaldi's church compositions – many of
which are less likely to have been composed for St Mark's
than was once thought, but rather for the newly built chapel
of the Pietà – are settings of the psalms *Dixit Dominus* and
Beatus vir, settings of the *Magnificat* and *Stabat mater*, several
fine solo motets, and two settings of the *Gloria*. All display
that style, not peculiar to Vivaldi but individually treated by
him, in which a predilection for melodic line is strongly influenced by the operatic style of the moment.

Vivaldi's *Gloria* is in twelve carefully and effectively contrasted movements, laid out in the manner of a cantata and,
broadly speaking, similar to the way in which Bach subdivided the same text in the B minor Mass (from which it differs

considerably, however, in its treatment). Venetian composers, like those at Bologna, were inspired – no doubt largely by the architecture of their churches – to experiment with musical colours and sonorities; Vivaldi's larger setting of the *Beatus vir* psalm, for instance, derives its particular effect from an antiphonal ritornello which runs throughout the work. In the *Gloria* it is the swift changes of mood and the kaleidoscope of instrumental and vocal colouring which is most striking. Its compactness, together with its cyclic form (so to speak), are sufficient evidence to suggest that this work was not intended as part of a complete mass, but rather composed as an entity in itself.

In the first section of the *Gloria* the four-part choir is supported by a string orchestra with an oboe and a trumpet; the unison opening which emphasises the tonic key in octave intervals is a favourite Vivaldi device, by which we can often distinguish his style from that of his many gifted Italian contemporaries. In the sequence of solos and choruses which follows, the composer achieves his composite picture not only by striking changes in texture and colour blends – he uses an oboe, for example, to accompany the tender 12/8 soprano solo 'Domine Deus' – but also in his choice of keys: D major and its relative B minor are reserved for the two opening and two closing numbers. For the remainder of the work Vivaldi takes us through G major, E minor and C major (these last two were favourite keys of his), F major, D minor and A minor. The double-fugue chorus 'Cum sancto spiritu' which ends the work is also present with slight alterations in Vivaldi's other *Gloria* (RV588). Originally, however, this music appears to have been the work of another Venetian, Giovanni Maria Ruggieri (*fl. c.*1690–1720).

© Nicholas Anderson

William Walton (1902–83)

Born in industrial Lancashire, Walton made an early escape to Oxford, becoming a chorister at Christ Church Cathedral, then staying on at Christ Church as an undergraduate. Here he had the good fortune to fall in with the literary Sitwell family (Edith, Sacheverell and Osbert), who supported him for ten years as well as introducing him to leading artists of the day. His *Façade* (1922) – a chic, jazzy entertainment for reciter and ensemble, to texts by Edith – caused a stir. The Viola Concerto (1928–9) soon followed, as did the cantata *Belshazzar's Feast* (1929–31), which quickly became a staple of the British choral societies. During the 1940s he produced film scores for, among others, Olivier's *Henry V* and *Hamlet*. Following his marriage in 1949 he and his wife Susana moved to Ischia, off the Naples coast. He also wrote concertos for violin (1938–9) and cello (1956–7), and showed a flair for occasional music, displayed in the marches *Crown Imperial* and *Orb and Sceptre* written for the coronations of George VI and Elizabeth II respectively.

❧ *Belshazzar's Feast* (1929–31; rev. 1931, 1948 and 1957)

When Walton began composing *Belshazzar's Feast*, he had in mind a different kind of work from the one that was to triumph at its first performance at the 1931 Leeds Festival. In August 1929 the BBC had commissioned the rising young composer to write a choral work for small forces, with an orchestra of 'not more than fifteen soloists'. Walton asked Osbert Sitwell to assemble the text of 'Nebuchadnezzar', or 'The Writing on the Wall', from Old and New Testament sources; and, while staying with the Sitwells in Amalfi during the following winter, he at least partly completed a setting of it (now lost) involving two soloists, a mezzo-soprano and a baritone, before grinding to a halt at the words 'Praise ye the god of gold'. Walton always liked to dramatise his propensity for writer's blocks, but this particular one was severe enough to bring about a startling change to the final result. A few months later *Belshazzar's Feast*, as it was now named, had transformed itself into a spectacular cantata, scored for forces much too large for the BBC's studio resources. Walton finished the score in the spring of 1931 and, when the BBC bowed out, the premiere passed to the Leeds Festival instead.

The Leeds Festival, at that time directed by Sir Thomas Beecham, was well used to mounting performances on a grand scale. According to Walton, Beecham suggested to him: 'As you'll never hear the thing again, my boy, why not throw in a couple of brass bands?' These twin ensembles of three trumpets, three trombones and a tuba, placed on either side of the orchestra, duly augment the cantata's scoring for baritone soloist, large double chorus, organ and an orchestra including saxophone and a sizeable percussion section.

The music's impact, however, relates to more than the tearing pace and huge decibel-level of the biggest passages. What counts just as much is Walton's skill in drawing together strikingly different musical resources into a single conception. The snappy cross-rhythms and gaudy instrumental colours of the Jazz Age rub shoulders with blocks of unaccompanied choral writing characteristic of the English choral tradition. The extravagant verve of the feast and finale is offset by Walton's instinct for thinking economically, as in the soloist's unaccompanied description of the splendours of Belshazzar's Babylon. And throughout the feast's hedonistic revelry, the needlepoint precision of the scoring (for woodwind in particular) is a Waltonian trademark.

A menacing, single-note fanfare on unison trombones introduces the cantata's opening statement: a harshly dissonant setting for male chorus of Isaiah's prophecy of the Israelites' exile in Babylon. Tremolo violas and mournful low strings then set the scene for the chorus's lament 'By the waters of Babylon'. This is punctuated by the fury of 'For they that wasted us', accompanied by spitting muted trumpets and trombones. The baritone soloist's passionate invocation 'If I forget thee, O Jerusalem' is followed by a second choral outburst at 'O daughter of Babylon, who art to be destroyed'. This ends in quiet despair.

Next comes the baritone's vivid unaccompanied narrative, 'Babylon was a great city', leading straight into the virtuoso choral and orchestral depiction of the feast. The point where the Babylonians thrillingly echo their king's exhortation 'Praise ye the god of gold' was where Walton 'got stuck' during the work's composition – not that one would guess as much from his solution. This is a rampant march, fizzing with cross-rhythms, while exotic percussion evokes the Babylonians' assorted pagan deities. (The extra brass bands, cunningly held back until now, make their first appearance between the gods of iron and wood.) A truncated orchestral climax leads to a reprise of the 'feast' music, culminating in the Babylonians' hysterical plea to their king to 'live for ever'.

A sudden hush – and the baritone soloist, again unaccompanied, tells of the appearance of the writing on the wall, evoked in the orchestra by shuddering low strings and sinister percussion sounds. Judgement is pronounced on Belshazzar; his death is marked by a choral shout (literally); and the orchestra begins a wild, rhythmically complex dance of joy, joined by the chorus with 'Then sing aloud to God our strength'. At 'Blow up the trumpet in the new moon', Walton the native Lancastrian, aware of the expertise of northern brass players available at the Leeds Festival, provided a scintillating opportunity for them.

Pace and perspective open out at 'While the Kings of the Earth lament', and an unaccompanied double semi-chorus describes how 'The trumpeters and pipers are silent' – a telling touch in a work which has told the story from the standpoint of the peoples of Israel and Babylon, rather than that of their rulers. Then the dance of triumph returns, growing increasingly frenetic in a torrent of repeated Alleluias. These lead towards a thunderous reprise of 'Then sing aloud', and a headlong rush towards the closing bars.

© Malcolm Hayes

Chronology of works

1845–6	*Elijah*, Op. 70 (rev. 1847)	Mendelssohn
1850–4	*The Childhood of Christ*, sacred trilogy, Op. 25	Berlioz
1855	*Te Deum*, Op. 22	Berlioz
1865–9	*A German Requiem*, Op. 45	Brahms
1866	Mass No. 2 in E minor (revised 1876, 1882)	Bruckner
1867–8	Mass No. 3 in F minor	Bruckner
1874	Requiem	Verdi
1876–7	*Stabat Mater*, Op. 58	Dvořák
1877	Requiem, Op. 48 (rev. 1887–94; orch. 1900)	Fauré
1878–80	*Das klagende Lied* (rev. 1892–3, 1898–9)	Mahler
1887	*Blest Pair of Sirens*	Parry
1888–97	*Four Sacred Pieces*	Verdi
1891–2	*Kullervo*, Op. 7	Sibelius
1899–1900	*The Dream of Gerontius*, Op. 38	Elgar
1900–11	*Gurrelieder*	Schoenberg
1901–6	*The Kingdom*, Op. 51	Elgar
1902	Coronation Anthem: *I Was Glad* (rev. 1911)	Parry
1902–3	*The Apostles*, Op. 49	Elgar
1903–4	*Sea Drift*	Delius
1903–9	*A Sea Symphony* (Symphony No. 1) (rev. 1918)	V. Williams
1905–6	*Toward the Unknown Region*	V. Williams
1913	*The Bells*, Op. 35	Rakhmaninov
1914–23	*Les noces*	Stravinsky
1915	*All-Night Vigil* (Vespers), Op. 37	Rakhmaninov
1916	*Jerusalem* (orch. Elgar, 1922)	Parry
1917	*The Hymn of Jesus*, Op. 37	Holst
1926	*Glagolitic Mass*	Janáček
1926–7	*Oedipus rex*, opera-oratorio in two acts	Stravinsky
1927	*The Rio Grande*	Lambert
1929–31	*Belshazzar's Feast* (rev. 1931, 1948, 1957)	Walton
1930	*Symphony of Psalms*	Stravinsky
1936	*Litanies à la vierge noire*	Poulenc
1936–7	*Cantata for the Twentieth Anniversary of the October Revolution*, Op. 74	Prokofiev
1937	*Carmina burana*	Orff
1938	*Serenade to Music*	V. Williams
1938–9	*Alexander Nevsky*, cantata, Op. 78	Prokofiev

1939–41	*A Child of Our Time*	Tippett
1947	Requiem, Op. 9	Duruflé
1947–8	Mass	Stravinsky
1948–9	*Spring Symphony*, Op. 44	Britten
1959	*Gloria*	Poulenc
1960–2	*Sept répons des ténèbres*	Poulenc
1961	*War Requiem*, Op. 66	Britten
1963–5	Requiem	Ligeti
1965	*Chichester Psalms*	Bernstein
1975–6	*Coro*	Berio
1980–1	*Harmonium*	Adams
1980–2	*The Mask of Time*	Tippett